DATE DUE

GAYLORD   PRINTED IN U.S.A.

OF LONG MEMORY

OF LONG MEMORY

MISSISSIPPI AND
THE MURDER OF
MEDGAR EVERS

Adam Nossiter

▲
▼▼
Addison-Wesley Publishing Company
Reading, Massachusetts   Menlo Park, California   New York
Don Mills, Ontario   Wokingham, England   Amsterdam   Bonn
Sydney   Singapore   Tokyo   Madrid   San Juan
Paris   Seoul   Milan   Mexico City   Taipei

Many of the designations used by manufacturers and sellers to distinguish their products are claimed as trademarks. Where those designations appear in this book and Addison-Wesley was aware of a trademark claim, the designations have been printed in initial capital letters (e.g., Plymouth Valiant).

Library of Congress Cataloging-in-Publishing Data

Nossiter, Adam.
    Of long memory : Mississippi and the murder of Medgar
Evers / Adam Nossiter.
        p.   cm.
    Includes bibliographical references and index.
    ISBN 0-201-60844-8
    1. Afro-American—Mississippi—Politics and govern-
ment. 2. Mississippi—Race relations. 3. Evers, Medgar Wiley, 1925–1963—Assassination. 4. Beckwith,
Byron de la. 5. Mississippi—Politics and government—
1951—   I. Title.
F350.N4N67   1994
323.1'1960730762—dc20   94-45
                                                          CIP

Jacket design by Diana Coe
Text design by Richard Oriolo
Set in 12-point Garamond 3 by G & S Typesetters, Inc.

1   2   3   4   5   6   7   8   9   10-ARM-9897969594
First printing, April 1994

TO THE MEMORY OF MY FATHER,
BERNARD NOSSITER,
1926–1992

CONTENTS

ADAM NOSSITER

ACKNOWLEDGMENTS

A s a non-Southerner and non-Mississippian, I labored under a double disadvantage in preparing this book. So I owe a great debt of gratitude to all my friends in the region who, over ten years, tolerated my ignorance and aided my stumbling attempts to overcome it.

This book would not have been written without the encouragement and advice of Robert Sherrill, a Southern journalist whose work remains unequaled.

In Mississippi, I owe much to many. I am especially grateful to my friends in Jackson, and in particular Sharon Stallworth and Wilson Carroll, for educating me about their native state. Everyone who writes about Mississippi is bound to be indebted to Bill Minor, one of the great American journalists, whose courage, doggedness, and acuity over more than forty years of reporting from Jackson are exemplary. I was especially fortunate to have worked beside Bill in the capital press room, and to have benefited from numerous conversations with him, formal and informal. Frank Smith, a former congressman, supplied me with most of my library and, from his rocking chair at Choctaw Books in Jackson, his humane wisdom about the state's history. Hob Bryan's wit and insights into Mississippi politics from his perch in the state senate have been valuable and entertaining.

A number of people were generous with their time in granting interviews—Bill Waller, Charles Evers, Ed King, and Bob Pritchard, in particular. No historian has keener insight into the state than Neil McMillen, and I am grateful to him for sharing his wisdom and for letting me speak with his students. My editor at the *Atlanta Journal-Constitution*, Plott Brice, gave me the freedom to roam over Mississippi for four years, and I am grateful to him. I owe much to the late Anna Cancogni; what I know about reading and interpretation I learned from her. The staffs of the Mississippi Department of Archives and History and the Amistad Research Center, at Tulane University, were always patient.

Gloria Loomis, my agent, was encouraging and sympathetic throughout. The suggestions of my editor at Addison-Wesley, Nancy Miller, were valuable and helpful.

I take full responsibility for any errors herein.

PREFACE:
OF LONG MEMORY

S hortly after midnight, on June 12, 1963, a watershed civil rights murder took place in Jackson, Mississippi. Medgar Evers, the chief representative of the National Association for the Advancement of Colored People (NAACP) in the state, was shot dead as he stepped out of his car to turn in for the evening. Evers was a principal leader of the growing civil rights movement in Jackson, the capital of Mississippi, which for 100 years had waged the South's most violent, unremitting campaign to suppress blacks' rights.

By June 1963, the civil rights movement had engulfed the entire South. But the murder of Evers stood out from the general conflagration for a number of reasons. He was the highest-ranking civil rights figure to be assassinated up to that point. In Mississippi alone, in the preceding eight years, three black men had been murdered for their work in attempting to register voters. But they had labored in obscurity, mostly unknown outside their home counties. Evers was a public figure. Even before his death, he was gaining recognition as a person of exceptional courage, fighting an often isolated battle under the most difficult circumstances imaginable. And so the murder itself drew unprecedented attention and condemnation, from President John F. Kennedy down to demonstrators in streets across the country. Even inside Mississippi, white officials felt it necessary—for the first time—to denounce a civil rights killing, though they were far from renouncing their resistance to Evers's goals.

A white man from the faded planter aristocracy, a mediocre fertilizer salesman, Byron de la Beckwith, was soon arrested for the murder. As a passionate racist, he had a strong motive for killing Evers. The physical evidence against him was strong. The prosecutor, a Mississippi white man, made clear early on that he would do his duty conscientiously, and he ultimately did so.

Still, Beckwith had every reason to expect a quick acquittal. This was the normal Mississippi verdict in such cases.

And yet through two mistrials in the winter and spring of 1964, juries of white men could not reach a unanimous verdict that Beckwith was innocent. Some actually voted for his guilt. True, Beckwith was eventually set free. But, critically, he was not acquitted. A turning point seemed to have been reached in the American state most violently committed to resisting black equality. It would nonetheless be many years before the full dimensions of this turning point were revealed.

This long span of years would have been entirely predictable in the days following Beckwith's triumphant ride home in the spring of 1964. Overt shifts in the dominant white majority's racial attitudes were slow in coming. And the Mississippi authorities could reasonably claim that they had already given the Beckwith case their best effort, and that there was no need to revisit it. Over the years, they certainly did make this claim.

But by the late 1980s, these arguments no longer seemed adequate. They never had been enough to satisfy those who felt that justice had not been served originally. The known murderer of Evers had, after all, gone unpunished. That the prosecutor in 1964 had performed honorably did not satisfy the people who felt moral anger about the outcome—in Mississippi, principally blacks, 35 percent of the state's population. What was decisive in the practical world—the world where judicial decisions were made and unmade—was that precious few whites shared their feelings.

There were good reasons for this. From within Mississippi, one would have needed a considerable moral and historical perspective to be troubled by the outcome of the Evers case, much less want to reopen it. An observer had to recognize that far more than a simple malfunctioning of the judicial system had taken place in 1964. The system—the police, the prosecutor, the judge—had performed adequately. The problem had been with the jurors, and thus with the larger world of white Mississippi that they represented. A majority of them had gone along with what was then the state's highest commandment: uphold the law of racial solidarity.

The jury's verdict simply gave voice to what white Mississippians were thinking about Beckwith: he was not guilty. Where the world outside white Mississippi saw clear and compelling evidence against Beckwith, a majority of jurors could not. One of the twelve jurors who sat and sweated with the case in 1964, John T. Hester, said many years later: "There was too many contradictions in the thing."[1] Seeing through whatever imagined "contradictions" the evidence assembled against Beckwith might appear to have thrown up meant condemning the jurors—agreeing that there was something very wrong with Mississippi society in that time and place.

More than a quarter century after the first mistrials, in December 1990, a singular event in Southern history occurred. Unprodded by the federal government, Mississippi reached back into its own past and reindicted Beckwith. Legally, the matter was relatively simple. Because of the mistrials, the case could still be reopened, and no statute of limitations applied to murder. Still, in the long catalogue of unpunished Southern civil rights murders, there was no precise parallel for this occurrence. Nor was there any easy way to interpret it. From the beginning, it seemed foolish to assign a simple meaning to Beckwith's reindictment—something on the order of, "My, look at how Mississippi has changed." That view temporarily replaced the rusty "My, look at how Mississippi hasn't changed" in many of the journalistic accounts. As the months dragged on to Beckwith's trial, through the grumbling of Mississippi whites and the cynicism of Mississippi blacks, these strategies seemed even less certain.

It was only when I looked back on it, in the context of the other things I knew about Mississippi, that the reindictment of Beckwith began to make sense. By then, I was in the fourth year of an assignment to cover Mississippi for the *Atlanta Journal-Constitution*. From the first day I set foot in the state, it was a place that seemed to me as culturally distinct from the rest of the South as the South seemed from the rest of the country. It had the distinctively Southern things, only more so: in particular, the physical closeness of black and white cultures that always formed a jarring counterpoint to persistent racial animosity. But it was also a place where the past jutted into the present to a startling degree, quite unlike other Southern states that I knew well.

I was immediately captivated by Mississippi. My time there resonated back to a childhood spent mostly in Europe, and to my memory of how echoes of the cataclysmic war resonated from so many aspects of daily living—relationships, buildings, conversations. World War II, which had been over for more than thirty years by the time I returned to the United States in the late 1970s, seemed to me, growing up, a kind of universal backdrop.

Mississippi had something of the same aura. Ten years after coming back to this country, I was roaming the state for my newspaper, following a Southern reporter's habitual round of racial disputes in small towns, labor fights in low-wage factories, and racially divided politics in the state capital. The past kept intruding into these stories. Mississippi came to seem like a laboratory, a continuous experiment in which people were forced to learn how to live with their past.

Beckwith's reindictment was a culmination of this experiment. It was by no means final proof of some decisive change. But it was the richest evidence yet in the ongoing process whereby a people tried to come to grips with their own tortured history.

To attempt an explanation of the new case against Beckwith in these terms is my object. To me, his reindictment was part of the larger story of how Mississippi, at the end of the 1980s, was transacting with its past. "I don't think it happened in a vacuum," said Ray Mabus, the former governor (see chapter 8). What had filled the vacuum? By fits and starts, over a period of many years, the ground had been made ready for a renewed attempt to expiate the crime. The political evolution of the state was clear, though not exclusive, evidence of this process. How the ground was readied, and why, are the main questions I attempt to answer. I am personally biased toward the examination of politics—in my mind, always a compelling mirror of larger movements beneath the surface. In the years I spent covering Mississippi, I was able to gain, or so it seemed to me, a fair sense of the state's mood by following the action around the state capitol in Jackson. So my principal tool in the following look into Mississippi's evolution is political history, with apologies to those whose bias runs toward other measures of social and cultural change.

CHAPTER ONE

CONFRONTING HISTORY IN MISSISSIPPI

A light drizzle fell over Jackson, Mississippi, the day in December 1990 when the papers announced that Byron de la Beckwith had been indicted again for murdering Medgar Evers. The city's low vistas of parking lots and fast-food joints and shopping strips were bathed in a grayish light, so that you had the feeling of being in a black-and-white photograph. For the next few days, the papers would be full of commentary about how this was one more piece of evidence that Mississippi was moving into the future, that it was irreversibly different, that people in the state were glad, in fact, that the crackpot white supremacist was going back into court and might even be convicted this time. The most thoughtful voices—the former governor William Winter, and a host of progressive politicians, black and white—were saying such things. It certainly was easy to see things that way. But for me, that gray day in Jackson seemed like a clear window on the past.

I had been coming here regularly for almost four years as a reporter. The old Jackson that I had somehow hoped to experience, of civil rights demonstrations and sit-ins and hatred so thick you could touch it, was not immediately evident—more difficult to conjure up than the German occupation in Paris. For one thing, people were generally lavishly friendly, anxious to show me, a blatant Yankee, how civilized they were. Nobody was going to let me feel like one of those vulnerable Northerners who had come down thirty years before to be harassed. And there seemed to be an entire class of people in their thirties and forties, some of whom I was friends with, who were painfully eager to apologize for the behavior of their parents. At a bar in a renovated downtown warehouse, the night Beckwith was indicted, the drunken young urbanites were almost gloating over the day's news and wishing all kinds of hell on Beckwith.

In months spent in the city, I had not witnessed much open hostility between blacks and whites, and certainly not any large-scale racial tension. Social life in Jackson is no more, and no less, segregated than it is anywhere else in the South. Blacks and whites are occasionally seen together in the city's bars and restaurants. But those sneering, racially tinged asides I had gotten used to from whites in Alabama, where I made my home, were rarer here. So the 1960s accounts from journalists and other writers that pictured Jackson as a queer, almost foreign little outpost planted on American soil seemed about as meaningful to the present as a nineteenth-century travel narrative.

Visually, the city had not changed much since the 1960s. A few feeble glass-and-steel homages to Dallas aside, there had not been enough money to change the city's look. The Mayflower and Primos restaurant signs still poked out of downtown blocks, bringing back the old newsreels. The old limestone insurance company towers still rose incongruously from moribund blocks of brick commercial buildings, just as they did in the late 1940s when John Gunther came through town for his book, *Inside U.S.A.*

And sometimes, the past echoed in Jackson in odd ways. Deep quiet enveloped the heart of the city by late in the afternoon and on weekends. On one late-August Saturday in 1987 downtown Jackson, intense afternoon heat had blasted every soul off the sidewalks, and it was possible to walk for blocks along the wide, silent streets without encountering anyone. A bedraggled, derelict black man wandered aimlessly on the empty streets, and an overweight white man, sweating through an undershirt, sat on his front porch watching his dog, which was miserably tethered to a porch pillar.

The empty city seemed an eerie stage set left over from the turmoil of a quarter century before. Still, though the unchanged landscape of Jackson evoked the past, I had to people the streets myself with imagined faces, mean-faced whites with crew cuts and beefy cops with truncheons, to bring the old city back.

But as I drove around town on that gray December afternoon after Beckwith had been reindicted, the day felt different. I sensed that the fabric of the present had been ruptured. It was as if the tense, seedy little Southern city of the 1960s black-and-white photographs and newsreels had, for a day at least, come flooding back. There were the matrons at the supermarket in the sedate Belhaven area, clucking their tongues over the folly of persecuting an elderly white gentleman for the sake of a long-dead black troublemaker. "It's ridiculous, bringing it up again," said a smartly dressed older white woman, the widow of a former state supreme court justice, as she tipped a black checkout clerk.

There were the white electricians in the down-home café inveighing with quiet fury against blacks in general and civil rights workers in particular, murmuring sympathetically for Byron de la Beckwith. "In some ways, you can see his point," one of them said, deliberately provocative. Blacks, he explained, were "doing a bunch of hollering without doing anything for it."

There were blacks in Medgar Evers' now-forlorn old neighborhood, full of fierce pride this day, the same that had pushed their parents (and, as children, them) out onto the streets to demonstrate thirty years earlier. This time, they vowed, the man who had killed Evers was going to get what was coming to him.

These feelings had been there all the time, of course. The revival of the old case was simply bringing them out of shadows. In fact, the day's headlines were forcing people all over the state, and in Jackson especially, to confront their past. It was not the first time this had happened. The film *Mississippi Burning*, for one thing, had induced similar mingled spasms of defensiveness and painful self-recognition (see chapter 8).

There were times when the entire state seemed to be living in the past—or if not in it, at least living with it. What had happened before—the lynchings, the beatings, the whole grim superstructure of white supremacy—hovers at the edge of encounters in Mississippi, particularly those with older people. Often, this amounts to a kind of set-jawed reliving of old battles.

Once, in the steamy little Delta town of Moorehead, a grizzled old white junk-store owner told me of a proud episode from his past: he had personally defied the Civil Rights Act of 1964 by chasing blacks from the movie theater he had owned at the time. Looking me up and down suspiciously, he said, "Who're you with, anyway? COFO?" The Council of Federated Organizations, COFO, was a name that lived on only in yellowing newspaper clippings and history books. An ephemeral organization from its start in 1962, COFO had been a fractious union of civil rights groups in Mississippi: the National Association for the Advancement of Colored People (NAACP), the Southern Christian Leadership Conference (SCLC), the Student Non-Violent Coordinating Committee (SNCC), and the Congress of Racial Equality (CORE). COFO had been out of existence for twenty-five years, ever since Mississippians like this man had done battle with it during the Freedom Summer of 1964. That had been COFO's finest hour—the flooding of Mississippi by hundreds of white Northern college students in the summer of 1964. They had tried, with varying degrees of success, to register voters, test segregation laws, and engage in other subversive activities. This nightmare was still vivid to the older generation, made all the more unnerving by disquieting memories of beards, unkempt hair, and black and white couples arm in arm. For good reason, COFO was still alive in the old man's mind, and he felt compelled to remain on the lookout for it.

Here was someone filled with the racial attitudes "of the old school," as an up-to-date Mississippian might put it with a deprecating laugh—someone who might look across the railroad tracks to where the blacks live and spit on the ground, just as the junk-store owner did. Beckwith himself was sometimes said to be "of the old school." It was easy enough to find such racism all over the state. "You're not from Mississippi, are you?" a store clerk had asked sharply. I had been making inquiries as to why some people in her

4

town of Macon, Mississippi, had found a discreet interracial church so objectionable that they had burned it to the ground. "If I had known about it, I would have carried some gasoline over there myself," said an old man whose house was behind the burnt-out church. "We don't need that kind of stuff going on here, mixing up with all the whites and niggers." The best that could be said was that there was rarely any attempt to conceal such feelings. "I've had niggers raised with me," the mayor of the Delta town of Pickens had said. "Ran a little country store. Wasn't anything but blacks around. If there's any racism in me . . . I may have some."

There was no revelation in discovering the persistence of these attitudes; what was striking was their relative impotence. They were so clearly no longer a dominating force in the politics of the state—could not be, with blacks making up a third of the voting age population by the end of the 1980s. Mississippi had more black officials than any other state. True, politics in 1990s Mississippi were as racially polarized as anywhere else in America. Whites, with few exceptions, voted solidly Republican in national elections; blacks, solidly Democratic.

But the picture was more complicated than this. For nearly twenty years, Mississippi had elected an unbroken string of moderate-progressive governors. The cycle was finally broken in the 1991 election, when the frustrated voters threw out the progressive-sounding but unskillful Ray Mabus for a right-wing businessman, Kirk Fordice, an unknown full of unexpected bluster and blunder.

Modern racial appeals played no more of a role in these elections than they did elsewhere. And, where it could be found, the old racism had to exist side by side with the realization that it had failed. This, ultimately, seemed the stronger feeling: the inescapable memories of all those fruitless contortions of the 1950s and 1960s. The pitiful situations of Beckwith's old Ku Klux Klan buddies was a telling indicator of how futile their old exertions had been. Clutching a Styrofoam cup of bourbon at midmorning outside his suburban Jackson home, one greeted me amiably. Another faced a pile of bills with no money and was being hounded by the IRS. "Remember now, if you get involved in a struggle, make sure you pick the winning side," he had said, wryly closing an interview.

An outsider triggers these memories of past failures. The outsider is a mirror, and what people see reflected is not exactly themselves, but their past. Thus, with whites, the presence of the past is often invoked with a defensive question such as, "You're not going to write anything bad about us, are you?" (If the person is hostile the question becomes a statement of fact.) With the bit players of the 1960s, minor white politicos who were cogs in the machinery of segregation, one detects defensiveness and often a hint of guilt. "That was just a hard period we had to go through," I was told by Charlie Jacobs, a powerful segregationist state representative in the 1960s, a man who had once denounced a state house colleague as "a renegade disgrace to the white race in general."[1] He is now an obscure country lawyer. "It turned out maybe he was right, and I was wrong," Jacobs said, referring to one of the only two liberals in the legislature in the early 1960s. But that was all he wanted to say on the subject, which seemed too painful.

With blacks, the past is the backdrop, sometimes spoken, sometimes not, to any narration of present experience.

This involuntary immersion in history was an ironic fate. So recently, Mississippi had been condemned for clinging murderously to the Jim Crow structures erected after Reconstruction—for literally living in the past. The popular historian Walter Lord entitled his account of the 1962 riot over James Meredith's attempt to integrate the University of Mississippi, when much of white Mississippi seethed with insurrectionary fervor, *The Past That Would Not Die*. Now Mississippi was saddled with the overwhelming memory of its own recent violence, condemned to live uncomfortably with its past.

Living with the past had produced an apathy about it, too—a "numbness" among whites, as one of the more thoughtful members of the present-day legislature said. For some older black Mississippians, veterans of the civil rights movement, the apathy had taken a different form. Aaron Henry, the state president of the NAACP for over thirty years and someone who knew Medgar Evers well, sometimes exhibits impatience with memories of those years.

In some ways Henry seems to feel the history as a personal dead weight, which is perhaps why, early in 1978, he announced a surprising development: he had ascertained that the aging segre-

gationist Sen. James O. Eastland had undergone a miraculous conversion. Shock waves rippled through the black political leadership. It was the way Henry talked about his new relationship with
the balding, cigar-chomping old "seg" that surprised people most.
Henry spoke of his "romance" with the senator and said Eastland
was a "very sensitive man." The NAACP leader was then in his late
fifties, but he seemed not to notice when Eastland in his turn addressed Henry as "son."[2]

Henry's willingness to forget was a mirror image of the older
white politicians' desire to do the same, and that inclination contributed to the general numbness. In the late 1980s, a series of jolts
shook this apathy and culminated in the Beckwith reindictment.
For blacks and whites, the phenomenon of *Mississippi Burning* was
a qualitatively different experience from the routine living with history. The reindictment of Beckwith was a still more brutal confrontation with the past. It was not a question this time of some
outsider, a writer or a filmmaker, lecturing people about their previous iniquities. And it was not like when the new breed of Mississippi politicians got up and made a speech obliquely apologizing
for what had happened thirty years ago. People were sullenly getting used to that, at least.

No. Here, for the first time, history was going to be yanked
out of the safety of the documentaries and the textbooks and the
politicians' speeches, and relived. A terrible crime and the blatant
injustice that had followed it in Beckwith's mistrials—all this was
going to be served up hot and steaming, day after day. Many people
clearly were not thrilled about the idea. Apprehension, resentment,
and feelings of vindication were in the air.

"What the hell is wrong with Mississippi?" Thelma Beckwith
had cried as her husband was being deported back to his native
state early in 1991. It was easy enough to see, glancing around the
time warp of their mountain retreat outside Chattanooga, Tennessee, why she was so bewildered. The porch was draped with a Confederate flag, and Beckwith's study was strewn with pamphlets and
newsletters from obscure far-right organizations. The "Jewsmedia,"
the "Jew money power," fluoridation, interracial dating, and the
"Kosher food conspiracy" were the favored targets. A leather-bound
copy of *Protocols of the Elders of Zion* sat on the bookshelf.

Yet Thelma Beckwith had somehow hit on the question of the hour: What *was* wrong with Mississippi? Clearly, something was now different about the state that had been so safe for her husband for so many years.

To be sure, white Mississippi was choking a little on the first doses of this new medicine. And it would choke some more as the legal process dragged on through 1991, 1992, and 1993, and out-croppings of sympathy built for the sickly old man waiting for his trial in a tiny jail cell. Angry calls came in to the district attorney's office, and white Jackson grew tremulous at the thought of what black Jackson would do if Beckwith was released. There were re-ports of teachers being sent home early and offices being let out on the day the state supreme court was to decide whether Beckwith's trial should go forward. Clearly, vestigial fears of the coming servile insurrection, for long a part of segregationist mythology, remained.

But this discomfort had been, on the whole, quiet. Beckwith was very obviously no longer the white folk hero he had been in the mid-1960s. Accounts of his lunatic courtroom behavior filled the local media after his reindictment in December 1990. In one such appearance, he stood erect in a frayed pinstripe suit and tie, the ex-marine addressing the judge with exaggerated politeness, a Holly-wood Colonel Reb with a deeply Southern accent: "I'm delighted I'll be able to stay here, so I can continue fighting this process," he said grandly, looking around the courtroom. "I thank the court." It was as though the bemused-looking judge had invited him to a tea party. "How many Jews are among you? I see one nigra man," he called out to spectators at one hearing. Scenes like these were af-fecting public opinion.

Shreds of the courtly gentleman facade still clung to the pub-lic Beckwith, making him barely palatable. In private, these tatters were not much in evidence. I discovered this for myself one rainy Saturday morning in July 1992. At that juncture, Beckwith was being held in the Hinds County Detention Center in downtown Jackson, and that is where I met the old man.

I was brought to the jail by one of Beckwith's old friends and Ku Klux Klan colleagues, a man I had met at a court hearing the day before. He had helped Beckwith in the latter's bizarre excursion into electoral politics, in the 1967 lieutenant governor's race. The man was friendly enough, in a sheepish way. That Saturday morning, he told me he had to take Beckwith a few things and invited me to come along.

Knowing that Beckwith had been demanding cash for talk, I said yes. This could be my only chance to see him up close.

We met outside the courthouse and proceeded around the corner to the jail entrance. Beckwith's friend began to get nervous.

"Need to ask you a few questions."

"Sure."

"You Jewish?"

"Yeah."

"Hunh. Well, just don't tell Beckwith that. We'll tell him you're Catholic."

"Oh. Okay."

I did not like it, but I was not going to argue. I wanted to hear what Beckwith had to say. And I knew he would not say anything if he found out I was Jewish.

Besides, Beckwith had deigned to shake my hand at the hearing the day before. Grinning, he had given me one of those lines the reporters scribble down to add color to their stories: "Anything you write to help me, good. But if you fart around like a damn nigger or a Jew, God will punish you for messing with a Christian." Fine. This was vintage Beckwith.

We went into the jail, signed in with no problems (I did not even get a suspicious glance from the drowsy, overweight guard), and went down the corridor to Beckwith's cell.

He knocked. "Delay. Delay!" (This is what Beckwith's friends call him.)

Beckwith opened the door. He was the gracious Southern gentleman, smilingly welcoming us into his parlor. "Come in, Come in. Sure, I remember you. Glad you could make it." We shook hands all around.

I sat down on a stool, and Beckwith immediately slumped back onto his cot. He looked terrible, deathly ill behind his thick glasses. He had had major heart surgery, and lately there had been speculation about whether he could even survive until his trial.

The cramped, stuffy little cell was a sight. There were stacks of *The Spotlight*, the anti-Semitic newspaper of the far-right Liberty Lobby, all over the floor and on the thin cot. Beckwith's scribbled sayings, generally wishing death to blacks and liberals, were taped to the walls. In the little bookshelf were several Bibles and a concordance. A David Duke sticker hung on the wall, along with a sympathizer's ham-fisted cartoon purportedly illustrating Beckwith's plight. He immediately gave me a copy.

The friend was standing awkwardly in the far corner, just out of my sight. He had brought a roll of plastic baggies so Beckwith could package his appeals for money and Liberty Lobby material together. (These would later end up on the lawns of the citizens of Panola County, hundreds of miles to the north. The judge moved jury selection there, at the request of Beckwith's lawyers, in hopes of finding jurors who had not read about the case. Beckwith, with the help of his friends, the Liberty Lobby, and the plastic baggies, was going to launch a preemptive strike of his own to influence the Panola County jurors.)

"Delay, this here is a good old Catholic boy from Looziana."

"Fine, fine. Those Catholic boys sure saved my ass down in Looziana." He chuckled. In the 1970s, Beckwith had tried to bomb the home of the Anti-Defamation League head in New Orleans and had subsequently been imprisoned in the Louisiana State Penitentiary at Angola (see chapter 4). The black prisoners had threatened to boil him for soup.

Beckwith looked at me. "Say the Hail Mary for me."

I got a sinking feeling. This was not going to work.

"Can't. Don't know it."

Instantly, the look on Beckwith's face changed. He began to stare at me, hard.

"I've never met any Catholic who couldn't say the Hail Mary. You sure you're a Catholic?" His face was twisted with anger. "What was your grandfather's name? You're not a Catholic. You're a damn Jew!"

Beckwith lurched into a frenzied, disconnected series of rapid monologues, several of them invoking Jesus. The friend still stood in the corner, occasionally interjecting an imploring "Delay! Now, Delay!"

From Beckwith there was a deliberate, graphic description of hog-killing time in the country: "You shoot him in the back of the head. You cut him open, down the belly. Then you string him up. 'Course, you wouldn't know. You're a Jew."

He talked about having joined the Greenwood Country Club after he had gotten out of the marines in World War II, pathetically adding that he had been unable to pay the dues: "Shit, man, country club's the only way to go."

There were imprecations against Jewish publishers and Jewish newspapermen.

Vehemently, he said: "Jesus Christ was not a Jew." He wanted me to understand this. "Haven't you ever heard of the Twelve Tribes of Judea? Say the Kol Nidrei. How much do you know about the Jews? Shit, these Northern boys are smart."

For an instant, he seemed to be lost in dreamy speculation. "The Ku Klux Klan, the Identity Church [a violent anti-Semitic sect to which he belongs], nothing but a centrifuge. The Jews, the niggers . . ."

I tried to ask him a question. He became more infuriated. "I'm not answering any of your damn questions. You're a damn Jew. Get out. Get out!"

He jumped off his cot and stood next to me. "I may not look it, but I can handle you. Get out!"

Arguing was futile. Instantly, with no provocation, he had conceived a deep hatred for me.

I left the cell and stood outside in the hall, then listened. Inside, Beckwith was continuing his tirade against Jews.

"You can smell them anywhere! We've got to get these people out of the country!"

The face of the man in the cell next to Beckwith's was pressed to the glass. I could see him grinning.

Beckwith and his friend emerged. Beckwith delivered a fragmentary religion-tinged harangue about Jesus advocating the decapitation of all Jews. There would be blood. He, Beckwith, was in general agreement with this plan of action.

We left.

"I'm so embarrassed. That was so embarrassing," the friend said, over and over.

Clearly, he was mortified. I tried to comfort him. But I was a little stunned by this performance.

In the drizzle, we sat on the courthouse steps. Beckwith's friend continued to apologize. He had known Beckwith for years, and the two had shared a passion for guns. He had remained loyal. This puzzled me.

I wanted to comfort him. "Well, he's just a mean-spirited old man," I said. "Don't you think?"

"No, not really," the friend replied. "To you he was, maybe." After a little more desultory talk, we drove off.

Three days later, Beckwith wrote a letter to Reed Massengill, the nephew of his first wife, describing our meeting:

> I just threw the snotty-nosed, 6'4", yellow-skinned, mongrel, damned-by-God, stinking son-of-a-bitch Jew out of my comfortable chamber as he crept in with a long-time true friend of mine here.
>
> He's been writing an anti-Delay, anti-white, anti-Christian, anti-Dixie book—one mother-defiler, Adam Nossiter, who months ago had the gall to ask me to release my FIA FBI file to him! All of which is normal for a Jew and all who associate with Jews—for Jews pleasures are worse than the Jews—*so says Jesus! Who is very God, dontcha know* Jesus is on their ass, and *me too.* I've had a file on him for several years.
>
> He slithered in Thelma's home, and that could be the end of a happy marriage—my wife letting a God-damned obvious Jew in to her home where we live!!! Shit Shit Shit.[3]

Prosecuting such a man for what he represents now—senile, lunatic race hatred—would have been of limited significance. His far-out ranting made the Beckwith of 1992 a figure of only marginal interest. But in fact, it was the Beckwith of the early 1960s—the representative man—that the state of Mississippi was now going after, with at least the grudging approbation of the state's citizenry. Why?

Some months after the indictment, in early 1991, I went to see Bobby DeLaughter, the earnest young assistant district attorney who was prosecuting Beckwith (see chapter 7). He is white, and his parents were both working people. I knew that almost before he told me: the South is like England in that it is still, disconcertingly, possible to accurately guess someone's social origins from his or her accent. He speaks with a slight country twang, and in the formal language of unquestioning respect for law enforcement and prosecution. Not exactly a civil rights crusader.

Yet he said to me: "An uncleansed wound never heals. It just keeps festering. I don't think this case would ever have 'gone away.' It's an uncleansed wound in society.

"Assassinating someone for what they believe in, I think that just lays one heck of a gash in humanity and in society as a whole. When the person is not held accountable, I don't think the wound ever heals, it just keeps on festering."

How had someone like this young prosecutor come around to saying these things?

The short and cynical answer, one on the lips of many black politicians and some racist whites, was political expediency. Hinds County now had a tiny black majority; DeLaughter, in his quiet way, is an ambitious man. But there was more to it than politics. An earnest schoolboy manner and the testimony of people who knew DeLaughter provided evidence that the prosecutor believed what he was saying. What was the nature of the wound DeLaughter spoke of? The answer to that question would go far toward solving the mystery of that December afternoon when Beckwith was reindicted.

The mystery did not revolve around Beckwith's guilt; the evidence against him had always been overwhelming. Most people accepted that only the hold of white supremacy had allowed him to escape punishment twenty-six years before. As the late Al Binder, the Jackson lawyer and power broker who was one of DeLaughter's mentors (see chapter 4) put it: "I mean hell, everybody knows Beckwith killed Evers."

Beckwith's case was a murder mystery without the mystery, just as Beckwith himself was the murderer who claimed, with a sly wink and a nod, that he was not one. Another of Beckwith's old Klan friends, capturing the spirit if not the actual letter of his friend's discourse on the subject, put it this way: "Where he screwed up on the Evers deal was, he never denied it. He wanted to be a hero."

So the important question raised by Beckwith's reindictment was this: Why, in fact, was official Mississippi bothering to revive the Medgar Evers case at all?

Ever since the mistrials of 1964, the state had chosen to ignore the case, and few people seemed to care. There was no cost in continuing to pretend that justice had already been served. True, new evidence surfaced in mid-1989 implicating the long-defunct, 1950s-era agency in charge of defending segregation, the State Sovereignty Commission, in Beckwith's eventual liberation. The Jackson *Clarion-Ledger* and a handful of black politicians expressed outrage, but such responses were not novel and usually had not influenced official policy in any major way. All the clamoring could have been dismissed with the favored bland formulation, which had been deployed often before: Look to the future instead of dwelling on the past. This time, although the phrase was invoked, it did not end the matter. The legal process was going to go forward. Some shift in attitude seemed to have taken place.

For years, Mississippi had been forced to change its present. Ever so grudgingly it had given up the customs and laws that bound it to the past. But that past itself remained fixed, largely unexamined by a citizenry and officialdom grown sullen from constant reproach by the outside world. The official two-volume state history, published in 1973, devotes twice as many pages to the history of medicine in Mississippi as to the civil rights movement.

In the schools, the situation was no better. The state's education establishment had willfully turned away from a critical look at the recent past, so white Mississippi high school students were sometimes ignorant about their state's true history. My own contemporaries in Mississippi, people born around 1960, often seemed shocked to learn of events that had been on the front pages of national newspapers thirty years before. They were dimly aware, from listening to their parents on the subject, that there had been unpleasantness during the 1960s. But the sheer ugliness of the white backlash eluded them: the thought control exercised by the Citizens' Council, the powerful segregationist organization that dominated political life in the first few years of the decade; the mobs of students at Ole Miss in 1962; the brutal suppression of demonstrations in Greenwood and Jackson in 1963.

School history texts were partly to blame for their ignorance. "A Negro who had been giving trouble in a community might awaken some night to find a ghost-clad figure standing by his bed," is the gentle beginning to a discussion of the Reconstruction Ku Klux Klan in *The Mississippi Story*, a textbook published in 1959. Later texts barely mentioned the civil rights movement. "In time white politicians quit running on the race issue," John K. Bettersworth wrote airily in *Your Mississippi*, the standard book of the 1960s and 1970s. In the 1975 revision, Bettersworth's cursory treatment of civil rights contains virtually no discussion of white violence. It begins with the remarkable conclusion that "gradually Mississippians, black and white, found that they could get along together—as they always had."[4]

In the mid-1970s, a group of professors and students at Tougaloo and Millsaps colleges, two liberal institutions in Jackson, attempted to change this. They published a frank high school history textbook, *Mississippi: Conflict and Change*. Unlike most American school texts, the book pulled no punches: its treatment of Mississippi's brutal heritage of white supremacy and racial oppression remains among the most powerful ever written, and it won prizes and praise from authorities like the psychiatrist and writer Robert Coles.

But few people in Mississippi ever saw it. The state textbook committee rejected the book in 1974. It had found this new textbook deeply offensive, as a subsequent lawsuit by the authors of *Conflict and Change* made clear. "Excessive use of racism as a theme" was one of the committee's complaints; "[would] cause hard feelings between black and white students" was another. One committee member objected to a picture of a slave being whipped, and to a famous photograph of a lynching.[5] For six years, while *Your Mississippi* kept a generation of young Mississippians in the dark, the state fought the authors of *Conflict and Change* in court. Finally, in 1980, a federal judge in Greenville, Mississippi, ordered the textbook committee to put the book on the state-approved list. But not many districts adopted it, and it is now out of print. New books have replaced *Your Mississippi*; they are an improvement, but they are not as good as *Conflict and Change*.

Clearly, facing up squarely to the whole past, not isolated bits and pieces of it, has remained painful for many white Mississippians. An elderly man, a high school history teacher living in his wife's ancestral mansion at the edge of the Delta, worked himself into a quiet fury at dinner one frigid winter night over the too "liberal" *Conflict and Change,* which he and many of his colleagues had refused to use.

In contrast, in Neil McMillen's black history class at the University of Southern Mississippi in Hattiesburg, the anger is visible on the faces of the black students, year after year, when the professor launches into his special field: black life under Jim Crow. The few white students, meanwhile, become quietly withdrawn or loudly defensive. But in general the students have been "hungry" for what he has been teaching, the professor reported.[6]

McMillen's black students may be angry, but they are generally not surprised by the story he tells them. These students are required to read the professor's searing history of Mississippi's Jim Crow era, *Dark Journey.* It is a grim narrative of brutality, lynchings, economic exploitation, and legalized injustice stretching over fifty years, from the 1880s to the 1930s. In an environment where the dissemination of historical fact is haphazard, history is sometimes a shock. So *Dark Journey* was too painful for Pam McElroy, a twenty-one-year-old black undergraduate from Jackson who was one of McMillen's students during the 1992–1993 school year. "I had to put it down," she said, during an informal discussion I had with a group of students from the class one spring afternoon in 1993. The book had caused her to treat white friends "differently," had made her "snap at them."

Pam McElroy's family had never told her the stories of brutality that are the birthright of black Mississippians, but she was an exception. Among McMillen's other black students—there were fourteen in a class of twenty-two—there was a shock of recognition, not of horror, on reading *Dark Journey*. These students were calm.

"When I read in the book, I could hear my father talking," said Jerry Beatty, an amiable twenty-three-year-old from Houston, Mississippi. "It really wasn't shocking to me. I've already heard the stories from my grandmother," said Jackie Ledger, nineteen, from Grenada.

McMillen's disquieting story may have been familiar, but it was most definitely a *story*—"folklore," as one of the black students put it. It chronicled things that had happened in the past, things in many respects unimaginable as conditions of daily living in the 1990s. The students were connected to the story only through the memories of parents and grandparents, and through what they saw as a certain fear and defensiveness among these elders. "Sitting back now in '93, you say, 'Man, how did these people put up with this for so long?'" said Kelsey Rushing, a serious-minded twenty-one-year-old from Carthage, Mississippi.

The discussion that spring afternoon turned to current conditions, inevitably of more pressing concern. There was mention of casual racial slights and condescensions. Some of the students had been called "nigger." A few spoke of the difficulties involved in interracial dating—it could be done, but quietly. A girl from Philadelphia, Mississippi, once heard a white high school teacher make a slighting remark about the hair of black people. Another young woman, who had worked as a part-time ticket clerk at a movie house in McComb, remembered that older whites had thrown their money at her, but that younger ones had treated her "fine." In high school, Jerry Beatty had been pursued by a white girl whose father was an implacable racist, a situation he found paradoxical. Although he had experienced the racism of whites, he insisted, "I still say I like Mississippi the best." And that feeling too was not uncommon.

Three white students listened quietly to these remarks and did not protest any of them. One found it "surprising" that they had not learned more about Jim Crow in high school, and another recalled that only one day during the four years of high school history classes had been spent on the civil rights movement. McMillen's stories had a ring of familiarity to them, as well. These whites, however, were exceptional in the larger student body: their white fellow collegians often expressed astonishment at the idea that they were taking a black history course. "You should see the reactions," twenty-four-year-old Rob McReary said. These ranged from: "'Why are you taking a black history class?'" to "'Why do you need to know [about that]?'"

McCreary's remarks were borne out in a visit with his fraternity brothers at Sigma Chi, at the other end of the University of Southern Mississippi campus. These young men, whites, had never gone near a black history class, nor were they contemplating it. They were perfectly willing to concede, as twenty-two-year-old Ladd Monk put it, that "the way things were done then was wrong, with people killing black people," and that "there were mistakes made," in the words of another twenty-two-year-old, Chris Thomas. But the vagueness of these admissions was an indication that for these young whites, reminders of the precise dimensions of the "mistakes" were, if not exactly unwelcome, at the least uninteresting.

The fraternity boys' disengagement was no real surprise. And that some gnashing of teeth over the integrated present was going on in the sanctity of their parents' living rooms could be taken for granted. What seemed significant was that teeth gnashing no longer guided the public discourse on the past. A whole series of occurrences, official and unofficial, at the end of the 1980s appeared to signal a change in that discourse, and the most significant indicator was the reindictment of Beckwith.

But there had also been an overturning of the old-guard political leadership, the election of a governor who made frequent references to the past, the reaction to *Mississippi Burning,* the penitential twenty-fifth-year commemoration of the murders of the civil rights workers at Philadelphia, a small groundswell to reopen the Sovereignty Commission files (all discussed in later chapters), and the generally favorable reaction to McMillen's new book. Some twenty years before, this reserved, soft-spoken history professor had written a trenchant study of the Citizens' Council, then still a force in Mississippi, and the reaction in the state had been decidedly cool. Now, he felt, there was "quite a bit of pride" in *Dark Journey*: the president of the University of Southern Mississippi, in the 1960s a bastion of reaction in the state, had told the university public relations department to "put on a full court press" for the book, and the newspaper in Hattiesburg had featured him on its front page.[7] Still, the pain and ambiguity in the new attitude was brought home to McMillen by a white lady who told him she could not decide whether to weep for shame at his new book's revelations or cry out in rage against him.

White Mississippians, the insurgent University of Mississippi history professor James Silver had written in 1963 (see chapter 3), were obsessed with the past, but they saw legend rather than history. Indeed, the Mississippians' mythic vision of the past was essential to the maintenance of white supremacy, in Silver's view.[8] Since the mid-1960s, Silver's angry vision, as enunciated in *Mississippi: The Closed Society*, has been a defining one. Within Mississippi, he was the target of threats and scorn for his views. The atmosphere was decidedly uncomfortable when Silver left the state for good in 1965.

In the fall of 1984, a reception was held in the now-retired professor's honor at the old capitol in downtown Jackson. A former segregationist governor, J. P. Coleman, was a featured speaker.[9] What if people in Mississippi were now, at last, seeing history rather than legend? Clearly, this would be a change as significant as the tidal wave of legal and political transformations that had been washing over the state for three decades.

But those changes had been forced by agents of the outside world—the Justice Department, the civil rights lawyers, and the legions of young activists who flooded into the state for over a decade. The deeper change, a mirror of the more obvious changes, had taken place beneath the surface, and it had been in the works for some time. The one-paragraph indictment of Beckwith handed down on a chilly December evening in 1990 did not spring full-grown from the heads of the eighteen bleary-eyed grand jurors, eight of them white. Where had it come from? What, or who, had been its agents?

Grotesquely mocking his interviewers, Beckwith likes to say now, "That nigger sure is dead." It's all a big joke. Why make such a fuss? Beckwith is consigning the dead Evers to the same anonymous mass grave where murdered black Mississippians were dumped for generations: lives without histories, and deaths without consequences.

But in fact, the murder of Medgar Evers was a watershed. When he was killed, white Mississippi, forced to look at itself, was confronted with the ultimate logic of the white supremacist state: political assassination. This logic seemed too much even for official Mississippi. For the first time, some powerful whites went out of their way to condemn a racial killing. The segregationist officials who had most bitterly opposed Evers felt the need to profess shock at the murder. The mayor in Jackson pronounced himself "dreadfully shocked, humiliated, and sick at heart" and canceled a Florida vacation because of it.[10] True, the tide of official race hatred quickly washed over this brief emergence of conscience. Mississippi had not by any means seen the last of racist violence.

But the murder began a long process of internal unraveling in the state that entailed nothing less than the downfall of respectability for the Beckwith worldview. Through two mistrials, nine white men out of twenty-four voted to convict him for killing a black man. Bill Waller, the white prosecutor, was not run out on a rail for trying hard to put Beckwith in jail. And Beckwith himself reached his apogee sitting in the courtroom at Jackson in 1964. A white folk hero at that moment, showered with contributions, goodwill gifts, and letters of support, Beckwith would never have it so good again.

Not coincidentally, Evers's murder set in motion the careers of three men who would be agents of change in the state. They were not the only such agents, but they were among the most important because they had that common starting point: the flashpoint when white Mississippi looked in the mirror. The journeys of Waller (see chapter 5), Medgar's brother Charles (see chapter 6), and Beckwith himself (see chapter 4) through the pivotal years from the mid-1960s to the mid-1970s were defined by that moment.

What happened to them, and the actions they took, can help us understand the deeper change that took place in Mississippi during those years. It is not that these men helped change racial attitudes, although in some measure they did so. In the rural towns,

white parents were still sending their children to segregation academies, and still cursing "niggers" at the country club throughout
this period. Nor could the claim be made that they helped elimi-
nate racism—not Beckwith through his extremism; Waller, his
moderation; or Charles Evers, his toughness. Finding white people
who will say "nigger" unhesitatingly is still easy in all corners of
the state.

No. The real contributions of these men—Waller and Evers
in a positive sense, Beckwith in a negative one—lie elsewhere: they
helped make integration a fact. They made an idea that had seemed
extraordinary in Mississippi—the idea of whites sharing social and
political institutions with blacks as coequals—ordinary. Until this
idea became a part of everyday life, whites could not begin to have
a perspective on what had happened during the long era when
blacks' rights had been suppressed.

Waller was not too keen on the integrationist goals of the civil
rights movement, but Jim Crow disturbed his ideals of justice
and fair play. As a prosecutor, and later as the governor, he bulled
through old restrictions. He came along at a moment when, because of intensive black voter registration, the politics of his convictions were plausible. Charles Evers helped create that moment. He
turned his own murderous fury over his brother's killing into a hybrid political movement, scaring the hell out of whites and signing
up thousands of new voters. A tough, physically imposing man, he
became the undisputed focal point of Mississippi's black leadership.
Paradoxically, the downward spiral of his career was important for
statewide integration because it meant the end of that brief era
when black politicians were regarded as somehow extraordinary
and thus outside the mainstream. Beckwith's marginalization—
finally even his old allies were forced to cluck their tongues over
him—signaled a parallel change.

These men laid the groundwork for a new look at the past.
How true was it that the old wounds remained unhealed? Confir-
mation seemed to lie all around, not least in the memories of the
principals in the Beckwith case themselves.

Beckwith's mistrials and the official closing of the case in 1969
resolved nothing. The old white supremacist was still running
around loose, making crazy and provocative statements. Other wit-

nesses and participants made occasional ritualistic expressions of
homage to Medgar Evers. Mostly, for a quarter century, they had
kept their own counsel.

Waller had returned to private law practice in 1976, with an
office shrewdly positioned on a central corner in downtown Jackson.
It is difficult to miss for anybody coming through the state capital,
and the burly attorney rakes in more than his share of lucrative
small cases for divorce or personal injury. True to his populist roots,
he is a "street-level" lawyer, as one of his colleagues in the Jackson
bar puts it: you don't have to take an elevator in one of the city's
handful of fancy high-rises to see him, which may explain the
steady traffic of casually dressed working people in and out of his
offices.

Waller rarely talked about the case now. He had his own theories—how Beckwith, for instance, had almost certainly not acted
alone, how the witnesses who provided Beckwith's crucial alibi may
have been in on it—but he kept them to himself. He had not been
able to prove these suppositions during the trials, so it seemed best
to let them lie undisturbed and unmentioned.

Evers's old associates in the Jackson civil rights movement remember him with sadness and longing. Two miles from Waller's
office, in the heart of an old black middle-class neighborhood, with
houses neatly spaced along pleasant tree-lined streets, Doris Allison
pulled snapshots of Evers from her yellowing file folders. As the
NAACP chapter president in Jackson in the early 1960s, she knew
him well. Girlishly dressed in a bright purple frock, Allison was
as coltish as friends remember her from thirty years ago. But her
mood darkened when she looked at the old pictures of a beaming,
heavily muscled young man whose face is radiant with optimism.
She idolized him. Years ago, on one of the photographs, Allison had
scribbled: "the greatest."

A few blocks away, in the shadow of giant, rusting cotton-
seed silos, tears welled up in R. L. T. Smith's eyes when he was
asked to remember a man who was "like a son" to him. Evers could
have been his son: Smith, a courageous pioneering black congressional candidate in the early 1960s, was in his nineties when Beckwith was reindicted. (He died in the fall of 1993.) "The finest man
I ever knew," he whispered in the quiet of his dark living room,
illuminated only by a single bulb.

Up in the Delta, in Greenwood, Hardy Lott's sentiments about the hometown boy Beckwith were hardly less paternal. In his eighties now, Lott was defensive, in a quavering sort of way, about his past as the president of the local Citizens' Council chapter and the attorney for Beckwith. (See chapter 3 for details on the formation of the Citizens' Council.) No quotes allowed, no mention that he remained a law partner of one of the Delta's better known lawyers and a former U.S. congressman, Webb Franklin (could be bad for business). Lott grew more assertive as the chat progressed. He maintained his old client's innocence, stoutly, like he did more than a quarter century ago. These thoughts led him into a tirade against the evils that integration has wrought on the Delta: blacks filling the schools, whites fleeing the towns. He ended the conversation feeling vindicated.

But Lott is a dinosaur, a fact he quietly acknowledged in his reticence. Here lies the paradox of contemporary Mississippi: a relatively integrated present, one that would have been unfathomable a generation ago, and a past that has seen no resolution. Only the wounds themselves—the uncontestable facts of Mississippi's turbulent recent history—provided common ground.

At the center of the story is the life and death of Medgar Evers. In his life, he recorded the death agonies of the white supremacist state, and he witnessed the full viciousness of this state. His murder revealed flaws in the edifice. And the memory of the murder was one of the seeds from which grew the changed outlook of latter-day Mississippi.

CHAPTER TWO

MEDGAR EVERS

During the early 1990s, in the front entrance of the Smith-Robertson Museum in downtown Jackson, the photographic portrait of a young man was displayed on an ornate stand—a tribute much like what grieving parents might set up in a funeral home. Blacks of a certain generation are inclined to remember the young man whose picture this is, Medgar Evers, like a long-lost son.

In truth, some self-deception dwells in that memory of Evers. His real place in the consciousness of black Mississippians is revealed more by the location of the picture—the Smith-Robertson Museum—than by its reverent display. The museum, a crumbling old former school building, houses relics of a vanished era, of black Jackson under Jim Crow. Evers, in the unconscious memory of many, is also a relic from that era. He is a martyr-symbol, a man the memory of whose real achievements has become so greatly attenuated, they seem barely to have happened at all. He is piously recalled in some public commemorations of the civil rights era, but in a lifeless, cliché-ridden way. On a stifling summer day in 1992, there was an official ceremony for the unveiling of a bronze statue of Evers in Jackson. The ceremony was strangely off-key: a succession of bland speeches, the "Pomp and Circumstance" march, a dramatic declaiming of William Ernest Henley's "Invictus." It could have been the homecoming tribute to some local boy made good in a country high school. The citizens are "a little vague" as to what Evers actually did, says one of Jackson's leading black politicians, the city councilman Louis Armstrong (see Epilogue). Partly, this reflects Evers's isolation in middle-class black Jackson during his lifetime. Also, it was dangerous to be associated with him, or so many people thought. But partly, too, it reflects something about Evers himself.

In the picture an innocence marks the face of this eternally young man. It is a face that seems to dream of all the possibilities envisaged by the early integration movement. The picture belongs to a distant era. It increases the distance between us and a man who, though his name is frequently invoked in latter-day roll calls of 1960s civil rights martyrs, remains perhaps the least known of all of them. Unlike the Rev. Martin Luther King, Jr., Evers left behind no great body of speeches; the few that have survived are awkward and cliché-ridden.

His martyrdom has colored the remembrances of those who knew him, and he emerges from these recollections a saintlike figure. The public writings he left behind—principally the field reports he sent to NAACP headquarters in New York—are conscientious documents, deliberately restrained and unemotional, hardly revealing of any inner turmoil.

There are no pictures of him at the head of a great, epoch-making march; his image is preserved in a few dozen grainy group shots with other speakers on a podium, meeting NAACP officials at the airport or, sleeves rolled up, taking notes in the field. There are few newsreels of him. One of the better known, a dark and jerky sequence of under thirty seconds in which he urges blacks to boycott stores on Capitol Street, conveys nothing of the heroic qualities imputed to him after his death.

The images of Evers's death in June 1963 are the best known of all: the long, mournful memorial march under a blazing sun in Jackson; the riot that followed; the open casket; the widow's tear-streaked face; the burial at Arlington National Cemetery.

Images like these were to become familiar during the next five years, through the murders of the Kennedys and King. The killing of Evers, the first of the decade's political assassinations, provided a kind of painful initiation into them. For the first time, a civil rights killing had a truly national impact. It was the lead story in the next day's *New York Times*. Hundreds of people demonstrated at the courthouse in Wichita, Kansas, and hundreds more were on the steps of the state capitol in Topeka. Blacks marched through downtown Fresno, California, and church bells tolled in Plymouth, New Hampshire. In Springfield, Illinois, blacks and whites gathered under the statue of Abraham Lincoln. In Atlanta, a crowd gathered mournfully at the train station to sing and pray as the train carrying Evers's body to Washington, D.C., passed through. In the capital, eight hundred people followed the casket from Union Station to the McGuire Funeral Home. "Men bared their heads and women wept openly as the hearse rolled by," the *Washington Post* reported. As the procession made its way to Arlington, hundreds of people, mostly whites, heads bowed solemnly, lined the streets. This civil rights murder soon penetrated popular consciousness, the first to do so. Not long after it occurred, Bob Dylan wrote a mournful, if imprecise, song about it.

Here was a man who had spent his working life peacefully burrowing away against segregation. He was the paid representative in Mississippi for that most unradical of organizations, the NAACP. He had critical words, the kind his bosses wanted to hear, for the brash young people in the Student Non-Violent Coordinating Committee (SNCC), and for the upstart Martin Luther King, Jr.'s Southern Christian Leadership Conference (SCLC). The most important part of his job was investigating and publicizing the indignities, routine and horrific, that Jim Crow inflicted on the black citizens of Mississippi. He did this carefully and methodically. The reporters for the mainstream Southern newspapers trusted Evers not to exaggerate when he called them in the middle of the night with a tip.

The NAACP, in its bureaucratic fashion, gave Evers and his equivalents in other states the imposing title of "field secretary." But much of his time was spent in mundane tasks such as recruiting members, collecting dues, and setting up new chapters.

Unlike other civil rights leaders in the 1960s, Evers had thoroughly American, thoroughly middle-class aspirations. As a college student working the Chicago meatpacking plants during the summer, he knew few greater pleasures than driving out to the Evanston suburbs to gaze covetously at the grand suburban mansions.[1] "He wanted all the things America had to offer, for everybody," his brother, Charles, said many years later.[2]

He saw himself as that most fundamentally American of all beings, a New Man, a champion of technology and of modern modes of living. The separate-but-equal doctrine is "as archaic as the horse and buggy age, as detrimental to democracy as the atheistic ideology of communism," he told a Milwaukee NAACP audience in 1958.

Yet Medgar Evers was murdered for his pains. During his lifetime, if the outside world knew him at all, it was as an unspectacular "quiet integrationist," as the *New York Times* profile of him ten days before his death put it, one who "talks quietly and attends to small details." And so it was his death that made him a hero: an all-American boy (the burial at Arlington symbolized this) who played college football; earned medals in the Normandy invasion and the campaign in northern France; wore conservative suits; had a wife, children, and a mortgage; and went about his work as if it were a business. The nation, fully awakened by mid-June of 1963 to the unfolding drama in the South, found his death un-American and shocking. There were speeches on the floor of Congress, the *New York Times* spoke in an editorial of "revulsion universally felt," and President Kennedy himself sent Evers's widow a message in which he spoke of "the justice of the cause for which your husband gave his life."[3]

Still, the respectable public persona, the one revealed in the *New York Times* profile and to visiting interviewers, gave hardly a clue about one of the dominating aspects of Evers's life: more than any other man in the history of Mississippi, he had exposed himself to white supremacy's most jagged edge. For his one-man NAACP investigations, Evers had literally inspected the mangled bodies of

Mack Charles Parker, lynched in 1959 after being dragged from his cell in southern Mississippi; Emmett Till, beaten, shot, bound to a cotton gin fan with barbed wire, and dumped in the Tallahatchie River in 1955; Edward Duckworth in 1956, shot by a white man who claimed self-defense. "We were able to get exclusive pictures of the body in its gruesome state," he wrote proudly in a monthly report of May 21, 1959, detailing his investigation of the Parker case.[4]

And Evers himself was exposed, more than any other black man ever had been in Mississippi, to the collective wrath of the state's white population. The proof of that would come the night of June 11, 1963, when a lone white man easily found his way to Evers's house in Jackson, lay in wait for him undisturbed, and made an untroubled getaway after shooting him in the back. Evers's attempt at a middle-class existence had made him peculiarly vulnerable. In Jackson, Evers's office address and phone number were listed. Even when he went to buy supplies for that office, he made no attempt to conceal his employer: the sales receipts from Jackson emporia, which he dutifully sent to the headquarters in New York, bear the NAACP name. With a house in the only black subdivision in town, he could be found, unlike the shadowy SNCC workers, who moved from place to place.

Evers had assumed a role never before undertaken by a black Mississippian. By the time of his death, he had become something of a public figure. He was by then known and written about statewide, as a man directly challenging the segregationist edifice. It was one thing for a local leader to take a stand in his home county; that had begun to happen in Mississippi during the 1950s. But Evers was standing all over Mississippi, identified as the "head nigger," as one of the anonymous phone callers to his house put it.[5] For more than six years, from the time he took over the NAACP job at the end of 1954 until March 1961 when nine black Tougaloo College students sat in at the public library in Jackson, Evers *was* the civil rights movement in Mississippi. There were no grassroots organizations, no demonstrators in the streets—there was just Medgar Evers.

As a civil rights leader, he was by definition to be ignored by the news organs of the segregationist state—the daily newspapers in Jackson; the television stations; and the *Citizens' Council,* the monthly newspaper of the militantly segregationist group of the same name. But when his name was invoked, it was with venom. Four years after he took over his job, in November 1958, the *Citizens' Council* mocked Evers on its front page, quoting from a recent *Ebony* magazine profile in which the NAACP man had discussed his youthful dream of a Mississippi Mau-Mau band. "Nuf Said?" was the headline above the short item, and above both was a grotesque cartoon of a spear-carrying African savage. Beckwith's name had appeared in the same publication the previous year, under a letter trumpeting the council's virtues.

Still, it seems probable that until his final month, Evers was an obscure figure to a majority of white Mississippians. Three weeks before he was killed, he gave an unprecedented television speech enumerating the demands of the integrationists (as described in more detail later in this chapter). Of twenty-nine viewers who immediately called to complain, only one seemed to know who Evers was; eight indignantly demanded the impertinent black man's name. In going before the television cameras that night, Evers had entered a new, ultimately fatal zone of notoriety. The shock of one woman who turned on her television set expecting "The Price is Right," and instead saw the black integrationist, is audible: "Is 'The Price is Right' not going to be on?" she asked plaintively. "It'll be joined about seventeen minutes after the hour," the operator answered. "Well, heck, they're going to put that nigger on then, huh?" "Yes, ma'am." For whites, his existence was now irrefutably confirmed. Evers provoked near-hysteria in station WLBT's white viewers. "Will you please get the damn nigger off the air?" an older woman pleaded; menacingly, a man stated: "They better get his black ass off, or I'm going to come up there and take him off. . . . This is in the South; this is below the Mason-Dixon line. You don't have to put these black jungle bunnies on TV."[6]

Throughout his life, Evers had experienced hatred like this. It could easily have turned him toward separatism, could have made him hate white people, yet it did not. His fundamental belief was so old-fashioned that the young revolutionaries in SNCC found him an unremarkable, though worthy, member of the civil rights fraternity: Hollis Watkins, one of the young SNCC firebrands, considered him "just another community person." Evers never lost a kind of frank cheerfulness, and he never despaired of converting whites to his cause. He "always envisioned a genuinely integrated society," remembered John Salter, his close colleague in the civil rights demonstrations that engulfed Jackson in the spring of 1963.[7] "He was a man who'd been through a great deal and in no way was a hater. He was just not a hater."[8]

With Evers, optimism about the future was as intrinsic as in any other successful suburban householder. On June 1, 1963, Evers assured a *New York Times* interviewer that Jackson would one day be a better place to raise children than New York City. The writer Walter Lord had glimpsed this side of Evers the previous January, when Lord saw "a wiry young man of immense energy, a quick smile and the most impressive set of teeth since Theodore Roosevelt. Sitting in his cluttered green office, practically welded to the telephone, he seemed in a million things at once, and delighted to be in them all. He was made of optimism, and he needed it."[9]

Evers's whole life, right up until the moment of his death, played out this uneasy counterpoint. On the one hand, he strove for, and in some degree achieved, an ordinary American existence; on the other, as a black man determined never to avert his eyes from the reality of white supremacy, he could never succeed. It was a contradiction that seems destined to have led to his death.

Medgar Evers was born July 2, 1925, outside the central Mississippi lumber town of Decatur, the son of a hardworking, taciturn sawmill worker named James Evers and his deeply religious wife, Jessie. Today, Decatur looks like any small town in Mississippi, with its drab, somnolent main street of faltering businesses, its railroad tracks running hard by the downtown, and its black section of small cottages and shacks. Evers's childhood in this unremarkable place armed the sensitive boy with the inspiration that was to spur his life's work: Mississippi's way of life must be overturned. But only two things obviously connect Decatur to a man whose early lessons in Jim Crow were gathered here: a narrow blacktop winding through his old neighborhood, now named Medgar Evers Circle; and a phone number on a billboard planted in a weed-filled lot. On this ground once stood the old frame house belonging to James

Evers. The lot was for sale in the early 1990s, and the phone number belonged to Medgar's sister, Elizabeth, who lives in Chicago.

Sixty years ago, when Medgar was growing up, Decatur was a
place of some bustle. It was home to a new junior college and several sawmills, and it was the market center for all of the area's small
farmers and planters. The stores, long since abandoned, did a busy
trade, and construction of a new highway through town kept
people in jobs. Looked at through one lens, Medgar's was almost a
Huck Finn childhood, hardly different from the life led by millions
of other poor children in rural Depression-era America. Deep in the
country, thirty miles from Meridian, the nearest city of any size, life
in a rural town like Decatur allowed black children the free exercise
of pursuits that might have been more circumscribed in an urban
area. For Evers, there were summertime swimming expeditions to
"the deepest hole we could find," as Evers's childhood friend C. B.
Needham remembered it. The two boys would roust the snakes out
before plunging in the water.[10] In summer the fields were rank and
lush, and the hillsides thickly covered with kudzu. There were
hunts for muscadines, the grapes that grow wild in the Mississippi
woods, and furtive efforts with his brother, Charles (two years older
than Medgar), to make blackberry wine.[11] Medgar liked to hunt
possum and squirrel, and go fishing.[12] He boxed and wrestled with
Charles, his close companion during boyhood.

In many ways it was as wholesome a boyhood as can be imagined, kept that way by rigid, but not unloving, parents. Later in
life, his civil rights colleagues admired him for his self-discipline
and spartan ways. Medgar learned these traits young. His deeply
religious mother, Jessie, allowed no alcohol or tobacco in the house,
and meals began with grace. There were family prayers on Sunday,
and trips to revivals three months of the year.[13] The household was
poor—Charles remembers two pairs of shoes every two years, and
hardly ever a change of clothes—[14] but James always made enough
to put food on the table. As in many rural families, the diet was
supplemented from the Evers's cows, pigs, and chickens. Medgar's
task was to milk the cows and bring them in from the pasture at
night, and to slaughter the hogs for bacon.[15]

In many respects, Medgar's early environment was a narrow,
closed-off world. For one thing, his father's world was of necessity

circumscribed. He never learned to read and write. And as a lumber stacker and contractor, he had to deal constantly with the white world and be careful about his pronouncements. Yet James, hardly an Uncle Tom, was known as a man who would not easily tolerate disrespect, whether from whites or blacks. And as the owner of his own house and of a considerable amount of land, he had more independence than most blacks. "The limbs wasn't big enough," the lynching limbs, for big Jim Evers, says Needham.

Still, James never lost his belief in the superiority of whites.[16] Jessie, on the other hand, living mostly in the private, domestic sphere, was under fewer constraints. She was more outspoken about the outside world, and she had ambitions for her children. Unlike many other black parents, she insisted on keeping them in school during cotton-picking season.

The young Medgar emerges from these recollections a saintly figure, yet there is enough unanimity in these memories to give them plausibility. "The saint of our family," Charles calls him, quite unlike his own delinquent and rambunctious self.[17] Medgar performed mundane chores ungrudgingly. He was the one who helped his mother with the laundry she took in from white families, and from the local community college. He would see that the water was hot, and he would transfer the hot water to the pot. He helped his sisters clean house.[18] When Charles cooked up a scheme to steal pecans from a white woman the two boys were ostensibly helping, Medgar was uneasy.[19]

"There was always a little something different about Medgar." That's how a high school friend, Y. Z. Walker, remembers the quiet boy, the most studious among all his fellows. Looking back fifty years, the young Medgar Evers seems a natural leader to some of his old schoolmates. The other schoolboys would "fool around, get us a can of beer." Not Medgar. "We'd get us a little toddy, homebrew," remembers Walker. "He would just chastise us for it." Swearing and cussing—again, Medgar took no part. Boys would get into a fight, and Medgar would approach them and try to settle the dispute. Sometimes, his older sister Liz would catch him whittling a stick and staring far off into the distance, lost in thought. Their mother called him her "odd" child because when he was younger, he liked to play by himself.[20]

33

It's almost the portrait of a goody-two-shoes, a priss, but for the admissions that Medgar liked to shoot pool and impress girls on the dance floor. Still, his old friends swear that the teenage Medgar, with his calm, quiet air of authority, was a figure of respect among his peers. The young Medgar was more studious; but, more importantly, he had an unusually deep appreciation of the humiliations that white supremacy inflicted on blacks, and an unusually fierce desire to do something about it.

If Evers's childhood was full of the normal things of an American country boyhood, it was also an education in hatred, violence, and discrimination. On Saturday evenings, gangs of whites would come into downtown Decatur and drive blacks off the streets. At Christmas, Jessie would not let her children go downtown because white children threw firecrackers at blacks.[21] A handful of lynchings punctuated Medgar's childhood, and they deeply impressed the young boy. One victim, a friend of his father's named William Tingle, was tied to a wagon, dragged through the streets of Decatur, and hung from a tree in a nearby field. For months, his blood-stained clothes lay in the field, and Charles and Medgar would pass them every day. James himself narrowly escaped a mob of angry whites after he ran into a white woman's car. Only the intervention of the benevolent white sheriff saved him.[22] Once, the elder Evers faced down a white storeowner in Decatur who had accused him of not paying his bill, and picked up the man while the two frightened and awestruck young boys, Medgar and Charles, looked on.[23] "The rope was all around" says Needham, the childhood friend.

For many of Medgar's contemporaries the lessons may have been obvious, but they went largely unacknowledged. To get along, blacks had to accept the looming, ever-present specter of violence or at least humiliation. And acceptance was the route followed by most blacks in Decatur. Y. Z. Walker, for instance, admits that things that bothered Medgar did not upset him much.

Why was Medgar different? It had to do with a special quality, one that truly marked him from his contemporaries, and even members of his own family. He had a capacity for sympathizing with the underdog, the one who was oppressed, a natural instinct to help people who were in trouble. For his brother Charles, Medgar was "more sympathetic" than the average being. "He'd sit here for two hours saying he didn't mean no harm by not opening the door for you." In his own little world, this meant helping out other students who were struggling with their lessons. He would even slip a student help during a test, if he could.[24]

But in the larger world of Jim Crow Mississippi, Medgar Evers could not put out of his mind—siblings and old friends remember him mentioning it repeatedly—that white children rode to school in buses while they had to walk twelve miles each way and get splashed with mud when the bus passed on a rainy day. Sometimes, the white children would spit on Medgar and his brother, and throw rocks at them. In winter, the schoolroom was cold, and the children would have to stand around the wood-burning stove to dry off. And it bothered Medgar that, to get a hamburger at John Henry Robert's stand in downtown Newton, he had to go around to the alley in the back.

Of course, it was not as though the young Medgar Evers went around all day thinking about the evils of segregation. He had the normal American material aspirations. He would see cars or houses in magazines, draw them, take the drawings to school, and tell his classmates: "Well, me and my wife are gonna own a car just like that." He'd tell them: "You've got to always plan for it."[25]

If anything, these desires made him even more acutely conscious of his own people's poverty and oppression. His father, one generation removed from slavery, counseled his boys to be patient, hang back, and accept what seemed to be the fixed realities. It was impossible for Charles and Medgar to go along. Their frustrations led them into acts that were part boyish pranks, part low-intensity gestures of defiance against the white world. Charles and Medgar took revenge on the daily insult of the speeding white school bus: armed with rocks, they would wait for it on opposite sides of the road, and when it passed, would hurl the rocks in unison. Other times, infuriated by the roving white junk merchants who came into black neighborhoods to con gullible housewives into their wares, the two boys would sabotage the merchants' trucks. By the time Medgar was in his late teens, anger and resentment at whites was turning into hatred. He and Charles had formed a half-serious pact: they would go into the army, and there they would learn how to kill white people.[26]

The lessons Medgar learned in the U.S. Army turned out to be quite different from those he and Charles sought. At seventeen, Medgar quit school to sign on in a segregated unit in the Transportation Corps in England and, after the Normandy invasion, on the Continent. The officers were white and many were racists; and the worst jobs, such as cleaning latrines, were reserved for blacks. But mostly, the war experience taught Medgar that integration was not simply an abstraction. He served under a sympathetic white lieutenant who recognized his intelligence, he dated a French girl,[27] and he found himself treated by white Europeans like he had never been treated by white people before. "They treated him just like he was one of the people," his sister, Liz Evers Jordan, says. "Not black or white."

His encounter with Nazism also provided him a kind of defining metaphor for the white supremacist regime he was to do battle with later. The Nazi image was to recur frequently in his speeches and reports. When he returned home from the war, "he was altogether different," his sister remembers. More than ever, his father's admonitions to stay out of trouble chafed. In the army he had engaged in that most taboo-breaking of all activities—going out with a white girl. Now, back in Decatur, he could not even sit in the restaurant downtown. "Something's going to need to be done," he would say to his sister. In the fall of 1946, when Medgar was twenty-one, he made a push at white supremacy's tenderest spot. With Charles and three buddies, including his childhood friend C. B. Needham, he set out from the family house for the county courthouse to vote. This was not at all like the more typical black voting attempts of that era—a frightened middle-aged school-teacher or minister, say, meekly exercising the voting privilege. Here were five young black men with change on their minds, and everybody knew it.

By the time they reached the old courthouse, now demolished, angry whites had blocked all four of the entrances.[28] Eventually, they made their way into the clerk's office, and as they did, armed white men came up behind them.[29] Charles wanted to push on through, but Medgar said, "No, Charley, don't try. It ain't worth it."

That early challenge to the system was unusual. For much of the next decade Medgar would follow a more conventional path.

He finished high school at a state-supported laboratory school for blacks that was attached to Alcorn A&M College, in an isolated spot near the Mississippi River above Natchez.[30] In 1948, Medgar entered Alcorn to major in business administration. He was a campus leader, "studious and disciplined," Charles remembered, a member of the debate team, the college choir, and the football and track teams. For two years he served as the editor of the campus newspaper, and in 1951 he edited the yearbook. He even made it into *Who's Who in American Colleges.*[31] In the summers he and Charles would drive in a broken-down car to Chicago and endure the humiliations of Jim Crow bathrooms on the way. Once there, the brothers earned money by working the meatpacking plants and construction jobs.[32]

By the time Medgar was ready to graduate, everything pointed to a swift departure from Mississippi. That was the time-honored way, especially for blacks who had had the unusual good fortune of getting a college education. But to the horror of his young wife Myrlie, whose fragile sense of middle-class status was threatened by the poverty and degradation all around her, Medgar decided to stay. (With his serious, refined air, Medgar had stood out from the crowd when the prim freshwoman first spotted him at Alcorn.[33]) In later years he would tell interviewers of his visceral attachment to the very soil of Mississippi: "There's land here, where a man can raise cattle, and I'm going to do that someday. There are lakes where a man can sink a hook and fight bass."[34]

It was more than that: he had a vision for transforming the state. The next two years of his life provided Medgar Evers with ample proof, if he needed any more, that this was an urgent necessity. He took a coveted job with the Magnolia Mutual life insurance company—coveted because it was one of the few black-owned companies in Mississippi, and it offered black college graduates a rare avenue into business.

The company was headquartered in Mound Bayou, an all-black town in the heart of the Mississippi Delta, the poorest region in the nation. As isolated as a tiny village in the Delta could be, Mound Bayou today seems barely to breathe, a town populated at noonday by unemployed men hanging out on the main street. Its federally funded city hall building, hung with portraits of civil rights leaders, is a sad counterpoint to the town's moribund state.

Municipal finances hover constantly on the verge of bankruptcy. Even for the Delta (which remains the poorest area in the United States), this is a drowsy spot.

But things were different in Medgar Evers's day. Founded in 1887 by ex-slaves, in its earliest years, the black-run town was an agricultural settlement of some prosperity, the "Jewel of the Delta," in the phrase of the first settlers. This symbol of independence and pride experienced a sharp downturn with the decline in cotton prices around 1920.[35] But echoes of the old, proud feeling survived into the 1950s; the town's elite were anchored in a row of substantial turn-of-the-century brick homes, incongruously grand in this bleak setting.

It was here that Medgar Evers settled with his new wife, and it was from here that he roamed the Delta selling life insurance policies. She chafed under the primitiveness of her new surroundings. But for her husband, his two years in Mound Bayou proved to be one of the formative periods of his life. Evers was deeply disturbed by what he saw. The degradation of blacks in the Delta, of sharecroppers living in conditions of terrible squalor and misery, was on a different scale from what he was used to.

To the junior salesman riding around in the car with him, Evers would talk passionately about the new order which must come.[36] At home, his anger over what he had seen during his rounds boiled over. He dreamed of secretly organizing a local band of vigilantes to defend black rights, a Mississippi Mau-Mau modeled on that of Jomo Kenyatta, the Kenyan political leader, whom he greatly admired.[37]

Evers's decision to join Magnolia Mutual proved to be a fateful step not just because of the terrible conditions it exposed him to but because the man who had helped recruit him to the company was Aaron Henry, the company's secretary. Henry was a stolid, tenacious man, a druggist who was part of the Delta's tiny black middle class. When Evers first met him in the early 1950s, Henry had been a member of the NAACP for years. (Into the early 1990s, he remained the state president of the NAACP, in spite of younger members' grumblings.) Under him and the company's founder, the pioneering T. R. M. Howard, the line between promoting the interests of Mississippi's major black-owned company and doing civil rights work was thin.[38]

Spurred on by what he saw all around him, Evers began selling NAACP memberships among his insurance customers. He was a passionate but clear-thinking speaker, as persuasive a salesman of insurance and civil rights as anybody could remember. "He was very serious in his delivery," remembers a junior colleague in Magnolia Mutual, Thomas Moore. "He wasn't a radical type man. He was a man you knew was serious." Quietly but firmly, he persuaded people of the urgency of the NAACP cause. "He was actually a good salesman for the cause," says Moore. "This is how I viewed him, as a salesman, because he could talk to a group of people and get them to do something." It was a tough sell. In Mississippi, getting people to do anything for the NAACP was exceedingly difficult. Black teachers, the prime target of Evers's contribution drives, were uncomfortable with the very mention of the organization. They would only give money if their names were kept strictly confidential.

The national office of the NAACP considered Mississippi a lost cause. In the state that accounted for nearly 13 percent of the country's 3,786 lynchings between 1889 and 1945, the NAACP was always on the verge of extinction.[39]

This was particularly telling, because the organization's historic cautiousness had allowed it to maintain at least some open presence in the other Southern states. Several factors explained this cautiousness. The NAACP was operated for, and by, America's tiny black middle class. Throughout the 1930s and 1940s, it had pursued such unrevolutionary goals as antilynching legislation and abolition of the poll tax. The style of Roy Wilkins, the NAACP's executive secretary during the time Evers worked for the organization, was thoroughly unrevolutionary. Raised by an uncle in St. Paul, Minnesota, who had achieved middle-class status as a railroad butler, Wilkins worked as a journalist before joining the NAACP in 1931.[40] His autobiography, published the year after his death in 1981, reveals something of the same twin preoccupations that dominated Evers's life: the pursuit not only of equality for his race but also comfortable status for himself. When the thirty-year-old Wilkins was being considered for the NAACP job he so keenly wanted, he cautiously reined in his eagerness and wrote a letter back to the organization of scarcely believable reserve. Although consumed by the struggle for equal rights, he was stymied by a

salary offer lower than he had expected.[41] "Anything overeager, I
cautioned myself, might spoil my chances," he wrote in his autobiography. Wilkins's whole life, as it comes to us through his book,
was made up of this duality: the easy acceptance of bourgeois accou-
trements—a new Pontiac, a calfskin toilet case, a tuxedo—and at
the same time passionate devotion to the black cause.

There was another NAACP tradition: the organization's field
secretary and, later, executive secretary, Walter White, had bravely
conducted investigations of Southern lynchings in the darkest years
of the 1920s and 1930s. But the NAACP's natural terrain was the
courts; its respectable leadership looked and felt at home at the bar.
In 1943, Thurgood Marshall had won for the NAACP what was
probably the greatest civil rights victory of the first half of the
century—the *Smith v. Allwright* case, which outlawed all-white
Southern primary elections. By the mid-1940s, the NAACP was an
accepted part of the national political landscape, recognized as the
premier advocate for black advancement.

Not in Mississippi. There, it had the status of an outlaw organization. Under constant pressure because of economic and
physical threats against members, the out-migration of bolder
blacks, and the pervasive poverty of black Mississippians (even the
one-dollar annual membership fee was a strain), the NAACP's few
branches in the state found it impossible to remain active continuously. By 1940 there were only five branches and 377 members,
fewer than in any other Southern state. Since receiving NAACP
material in the mail was dangerous, the New York office sent it in
unmarked envelopes. "Even in the larger cities, the NAACP operated until well after World War II in an atmosphere of fear and
secrecy," Neil McMillen writes in *Dark Journey*, his study of black
Mississippians under Jim Crow.[42] After the war, there was steady
but very slow growth. By 1953 the state organization was still only
eight years old; there were twenty-one branches and 1,600 members.[43] In Mississippi, the organization's few leaders were all volunteers, in contrast to other parts of the South where there were a
few paid staff members.[44]

Although marginal, the NAACP was the only organized out-
let for civil rights work in Mississippi, and Evers naturally gravitated toward it. In the summer of 1953 he drove with Thomas

Moore around the Delta's dusty roads, photographing conditions in the region's woeful black schools. It was just before *Brown v. Board of Education,* and southern officials were increasingly sensitive about the separate-but-equal doctrine. Sometime that summer, one of Evers's first encounters with white officialdom took place. Howard, Moore, Evers, and another man from the company journeyed down Highway 61 to Rosedale to meet one of the most powerful men in Mississippi, Walter Sillers, Jr. Since 1944, Sillers had been the speaker of the Mississippi House of Representatives, and his word was law around the legislature. (For more on Sillers see chapter 5.)

He was the owner of a big Delta plantation, a Dixiecrat,[45] and a cotton man, and he certainly did not think too much of treating blacks as equals. During the entire meeting, Sillers stood at the window of his office in the old downtown brick Sillers Building, a block or two from the Mississippi River levee. He kept his back to the group, never once turning around, and never establishing eye contact with anyone.[46] In the end, he made lordly promises of new buildings, and the next year some simple block schoolhouses were built. But the deliberate humiliation of the episode left Evers and the others commenting bitterly on the treatment they had received. It was a lesson for the future.

Mississippi seemed hopeless as a candidate for transformation. But as a place where the extremism of segregation was always on display, the state held enormous propaganda potential. By the spring of 1954 another, more immediate reason had come up for hiring a permanent staff member in Mississippi: the Supreme Court's *Brown v. Board of Education* decision that May outlawing school segregation. There would have to be people on the ground in the most recalcitrant places—the Southern states—to begin the long slow fight to make the decision real. In the wake of the *Brown* decision, NAACP counsel Thurgood Marshall recommended that paid staff now be added in Florida, North Carolina, Georgia, Texas, and the toughest place of all, Mississippi.[47] Here would be someone to begin the fight in the schools, to call attention to brutalities, to sign up new members. As it happened, the second of those tasks turned out to be at least as important as the other two.

Mississippi would require someone of unusual toughness and

dedication. Evers looked as though he might be the right man. He had already proved his mettle through his recruiting efforts. And at the end of 1953, he had deeply impressed a local NAACP meeting in Mound Bayou by announcing, to the "complete devastation" of his fearful young wife Myrlie, that he would apply to the University of Mississippi law school, the first black to attempt to enter the university. Predictably, after nine months of evasions by the state, his application was rejected on a technicality. But not before the application itself had made headlines in the Jackson *Daily News* in January of 1954.[48] When talk of filling the new position—a field secretary, in the NAACP's bureaucratic jargon—began to grow in the fall of 1954, Henry and others strongly backed the young Evers, who was enthusiastic.

Gloster Current, the NAACP man in charge of local branches, wrote to Executive Secretary Roy Wilkins on November 19, 1954, in the stilted manner favored by the organization:"The applicant is not only qualified, but courageous and impressive." He was hired five days later, told to open an office in Jackson, and promised a starting salary of $4,500 a year. The governor of Mississippi, Hugh White, and the mayor of Jackson, Allen Thompson, were invited to the office opening in the recently constructed Masonic Temple building on Lynch Street in the heart of black Jackson. They did not come. There is something touching about the ingenuousness of this overture to white officialdom; the NAACP in Mississippi, as always, just wanted to be part of the established framework.

At the end of 1955, the thirty-year-old Evers sat in his office in the dun-colored brick building on Lynch Street and looked back on his first year in the job. He had spent it much as he would the last seven of his life, fully occupied in two principal duties: investigating racial brutalities and helping the NAACP publicize them, and trying to sign up new members for the organization. For headquarters in New York, he summed up, with painful naïveté, his year's efforts:

Little did I realize the far reaching affect [*sic*] the NAACP would have on the lives of thousands of Mississippi Negroes in the year 1955. The influence has been tremendous, the good cannot be worded. As each month passed, not into obscurity but into history, Negroes in Mississippi and America gasped with utter amazement at the almost unsurmountable accomplishments of the organization.[49]

Over the next seven years, he sent hundreds of other pages from the sparsely furnished two-room office in Jackson. In stilted, sometimes ungrammatical language his voice comes to us from a very dark place. His life as an NAACP man was a continuum of pressure, discouragement, resistance, and hostility. And yet the most remarkable aspect of this brief career is that Evers clung to the naïve optimism of his first year's report, in spite of the brutality he witnessed. The naïveté moderated somewhat in later years, but not much. Cliff Sessions, in 1958 a young United Press (UP) reporter in Jackson, remembers Evers's shocked tone in retelling the tale of his recent beating at the hands of white thugs on a Trailways bus: it was a tone of "Gee whiz, can you believe it?"

In the early fall of 1957, Evers's name appeared for the first time in the *New York Times,* in two tiny UP items buried in the depths of the newspaper. The second of these stories was a brief report on the Mississippi NAACP's annual meeting on November 8. "Total racial integration will be accomplished in Mississippi by 1963," the story quoted Evers as saying. But that burst of scarcely credible optimism was quickly tempered by more modest claims. "Mr. Evers said the Mississippi branch might not seem to be making much progress 'when you compare this state to some of the others.' But, he said, 'we are getting our feet on the ground, collecting information and making other preparations.'" The dichotomy recorded in this brief dispatch—open-hearted optimism, on the one hand, and inevitable realization of a tough road ahead, on the other—summarized Evers's entire career.

The reports Evers sent back to New York constantly echo this opposition. They are the best surviving record of the eight and a half years he spent as the Mississippi field secretary of the NAACP. A record of the enormous odds Evers was facing, these documents show first that, surrounded by blacks' fears of being associated in any way with this incautious advocate of civil rights, Evers was thoroughly isolated. Second, they reveal that all the while, he was in considerable personal danger. He was harassed and vilified at every level, from the common citizen to the police officer to the legislative committee. A reasonable man assessing these odds would conclude that his chances for succeeding were not good.

But the written record of Evers's NAACP career reveals a third important aspect, something else besides the bad odds: he would not be cowed. It reveals a man dedicated to his organization, his job, and the larger cause he served. The papers bespeak a man who did his job—particularly the work of finding and interviewing witnesses, and recording evidence—meticulously, even when this seemed futile.

It was not his treatment by racist whites that most severely isolated Evers. Rather, it was the black people's fear, born of the retributive power of white supremacy. In its death agonies, this supremacist ideology was entering its most violent phase.

Evers was required to see these final contortions up close for his new job. He was obliged to spend much of his life on the road, pulling into the small, bleak towns where the final dramas of the white supremacist state were being played out. In Money, Mississippi, in 1955, he investigated the murder of the fourteen-year-old Chicago boy Emmett Till, who had been shot and beaten for whistling at a white woman. It was the first Mississippi lynching to receive the full glare of national publicity, and Evers proudly reported that he had come up with two new witnesses. He went to Belzoni that same year to look into the murder of the local NAACP man, the Reverend George Lee, who had struggled to put ninety-two blacks on the voting rolls; two shotgun blasts in the face while he drove on a downtown street had been Lee's punishment. No arrest was ever made; the local sheriff said the lead pellets in Lee's mouth and face were dental fillings.[50] Later that year Evers went to Brookhaven, where Lamar Smith, a prosperous farmer, had been killed on the lawn of the county courthouse for encouraging blacks to vote.

In the first year alone, Evers traveled over thirteen thousand miles on the narrow two-lane highways, sometimes by himself, sometimes with his NAACP friend Sam Bailey for company. As unobtrusively as possible, they would creep into these towns, often dressed raggedly in old overalls or in army fatigues.

Evers depended on local blacks to talk to him. When they did not, he had no report. "There were persons on the scene who would not talk to us at all," Evers wrote in a report of January 27, 1956, on the death of Edward Duckworth, a black man shot five times in "self-defense." (The phrase is in quotation marks in Evers's report.) Fear shut mouths. "It was with extreme difficulty that this information was secured. . . . Much of this information is recorded from memory as the persons would cease talking when worker [sic] began writing," he reported earlier that year, after visiting Yazoo City to report on blacks who had been fired, forced to leave town, or otherwise harassed for signing a school integration petition. "The Negroes are so fearful they distrust each other and everyone else," Evers noted.[51] The NAACP man's notepad intimidated people. He developed a technique of hurrying back to his car after interviewing someone, to scribble down what he had heard.

And fear forced people out of the NAACP. It atomized the community, making any kind of association a frightening undertaking. Whites saw any grouping of blacks as a threat.

"The Negroes will not come together, and our former president has not cooperated at all," Evers wrote despairingly from the Delta town of Yazoo City in 1956. Blacks there had filed a petition to desegregate the schools, as they had in a number of other Mississippi towns, in the wake of the Supreme Court's desegregation decision in 1955. The Citizens' Council responded with a well-honed campaign of intimidation and published in the local newspaper the names of parents who had signed the petition. The people working for whites almost immediately lost their jobs, and soon all but two of the petition signers had backed down.[52]

The Citizens' Council had intimidated the local NAACP president to such a degree that the group could no longer hold meetings in Yazoo City. "It appears that they have gotten next to him and we just can't get any results, not even a call [sic] meeting. One thing, the people are afraid. I would say it is worse than being behind the Iron Curtain," reported Evers.

Even in Jackson, NAACP members faced intimidation. In

April 1956 police surrounded one routine meeting at the Masonic Temple building on Lynch Street in a deliberate attempt to scare the people inside, as Evers wrote back to New York. But there was always a hardy band in Mississippi's capital that would stick by the NAACP no matter what. This was certainly not true in the small towns, where in the mid- and late 1950s members dropped away rapidly. This unfortunate fact had to be communicated with great delicacy to bosses anxious about contributions. "We are still faced, especially in the smaller areas, with a great degree of intimidation tactics which ultimately make our smaller branches somewhat in-operative," Evers wrote back in 1957.

The fear that surrounded Evers meant isolation for him, and many blacks of his class viewed him as a dangerous man to know or be seen around—a sadly ironic circumstance for a man who wanted to fit in. "In his neighborhood lived many teachers," John Salter recalled three years after Evers's death. "Most would scarcely talk to him . . . scared to death to even see him. Many of the clergy-men in Jackson were afraid to exchange words with him." [53] Evers's old companion Sam Bailey is still bitter about the failure of much of Jackson's black bourgeoisie to support Evers. "The people that benefited, didn't do nothing," he says.

At one black-owned dance hall, Evers jumped on the stage during intermissions to encourage people to register to vote and join the NAACP. The elegantly dressed patrons were not amused. "I could see people squirm in their seats, sort of turn their noses up," Myrlie remembered years later. "You could hear little boos, 'Come on and sit down.'" [54]

Year by year, his notoriety grew; he was becoming a public man. When Evers criticized a new high school building for blacks as an "overcrowded and ill-equipped . . . barn," the local grand jury launched an investigation of him. "His cries attain no higher stat-ure than those of the most irresponsible child," the grand jury report concluded. The story appeared on the front page of the *Citi-zens' Council* newspaper, the surest forum for whipping up hate among the hard core. [55] Sitting in a corridor outside a Jackson grand jury room where testimony was being heard on police brutality in 1959, the police recognized him. Evers was there only as an observer; but the police were becoming increasingly expert in harassment techniques, and they served him a summons to testify immediately. Once, his new Oldsmobile broke down in northern Mississippi, in a town whose only garage was owned by the president of the local Citizens' Council. The man recognized white Mississippi's public enemy number one. Evers knew he was in trouble, yet he had no choice but to stay and get his car fixed. Half the village paraded by to glimpse the marooned agitator, though he was not attacked. Still, that was one of the few times Evers conceded fear, Salter remembered.

Although he downplayed the constant personal danger, he often would dutifully report back to New York that it had been too dangerous to stay overnight in the small towns where he had been conducting his investigation, as in January 1957 in the Delta town of Ruleville. "Because of the intensity of the search and the aroused feeling, the Field Secretary did not stay in town Wednesday night, however, Thursday morning, dressed in Army fatigues and boots, I was able to mill among a number of the Negro citizens without being too noticeably observed," Evers wrote from Ruleville.

Instead of staying overnight, he would drive the dark highways back to Jackson, foot pressed to the accelerator, sometimes trailed by cars. Often, Bailey would drive on the way back so Evers could sleep. "Don't let anybody pass us," Evers would tell his friend.[56] He was beaten up when he tried to integrate a Trailways bus as he was returning home from Meridian in 1958. In 1960 he was menaced by a white mob in Winona while trying to get a young NAACP man out of jail. When he finally succeded, the sheriff told him brusquely to make himself scarce. "Before we could get out of town three cars made it their business to check our every move, and as we proceeded to the city limits we were followed quite some distance by these cars," he reported. And in 1961 Evers was beaten by policemen outside a court hearing for the so-called Tougaloo Nine, the first civil rights demonstrators in Mississippi.

In Jackson, police watched his house constantly. Every car that passed by was a potential menace, every stranger on the street outside his house a potential spy. These were dangers that existed in reality as much as in his mind, though sometimes his fears got the better of him. Going home for lunch one day, he spotted two telephone workmen on a pole next to his house. He assumed they were installing bugging equipment, and he yelled something harsh at them. Later he was able to laugh about his paranoia in retelling this episode to Cliff Sessions, the United Press reporter.

During periods of high tension, the threats multiplied. One Saturday night in 1962 when the entire state was seething with the Ole Miss integration crisis, Salter and his wife visited the Evers household. A police dog was barking in the front yard. Salter knocked on the front door, and an unseen hand opened it a crack. Salter saw a gun. Warily, he called out his own name. Then, with relief, he heard Medgar's voice apologizing, and the Salters entered. In the room, furniture was piled up in front of all the windows, and there were a half dozen guns in the kitchen and the living room.[57] During the height of the civil rights demonstrations in Jackson in the spring of 1963, a firebomb was tossed into the Evers carport. Evers taught his children to drop to the floor at the sound of passing cars.

Still, nobody remembers him complaining or making plans to leave. "I may be going to heaven or hell," he told the *New York Times* interviewer shortly after the firebombing. "But I'll be going from Jackson." Offered a transfer to California, he declined.[58] His own account of the bus incident in 1958 is stoically precise: "[The assailant] struck me on the left side of my face or head, with such severity that it was instantly numb. His attempt to further molest me ceased after the bus driver told him he would have to get off the bus. My only action was an attempt to ward off the blows." That is all Medgar said about an incident that provoked his mercurial brother to jump in a car, shotgun in the back seat, and speed down the highway to Meridian to find Medgar's assailants. "Which one of you sons of bitches hit my brother?" Charles says he shouted on arriving at the bus station. "I'll blow your fucking brains out." Medgar "had a fit about it" when he found out about this later, Charles recalled.

For all his earnestness and sincerity, Evers was hardly a good advertisement for the NAACP's cause. The intimidation meted out to him inevitably reverberated in black communities around the state. He was working at cross-purposes. On the one hand, his job was to sell local memberships; on the other, it was to serve the NAACP's national cause by investigating racial atrocities in Mississippi and publicizing them. Before Evers's advent, scores of such incidents had left no more lasting trace than a few sarcastic para-graphs in the local newspaper, or the isolated story in a northern newspaper, at most. To make sure the world knew of such inci-dents, Evers would call the reporters—Sessions, with whom he had established an early rapport, was his favorite—at any hour with the details. But the more these episodes were broadcast, the more frightened Mississippi blacks became.

In fact, the first years of his tenure coincided with a dramatic drop in the number of black Mississippians in the organization—from 4,639 in 1955 to 1,716 in 1956.[59] His bosses were sympa-thetic, up to a point. "It is imperative that you sit down at once and forward us a complete review of the 1956 activities in the state," Current wrote to him sharply in September of that year.

They never allowed him to forget that he was above all an organization man. When he took the liberty of spending $382.70 to fix up his car in December 1956, after tens of thousands of miles on the road, he was roundly chastized by Wilkins's special assistant, and he even received a nasty letter from Wilkins himself. These reproaches had their effect, prompting occasional obsequious mea culpas from Evers. "The field secretary, having given a considerable amount of his working time to our registration and voting pro-gram, did not contribute the necessary time and know-how to the increase of our membership," he wrote in his 1958 annual report.

He was eager to please. Even the first effective civil rights demonstration in Mississippi history inspired Evers to the hopeful thought that it would prove to be an organizational boon. On March 27, 1961, nine students from all-black Tougaloo College sat down to read at the white Jackson Public Library. The police or-dered them to leave. The students refused and were taken to jail. The next day, the normally quiescent undergraduates at all-black Jackson State College held a mass meeting and tried to march to the city jail.[60] "This act of bravery and concern on the part of these nine young people has seemed to electrify Negroes [sic] desire for Freedom here in Mississippi, which will doubtless be shown in an increase in memberships and funds for 1961," Evers wrote to Wilkins in March.

The reproaches from his bosses were not necessary, given Evers's deep loyalty to them. He identified himself with the people who had hired him almost as much as with the cause itself. This was the product of his isolation in Mississippi as much as of his lack of radicalism. The people at the other end of the telephone line in New York and Atlanta—Current, Wilkins, and the regional secretary, Ruby Hurley—"for many years, particularly in the pre-1960–61 era, were his only links with the outside world," Salter remembered. "These were important people for Medgar Evers . . . so what these people said to Medgar carried an enormous amount of weight."[61]

Memberships and dues were not the only bureaucratic preoccupations at the NAACP headquarters. By the end of the 1950s, as Martin Luther King, Jr.'s ascendancy was beginning, there was also deep concern—"suspicion bordering on paranoia," as one historian called it—about potential inroads from newer, more vital civil rights organizations into what was considered NAACP territory.[62] Evers's comrades-in-arms in the Mississippi civil rights movement remember today what they consider his fundamental sympathy for the bravery of the students in the Student Non-Violent Coordinating Committee (SNCC). But for his bosses, Evers adopted their attitude of hostility to this and other groups.

In January 1958, when King, on behalf of the Southern Christian Leadership Conference, was showing an interest in Jackson, Evers wrote to Hurley in Atlanta: "We have naturally discouraged, 'tactfully,' any such movement here in Jackson." He had harsh words for the young SNCC workers when they undertook their daring 1961 voter registration campaign in McComb. "Much of the fear that has been generated in Walthall and Pike counties is due in the main to the activities of members of the Student Non-Violent Coordinating Committee, who have projected un-necessary publicity," Evers wrote. The result was "violence against themselves and threats of violence and economic reprisals against prospective registered voters."

A week later he compiled a "Special Report On Activities Of Other Civil Rights Organizations," noting with satisfaction that SNCC's efforts to organize on the Tougaloo College campus had not been successful because of the "strong" NAACP chapter there. There was no ambiguity in the attitude of Evers's bosses toward the other organizations: their activities were "going to be a continuing problem," Current wrote in a memo attached to Evers's report.

Still, the NAACP was vulnerable to such inroads. With its

devotion to the slow and cumbersome legal process, it ran the risk of seeming ineffective in the murderous Mississippi context. In the late 1950s, Mississippi seemed so hopeless that the NAACP was even reluctant to go into court against the white supremacist state. Evers complained bitterly to New York about this at the end of 1957: "The influence and persuasion that we have once had in the state have tended to recede because many feel that of all the legal action [*sic*] that have taken place in other states certainly one suit should have been filed here in Mississippi . . . We *must* get off center if we are to maintain our influence here in the state and get more financial support." He urged lawsuits on barriers to voter registration, just as he had urged the NAACP's attorney, Thurgood Marshall, earlier that year to support a challenge to segregated parks and other public facilities in Jackson. His pleas were unavailing. Not until 1962 was a lawsuit filed over Jackson's segregated parks. It was March of 1963 before a lawsuit was filed—by Medgar Evers, for his eight-year-old daughter Rena—against the city's segregated schools.[63] And it would be well into the 1960s before a combination of lawsuits and grassroots organizing put substantial numbers of black Mississippians on the voting rolls.

Evers's organizational loyalty only went so far. His job was his life; and the ideal he fought for was indistinguishable from his job. Any compromise would have been anathema to him. There are hints of this in the angry letter to New York.[64] His work as a whole is imbued with earnest, ingenuous resolve. In the germinal stages of the civil rights movement in Jackson, in the winter and early spring of 1963, the so-called mass meetings were really "tiny affairs," Salter remembered later. Yet Evers always "functioned as though the meetings were the last crucial ones before the revolution broke in Mississippi."[65]

The same spirit is evident in the awkward but moving passages of high-flown idealism in his speeches, and in the meticulous precision of his fieldwork. The NAACP put these qualities on display, as well as the Mississippi story itself, as it began sending Evers around the country to make speeches in the late 1950s—no one else knew it better.

In a 1958 speech before the NAACP's Milwaukee branch, Evers spoke sincerely, with a concrete sense of injustice behind his phrasing. He urgently catalogued the indignities inflicted on Mississippi blacks—*"now, today,"* as Evers put it in one example. And since he had seen the indignities firsthand, a strong visual sense marked his words, as when he described "a two room school, with potbellied stoves, housing some forty-five students to the room, with most of the window panes out," in a place "less than twenty-five miles from Jackson, the state capital of Mississippi." In the passionate peroration, Evers told his audience: "For two and one half years I endangered my life as many other Negro Americans [*sic*], on the far away battlefields, to safeguard America and Democracy, only to return to our native country and state and be denied the basic things for which we fought. . . . I have been told that 'resistance to tyranny is obedience to God,' and for that reason if for no other we shall not cease to press forward, relentlessly, until every vestige of segregation and discrimination in America becomes annihilated." But he always bolstered such rhetoric by presenting facts. For example, his televised speech of May 20, 1963, when he answered the Jackson mayor's bumbling attempt to calm his city down, is a detailed enumeration of all the things blacks did not have: access to downtown movies, lunch counters, libraries, parks, or playgrounds.

Those speeches, and others he gave, are simply extensions of his fieldwork. His field reports reveal someone who doggedly sought the facts, a man of investigative skill who took his job very seriously. Newsmen considered him among the most reliable of civil rights sources.[66] When a black man was killed or beaten, he knew the police would rarely record the facts, so his reports were the only things that stood between most such incidents and oblivion. "Duckworth was shot five times in 'self-defense,'" he wrote in 1956. "But what was very strange to me was the fact that his face showed three or four different scars which could have resulted from a beating though he is alleged to have been just shot to death."

His reasonableness was such that, a week after his death, he was almost missed by the segregationists—those in the establishment, at least. "I wouldn't say we were crazy about him," said Robert Nichols, Jr., the city attorney of Jackson. "But I, for one, certainly didn't hate his guts. He was just another opponent."[67] He had observed the Southern proprieties, habitually going out of his way to show politeness to his antagonists. A few days before his death, during the blazing hot weeks of early June 1963, Evers looked out the window and saw a pair of Jackson policemen watching the door of his Lynch Street office. He asked Ed King, the Tougaloo chaplain, to bring them some Coca-Colas. Sometimes, he used this politeness to subtly undermine the Jim Crow code by playing on Southern habits of courtesy. At demonstrations, he would proffer his hand to the police captain, A. L. Ray, his principal law-enforcement foe. Ray, without thinking, would shake Evers's hand in return.[68]

Even the arch-segregationist Gov. Ross Barnett obliquely acknowledged Evers's skills. In September 1959, Evers wrote Current on what to expect from the new governor. And he reported on what must have been a most extraordinary meeting. A month earlier, at a secret midnight rendezvous on the Mississippi Gulf Coast, candidate Barnett, who would become an enduring symbol of die-hard white supremacy, had tried through an intermediary to recruit for his campaign Evers, who would become the South's first great civil rights martyr.

By then, Evers was hardened from almost five years of direct exposure to the worst of the white supremacist state. Barnett's overtures would only have strengthened the steely resolve that had crept into Evers's words. Barnett's election frightened some blacks and gave others a cynical joy. As for himself, Evers coolly wrote to Current, "I would rather analyze his actions after some three or four months in office."[69]

In the early days, Evers's outrage had been free-flowing, barely containable. "The experience shall be of long memory," he wrote solemnly in December 1955 after returning from the Delta, where he had investigated the wanton gunning down of a gas station attendant, Clinton Melton. He cried after the acquittal of Emmett Till's lynchers in 1955.[70] When Rev. George Lee was killed in Belzoni that year, he brooded furiously around the house, striking the table with his fist.[71] To New York, he did not hesitate to display his own sense of hopelessness. "Honestly, Mr. Wilkins, for Yazoo City there doesn't seem to be very much hope," he wrote in 1956.

Those kinds of phrases would later disappear from his writings. His capacity for outrage did not.

The photographs from those early years show an open, almost naïve face. For those newly making his acquaintance, he hardly seemed equal to the task. That was Doris Allison's view when she first laid eyes on the young Evers at an NAACP meeting at the Masonic Temple in 1955. Wilkins was the star attraction that night, and after his speech the newly hired field secretary for Mississippi was introduced. "Medgar Evers, this young man, got up," remembers Allison, already a veteran NAACP member. "I said God Almighty, I'm ready to leave, right now. I said I'm going to get out of here because I don't want to give Roy Wilkins the satisfaction that he bring this young man. . . . I said what does he think this little boy can do with this system. I said here we go again, here we go." Reluctantly, she stayed to hear the young man. "So, I sweated it out. I reckon what he said was alright. But I was just so thoroughly disgusted."

Allison, the future head of Jackson's NAACP branch, did not stay that way long. In fact, she grew to have a kind of worshipful adoration for the young man. "You couldn't help it. He would do something to you," she remembers.

That feeling is shared by many people who recall Evers. There was a kind, patient air about him, which only seemed to deepen as he exposed himself to more brutality. He broke down in tears in front of hundreds of people at an NAACP banquet in Jackson in the late 1950s as he tried to tell the audience about Clyde Kennard, a young black man whose application to all-white Mississippi Southern College had ended in a trumped-up theft charge, seven years at hard labor in the state penitentiary and, eventually, early death from cancer.[72] In his dealings with the white world, Evers kept such anguish at bay and maintained a mild demeanor.

When the most vile abuse came at him over the telephone, Evers remained calm. 'He was cool on it," Bailey remembers. "I never could understand it. Whatever they said on the telephone or anything, he never act liked he was mad about it. They called him all kind of names on the telephone." Sometimes, there would be death threats. "I remember distinctly one individual calling with a pistol on the other end, and he hit the cylinder, and of course you could hear it was a revolver," Evers told a CBS correspondent in June 1962. "He said: 'This is for you.' And I said, 'Well, whenever my time comes, I'm ready.'"[73]

There was an "angelic quality" about him, remembers John Herbers, the UP bureau chief. "I just always had the feeling I was in the presence of a saint."

The students who were to form the shock troops of the civil rights movement in Mississippi were particularly drawn to him, Evers's skepticism about SNCC notwithstanding. "God, the young people, they would mob him. They just wanted to get close enough to him just to touch him," says Allison.

As students at Jackson State College, Joyce Ladner and her sister Dori would surreptitiously slip down Lynch Street to the NAACP office for chats about civil rights. They had to be quick: Evers was persona non grata on the conservative campus, and contact with him would have brought retribution. Joyce Ladner remembers a quiet, soft-spoken, modest man, someone who "didn't look down on you," who "listened to what you said." Evers played a decisive role in steering her toward the activism of the next few years of her life, which she spent in SNCC. "I can't convey enough the gentleness that I felt when I talked to him," she says." Ed King, the chaplain at Tougaloo College and a leader in the Jackson civil rights movement, remembers a similar patience. As a white student at Millsaps College in the 1950s, he went to see the NAACP man for discussions about the emerging campaign for civil rights. "I can remember how tolerant Medgar had been of my ignorance. He guided me along." Evers was one of the first black men to whom the young white man from Vicksburg had ever talked as an equal.

"He wasn't really an organizer," Salter wrote three years after Evers's death. "He was sort of a lone wolf who traveled lonely and mighty dangerous trails. . . . He was simply and in every sense of the word, a hell of a brave pioneer deep in the wilderness."[74]

Evers was a pioneer in ways that Salter might not have quite realized when he wrote those words. True, Evers served as a witness for racist crimes that otherwise would have gone unrecorded. But his effectiveness at communicating these crimes to the wider world is open to some doubt. His name appeared only twice in the *New York Times* during the 1950s, and then only very occasionally thereafter until the climactic months of 1963.

His greatest accomplishment is one that has left barely a trace: his simple presence, his standing up for the idea of racial justice, in a time and place when it was extremely dangerous to do so. He kept that idea alive in Mississippi, publicly, at a time when no one else did. When other civil rights workers came into the state in 1961, they were not carrying their message into virgin territory.

His moment was fading just as the southern civil rights movement began to develop in earnest. As a lone wolf, Evers bridged the older civil rights tradition with one that was just emerging. On the one hand, he was descended from the brave, solitary NAACP men like Walter White and Howard Kester, who in earlier decades of the century had probed Southern racial atrocities. On the other, he utilized what would prove to be the modern civil rights movement's most effective weapon, publicity. "He was visible in Jackson," Herbers remembers. "He learned how to get attention." So he was exposed in a way that the earlier men, who had gone undercover, were not; and as an isolated civil rights worker, working autonomously for an organization based thousands of miles away, he was out in the open in a way that the later, mass-movement workers of SNCC and the Congress of Racial Equality (CORE) also were not. It was a dangerous spot to be in.

By the early 1960s some Mississippi whites viewed Evers as the "head nigger." But that grotesquely flattering identification was just another example of how isolated and uninformed the populace was. By the time Evers heard that phrase on the other end of the telephone line (receiving it with a reasonableness that astonished his wife) civil rights efforts far more threatening to the Mississippi way of life than Evers's own were under way, most notably SNCC's voter registration drives.[75] True, the ugly phone call came in the midst of James Meredith's 1962 push for admission to the University of Mississippi, and the NAACP Legal Defense Fund supported this effort, as did Evers. But that was an individual's fight—an eccentric one's, at that—with a symbolic meaning, not immediately relevant to the unenfranchised, oppressed black Mississippians. It was this group that SNCC targeted with its mass-based, grassroots organizing efforts and that the middle class–oriented NAACP had largely ignored.

A tiny band of SNCC workers had been in the state since the charismatic Bob Moses had moved into tough southwestern Mississippi to register voters in the summer of 1961. Beating and harassment had not deterred them there, or in Greenwood, in the Delta, where the operation moved the following year. They did not have much success. But the vicious white backlash and its attendant national publicity were critical for the growing civil rights movement. SNCC's bravery was especially important for Jackson, inspiration for the young people who were the shock troops in the demonstrations of the spring of 1963. "You've given us inspiration in Jackson," Evers told a mass meeting at Greenwood's Wesley Chapel church in late March.[76]

In Jackson, in May and June 1963, old and new civil rights inspirations clashed. In the fulfilling moment of his career, Evers himself orchestrated the capital's protests, but this leadership came with personal costs. Evers was pulled painfully in different directions: one way by the clamoring students who looked up to him, and another by hesitant NAACP officials in New York. The recollections of the younger people at the forefront of the demonstrations in those days are clear: as the marching, flag-toting students confronted Jackson's blue-helmeted riot police in the June heat, NAACP officials flew down from New York to apply the "brakes" on the movement their man had helped start.[77]

If the outside media that had descended on Jackson saw Evers as the confident, undisputed spokesman, people inside the movement increasingly saw a troubled, weary man. "I felt sorry for him," says Joyce Ladner, "for what he was enduring, the kind of strait-jacket they were putting him in."

There was a kind of slow, grim crescendo to the end, with the strain of continuous demonstrations and conflicting impulses and orders entirely visible on his haggard face. "He was tired," remembers Bailey. "Everything he was doing looked like it wasn't getting nowhere."

That last month of his life was unlike any other Evers had lived through. Up until then Jackson had been dead, barely on the civil rights map, its small black middle class cowed and complacent. "Lots of fear, lots of apathy," Evers told Salter in the summer of 1962.[78] A months-old boycott of downtown stores, pushed by the impetuous twenty-nine-year-old Salter, was only modestly effective and had been largely ignored by the officials in New York. Imbued with an instinctive allegiance to the growing movement for racial justice, Salter—an Arizonan, an ex-Wobbly, and part American Indian—had a high sense of romance and adventure. Two years before, he had come to the state expecting and half wanting trouble. He taught sociology at Tougaloo and headed a small NAACP youth group in the city, but the hierarchy did not take his efforts very seriously.

Suddenly, after Martin Luther King, Jr.'s triumph in Birmingham and rumors that Jackson might be next on the SCLC agenda, everything changed. The downtown boycott became interesting to New York; Salter, the prime mover, was told by phone April 9 that Wilkins was "extremely interested" in what was happening in Jackson. But decades of caution had made the NAACP incapable of committing itself wholesale to protest in the streets. From then until Evers's assassination, Salter rode a roller coaster of hope and despair, alternately cursing the national NAACP office when it repeatedly backed off plans for demonstrations (as it did May 10, again two weeks later, according to Salter, and finally just before Evers's death) and jubilant when it agreed to move forward, as it did at various points in between.

Evers rode a personal roller coaster. From the reporters who began to descend on the city, and from Salter's memoir, emerge snapshots of him in that last month urging the growing crowd forward into the streets and watching disgustedly as the crowd members are herded into paddy wagons and the makeshift barbed-wire stockade at the Jackson Fairgrounds. And he collaborated on Salter's demand to state officials May 12 for an end to segregation in parks, playgrounds, libraries, and downtown stores and restaurants.[79]

The segregationists' response was a paternalist daydream: "We have some of the best facilities you can find anywhere," the mayor of Jackson, a Citizens' Council enthusiast named Allan Thompson, declaimed in a television speech. "Beautiful, wonderful schools, parks, playgrounds, libraries, and so many, many other things. Next, there are no slums. Have you ever thought about it?"[80] Evers's reply came in an unprecedented appearance on a local television station May 20, secured with the help of the Federal Communications Commission. Never before had a Mississippi black man been allowed this kind of response to the segregationists.

He shot the mayor's fantasy full of holes. For seventeen minutes, to viewers all over the state, Evers gave a summation of his outlook, one rooted in the concrete and the real. Where Martin Luther King, Jr. might have traded in abstractions about racial harmony and justice, Evers drew directly on his experience: the black man, looking about Mayor Thompson's urban idyll, "sees a city," Evers said, "where Negro citizens are refused admittance to the City Auditorium and the Coliseum; his children refused a ticket to a good movie in a downtown theater; his wife and children refused service at a lunch counter in a downtown store where they trade." He was acutely aware a historic turning point had been reached: "Whether Jackson and the state choose change or not, the years of change are upon us. In the racial picture things will never be as they once were."[81]

As a picture of truth, this was more than some Jackson whites could take. As noted earlier in this chapter, several callers to the television station went beyond registering shock at this apparition: they made a point of furiously denying the veracity of Evers's claims. "I'd just like to call in and tell you I think that's very horrible, this nigra on TV with all his lies that seem to be coming in," one man said. "Well, I won't . . . just don't even quote me. But this is the most ignorant display of ignorance I've ever heard in my life," a woman said.[82]

He had touched the most sensitive nerve. What made it all the more dangerous for him was that he did not then retreat. On May 28 he told the crowd at the Pearl Street A.M.E. Church that the day's bloody sit-in at the downtown Woolworth's was only the beginning, and he called for a "massive offensive against segregation."[83] The next day he angrily denounced Jackson's mayor for "talking out of two sides of his mouth and duping people" after the mayor reneged on an agreement to desegregate public facilities. On June 1, he and Roy Wilkins were arrested in a symbolic demon-

stration on Capitol Street. And Evers arrived at his office at seven
o'clock every morning and rushed all over the city to arrange bail
bond for jailed students, attended mass meetings, and met with
reporters.

But he entered this whirlwind with some ambivalence: he was
an NAACP man, and that organization never overcame its fear of
crowd action. In his wife's memoir, he was "neither approving or
disapproving" of the pivotal Woolworth sit-in.[84] A few days before,
he had exploded in anger at Salter's skepticism about the national
NAACP, and he urged caution among black youths who wanted to
demonstrate.[85] His wife remembers that he "had his doubts" about
demonstrations, although she says he was later "won over completely" by the students.[86]

The young people who worked with Evers feel sure about
where his true allegiance lay. "He was a direct action person, in
terms of where his heart was," remembers Steve Rutledge, a white
Tougaloo student who worked with Salter. It was a leaning that
Rutledge and his cohorts thought brought Evers directly into conflict with the conservative officials in New York.

By the middle of June's first week, reporters were beginning
to pull out of Jackson because of the palpable lessening of civil
rights activity. "Press releases and news conferences replaced mass
marches today," a dispatch datelined June 3 began.[87] Local organ-
izers like Salter thought the national office was rolling back the
campaign of demonstrations in Jackson. Just after his own arrest,
Wilkins called for a halt to the demonstrations. He quickly relented
after protests, but to Salter the message was clear.[88] "The feeling
we had was so obvious," remembers Rutledge. "They're not supporting us any more. The national officers came down and laid the
law down, limiting the demonstrations."

There is a strange convergence between the way people remember Evers at the end of his life, and his demise itself. Invariably
in these accounts he is worn out, exhausted, at a breaking point
emotionally and physically. He was even considering a break with
the NAACP, according to Salter and Ed King.

"He had aged ten years in the past two months," Myrlie
wrote. "Tired" is how Salter repeatedly describes the Medgar of the

final week. At home, at the sound of passing cars, he would jump out of bed and grab one of his many rifles in one motion.[89] Police cars followed him constantly. On the last afternoon of his life, Monday, June 11, he telephoned the FBI office in New Orleans and told the agents that three days before, a police car had tried to run him down as he was crossing Franklin Street. He had had to scramble back onto the sidewalk, at which the officers had laughed.[90] A few hours later, shortly before attending that night's meeting, Salter saw Evers standing in the nearly empty auditorium of the Masonic Temple on Lynch Street. "He was very tired and worn, with sharper lines in his face than before, and he seemed quietly sad."

In such remembrances it is as if the living, breathing Evers is being wound down by the people who knew him. An Evers stripped of vigor is an Evers with no further historical role in the present—an ironic fate for someone who saw himself as a man of action above all else. At least in people's memories, the transformation from activist to martyr-symbol had begun even before his death. To be sure, such memories must be, at least in part, a device to give comfort to people who were attached to Evers; these acquaintances are unconsciously making his murder a logical culmination for his life. But the perceived transformation is also a reflection of a sad reality: the end of his usefulness to the civil rights movement had preceded his death.

The evening of Tuesday, June 11, was warm and dry in Jackson. Myrlie was watching President Kennedy's unplanned, breakthrough civil rights speech, engendered in the heat of that day's showdown at the University of Alabama between Gov. George Wallace and the government, demonstrations and beatings in Virginia, and the ongoing crisis in Jackson. "We are confronted primarily with a moral issue," Kennedy had said. "It is as old as the Scriptures and as clear as the American Constitution." The words made Myrlie glad. Medgar, of course, was away at a rally, struggling to prop up the faltering Jackson civil rights campaign. The three Evers children had been allowed to wait up for him; their only chances to see him came late at night. Myrlie, reclining on the bed, drifted off, and the children argued over which program to switch to.[91]

At midnight, Myrlie heard the sound of tires in the driveway. Medgar was home. The car door slammed closed. Then, a much louder sound, so loud in the hot, quiet night that people all over the neighborhood heard it. The children hit the floor, as they had been trained to do.

Myrlie knew what the sound was. She knew what it meant. She rushed to the door and turned on the light. He was lying there, face down. She saw the keys in his hand, and she saw the trail of blood behind him. He had managed to drag himself thirty-nine feet. The sweatshirts he had been carrying, inscribed "Jim Crow Must Go," were scattered all over the driveway. Myrlie screamed, but he did not move. The children were around him, screaming, "Please, Daddy, please get up!"[92] Still he did not move. He had been hit with tremendous force by the bullet from a high-powered gun.

Later, the police would be struck by the large amount of blood on the driveway and the flesh spattered on the car. "It looked like somebody had butchered a hog at that point," Detective John Chamblee observed later. The bullet had struck Evers in the back, exited through his chest, crashed through his living room window, gone through another wall into the kitchen, ricocheted off the refrigerator, shattered a glass coffee pot on the sink, and landed on a cabinet.[93] By the time detectives recovered it, this bullet was badly battered. But of one thing they were certain: it could only have been fired from a .30/06 Enfield rifle.

Up the street Betty Coley had heard a "crunching sound," then the unmistakeable noise of someone running. Kenneth Adcock had heard leaves and branches crackling: someone running, fast.[94]

Evers had been wearing a white shirt, an easy target for the sniper. Neighbors and police lifted the dying man onto a mattress and loaded him into a station wagon. "Sit me up," Evers said. "Turn me loose." Those were his last words.[95]

In the riot that followed Evers's funeral, three days after his murder, four hundred young blacks hurled bricks, bottles, and insults at the Jackson police. "Shoot us, shoot us," the blacks cried.

"No one shot them," a still surprised Hodding Carter wrote a week later. "This was not the Mississippi of five years ago," he continued. "But in the wake of Medgar Evers' death, Jackson and the state of Mississippi are not what they have been in many respects."[96]

Carter was both prescient and right to hedge his assertion. Evers had been up against much more than just a lone racist hiding in a thicket. It became, in fact, unquestioned dogma in the Mississippi civil rights movement that the surrounding society had pulled the trigger of the .30/06 Enfield rifle. "The issue before the court was not the guilt or innocence of Delay [his nickname] Beckwith," Ed King wrote not long after Beckwith's trials in 1964, "but whether Medgar Evers was guilty enough in his agitation to deserve the death sentence which Beckwith, for all white Mississippi, had carried out."[97]

There is no evidence to suggest a conspiracy. But what is certain is that Evers and the other civil rights workers were up against a uniquely formidable force: the structures that made up the white supremacist state.

CHAPTER THREE

THE WHITE SUPREMACIST STATE

T he scene would not have been out of place in some small Latin American dictatorship: it was the fall of 1962, and Mississippi was in a roiling fever over James Meredith's attempt to enter the University of Mississippi, or Ole Miss. Thousands of boisterous, murmuring people lined Capitol Street in downtown Jackson. Mounted precariously on top of a cruising car, a bizarre *tableau vivant* held the restless crowd's attention: a military pup tent, and next to it a skillet. It had instant resonance for the turbulent mob. "Bring your flags, your tents and your skillets," Edwin P. Walker, an insubordinate former U.S. Army major general, had just announced over the radio, in a call to arms for all citizens who wanted to bar the black man from the university. All the while, through a bullhorn in the window of the Citizens' Council office, across the street from the Governor's Mansion, came violent excoriations of

President Kennedy and his men. Here were words of a sort that had not been heard publicly in these parts since the only insurrection ever against the United States government, a hundred years before.

Bob Pritchard, a young lawyer, stepped out of his office at that moment. Pritchard, the law partner of the man who would later prosecute Byron de la Beckwith, had seen a good deal that was odd in recent days. But this was too much. Pritchard and a fellow lawyer surveyed this scene for a moment in amazed silence, and then his friend said, "You know what these people are promoting?"

Pritchard replied: "I think I do. They're promoting a revolution."

"I don't know about you, but I'm going home," his friend said.

"I am too," replied Pritchard. "I fought for this country, and I'm not going to get at cross purposes with it."

Straining to convey the strangeness of that first half-decade of the 1960s in Jackson, people like Pritchard will reach into their storehouse of anecdotes. And then they will stop. "It's almost *indescribable*, to convey what it was like in Mississippi," says Joe Wroten, one of two dissenters who took lonely stands against the segregationists in the state legislature of the early 1960s. "You almost had to be there." There is a point at which the witnesses are frustrated with specific recollection. Language becomes inadequate.

"It was insane," Pritchard concludes. "It was a time of insanity." Pritchard and Wroten stayed on, but others disturbed by what they saw—Cliff Sessions, the UP reporter who had been Medgar Evers's friend, and Neil McMillen, then a graduate student in history (see chapter 1)—decided to have nothing further to do with the state. Today, back again in Mississippi, they speak of a pervasive oppressiveness in those years: it could boil down to something as simple as an ongoing tense standoff with relatives at the dinner table. They had felt compelled to leave. "Mississippi," the writer Willie Morris wrote in the mid-1960s, "may have been the only state in the Union (or certainly one of half-dozen in the South) which had produced a genuine set of exiles, almost in the European sense."[1]

Those who remained to battle the state authorities—the dissident whites, but much more so the crusading blacks like Evers—felt repressed and menaced, for good reasons: the suppression of dissent, the racial ideologues who ran state government, the police force that served racial aims—all were facts of daily life. This dark view seems even more justified now. With the opening in 1989 of some of the theretofore secret files of the State Sovereignty Commission came revelations about the inner workings of the white supremacist state. The remarkable documents provide an unparalleled look into the dirty war that official Mississippi waged to maintain segregation. (See pp. 95–103.)

At the same time, for people looking in from the outside, the place had a kind of lunatic edge. Mississippi's repression appeared too incompetent for the state to qualify in any sort of totalitarian big league. The state's authorities were using a blunderbuss to shoot birdshot at the world, and they were hitting everything from the civil rights workers to what they quaintly termed "beatniks" to FBI men to the president himself. The men who ran Mississippi in those years were buffoons, not to be taken seriously. From the perspective of thirty years later, both this latter view, and the darker one, seem correct.

To contemporary observers inside Mississippi, Nazi Germany was a favored image; even some conservative Mississippians invoked it. In the spring of 1961, as the Citizens' Council was tightening its grip on government and society in the state, the editor of the relatively moderate Jackson *State Times* wrote: "There is a growing belief in Mississippi that 'witch hunting' and 'book burning' procedures should be tolerated. . . . Book burning is as wrong when practiced by our state as when it was practiced by Hitler's Germans." The Citizens' Council had recently declared that the American Red Cross, the FBI, the Elks, the Jewish War Veterans, the Methodist church, the National Lutheran Council, the Department of the Air Force, the Interstate Commerce Commission and the YWCA were all subversive to the Mississippi way of life. "One questions whether the reading of the Bible soon is to be restricted in the same manner that Nazi Germany sought to rid the Reich of all 'subversive' influences, literary and otherwise," wrote the editor of the weekly newspaper in Batesville, in north-central Mississippi.[2]

The Hitlerite police state was not a historical abstraction to people whose own memories encompassed the war years. The spreading tentacles of thought conformity, police brutality, and state harassment in early 1960s Mississippi triggered the specter of what many had seen at firsthand less than twenty years before. The Nazi image was hyperbolic; this was not, after all, a rigidly organized totalitarian society. That it was frequently invoked, however, testifies to the gravity of prevailing perceptions.

For Evers, Nazism was a common reference point throughout his brief career. "The atmosphere perhaps parallels that under the Gestapo," he wrote in a report from Yazoo City in 1956. In a speech to a Milwaukee NAACP group in 1958, he spoke of the "Nazi-like activities of the White Citizens' Council."[3]

Later, on May 31, 1963, at the height of civil rights demonstrations in Jackson, six hundred black children marched from Farish Street, downtown to Capitol Street and straight into massed ranks of blue-helmeted riot police, state troopers, and sheriff's deputies—hundreds of them, three deep. With cold efficiency, the youngsters were shoved through the ranks of police, herded into waiting garbage trucks, and driven to the nearby state fairgrounds, which had been ringed with a sharp hog-wire fence. Evers was standing on the sidewalk, grimly watching it all with John Salter. "Just like Nazi Germany," Evers exclaimed. "Look at those storm troopers," the *New York Times* reporter heard him add as the Jackson police marched in rigid platoon formation from the scene.[4] "The oppression of Negroes here is an American phase of Hitlerism," Evers's boss Roy Wilkins said at a mass meeting the next day. "This city has added another touch to the Nazi spirit with the setting up of hog-wire concentration camps."[5]

The atmosphere around the state capitol in those years brought back haunting childhood memories for Wroten. "Two Lonely Red Flashes," the Jackson *Daily News* sneeringly called Wroten and his one colleague in open opposition, the New York–born Karl Wiesenburg, in an editorial in the fall of 1962—a double entendre on the red lights flashing on the legislative scoreboard when the two offered their lone nay votes. His colleagues called Wroten "nigger lover," but that was not as bad as the fear of being recognized out on the streets of Jackson. There were, he remembers, a lot of people with guns in those days.

Now in his late sixties, his historic role largely forgotten, Wroten is a bustling, stout federal court clerk in a small northern

Mississippi town. He still speaks with the methodical slowness of the Methodist preacher's son, and he preserves a quiet astonishment at that distant world of white mobs in the street and fulminating politicians.

"As a child in the late 1930s, a lot of times, at odd hours, I would listen to the radio," Wroten begins, trying to remember what it was like three decades ago in the Mississippi capitol's ornate marble chambers. "I would hear Hitler's voice, some of the speeches that he made. I absorbed some of the atmosphere of hate and bitterness that was emanating from Germany in those days." Slowly, the comparison builds. "I could equate that with some of the atmosphere, the voices, the rancor, the bitterness, of the Mississippi capitol building," he says.[6]

There was little other business but race, and Wroten's memory is dominated by the efforts at racial control in the legislature. His fellow legislators in those years were like dike builders, lunging every which way to contain the wash of integration seeping in from beyond Mississippi's borders. Once, for instance, the house of representatives voted that the entire state of Mississippi boycott the city of Memphis, which had integrated the lunch counters of its department stores. As one of the Mississippi legislators put it, "There's no use doing business with our enemies."[7] A state house committee chairman, presenting a new bill of doubtful constitutionality to restrict black voting, told his colleagues: "I think everyone should be reading this bill and avoid asking questions not absolutely necessary."[8]

For the world outside Mississippi, the state was a weird blend of opera buffa and high tragedy, punctuated by the grotesque antics of Gov. Ross Barnett, "America's leading segregationist," as the *Chicago Daily News* called him in 1964.[9] The state's most successful damage-suit lawyer, he had used race baiting to propel himself into the governor's office in 1959, at the height of integration frenzy. The world watched, bemused, as Barnett on the campaign trail stepped backward into a rotating airplane propeller. In office, a reporter gamely measuring the new governor's foreign affairs acumen asked his opinion of the crisis over Quemoy and Matsu; Barnett blandly replied he was sure there would be state jobs for those two fine fellows. He was proud that he was the first Mississippi governor to appoint two Miss Americas as honorary colonels. At Western Michigan University in the fall of 1963, he told his audience that "Hitler offered the people of Germany a short cut to human progress. He gained power by advocating human rights for minority groups." The reporters from outside heard the quaintly empty campaign slogans and chuckled: "Roll With Ross, He's for Segregation 100 percent, He's not a Mod'rate like Some other Gent" or "Stand Tall With Paul," for Barnett's successor, Paul Johnson, who in local mythos had "stood up to the Kennedys" at Ole Miss.

The words of these politicians have a dreamlike quality. Gov. Paul Johnson told a television interviewer in December 1964 that blacks in Mississippi were "very, very happy."[10] Allen Thompson, the mayor of Jackson, in a television address during the height of the city's racial crisis, told blacks: "You live in a city where you can work, where you can make a comfortable living. You are treated, no matter what anybody else tells you, with dignity, courtesy, and respect. Ah, what a wonderful thing it is to live in this city!"[11] Thompson, after meeting with a group of black ministers several weeks later, laughingly commented to reporters: "Coming in here and getting everything you want. Think of that! Just think of that! We've had such a good time. We've accomplished a lot. Aw, it's wonderful."[12] And the mayor of Greenwood, Charles Sampson, declared during voter registration demonstrations: "We give them everything. We're building them a new swimming pool. We work very close with the nigger civic league. They're very satisfied."[13]

For the writers, who came not to do battle but to look, Mississippi seemed equally peculiar and menacing. Horrified but fascinated, they peered into the state with increasing intensity. By the summer of 1964, during what came to be called Freedom Summer, legions of writers and reporters were trooping through—so many that it became impossible to find a hotel room or rent a car in Jackson.

In the past, it had been a semiexotic region for Northern travelers. Mississippi was studied in the 1930s by Northern anthropologists and sociologists—academics whose intensive studies of the peculiar racial mores infuriated local whites. When the Yale sociologist John Dollard went to Indianola, a cotton town in the heart of the Mississippi Delta, in the mid-1930s, he found an abundance of distinctive and queer Deep South customs. In his seminal 1937 book, *Caste and Class in a Southern Town*, Dollard wrote vividly on the "sexual gain," the continuous sexual advantage white men took over black women, and the "prestige gain," the ego-reinforcing deference blacks routinely paid whites. His scene-setting description of Indianola on a Saturday afternoon is an essay in foreign travel writing for his non-Southern readers: he described the "country Negroes," who "mill through the streets and talk excitedly," and the "rednecks," whose necks, he conscientiously pointed out, were "red, due to open shirts and daily exposure to the sun."[14]

But for all the peculiarity of the customs under review, Mississippi is still a region in America in Dollard's work, albeit a queer one. The scene setting notwithstanding, he told readers that he wanted to avoid exoticism: "The researcher, of course, is not interested in this town as an esoteric item in American civilization." Rather, the town is to be seen as nothing more than a typical specimen in a certain American region.[15] As a matter of both professional strategy and personal predilection, Dollard wanted as much as possible to suppress his status as an outsider: acutely conscious that his "presence raised a note of apprehension and fear," his desire is to be "rather settled into the life of the community."[16] He was conscious also of what he called his "sectional bias," and wanted as much as possible to avoid it.

The writers of the mid-1960s had an entirely different strategy and enthusiastically embraced the position of outsider. And Mississippi, as much as possible, was to be cast as a foreign land. "Northerners who were concerned with [race relations] felt, when they visited Mississippi, that they had strayed into another time, another country," *New York Times* reporter and columnist Anthony Lewis wrote in the mid-1960s.[17] A lawyer's office in 1963 Jackson was described as "modernistic" in a dispatch from Claude Sitton, the *New York Times* Southern correspondent—as if readers needed to be reminded that such an office could in fact be found in so backward a place. Writers arrived half-looking for a strange, foreign land right there on American soil. This strategy developed into a moral imperative of the times: Mississippi came to be seen as the dark mirror, America's worst self.

It was a lone renegade inside the state who played a crucial role in developing the picture of Mississippi as a land apart. The tall, saturnine figure of the University of Mississippi historian James Silver captured American imaginations in this period. He became a kind of oracle of Mississippi, quoted and written about everywhere.

There was, first of all, the historian's idea, which became the title of his best-selling book of 1964: Mississippi was a "closed society," a "hyper-orthodox social order in which the individual [had] no option except to be loyal to the will of the white majority. And the white majority . . . subscribed to an inflexible philosophy which [was] not based on fact, logic, or reason." That philosophy was white supremacy.[18]

This idea had germinated over Silver's teaching career of nearly thirty years in the state, beginning in 1936. Most of that career was placid, spent in unremarkable scholarship, coaching of the Ole Miss tennis team, and private dissent from prevailing orthodoxies. Silver was known as a liberal, but he had not stepped out in a public way. When the black journalist Carl Rowan came through Ole Miss in 1956, Silver "did not dare to have Rowan at [his] table or in the class," as he wrote later. He was embarrassed a few years later when the state NAACP president, Aaron Henry, hugged him at a meeting, with photographers around them.[19]

Silver was cut off from whatever small civil rights efforts were percolating in Mississippi. "I didn't really know when Moses came into the state," he told an interviewer in 1981, referring to Bob Moses, the courageous SNCC field secretary who began registering voters in Mississippi in 1961. "I was isolated. There wasn't much in the papers. I heard about the violence, the shooting. I remember that somebody was shot in the neck over there in the Delta, I don't know who it was."[20]

But he changed, becoming, as he put it later, "radicalized" on the race issue, with the intensification of the state's racial militancy. The Ole Miss integration riot of 1962 provided the catalyst for Silver's "closed society" idea. The events themselves shocked him deeply. Almost twenty years later, he was still haunted by the look on his son's face after the riot. "He [Bill Silver] came home and at supper he was, his face was white. I guess he still had romantic ideas about southern women, but he had heard these co-eds at Ole Miss shouting these obscenities at Meredith when he came in, and he was shaken. Here he was a Harvard graduate, and that bothered me. I still think about it. I can still see him at the table."[21] And then there was the professor's rage over the false story Mississippi was telling itself about what happened that night: that President Kennedy's federal marshals had actually provoked the riot. Because of its need to maintain white supremacy, Mississippi was incapable of telling itself the truth about either its past or present, Silver reasoned.

He brought the "closed society" idea into the world in a powerful speech to the Southern Historical Association, of which he was president, at Asheville, North Carolina, on November 7, 1963. Mississippi, Silver declared, was a "totalitarian society." He continued: "The Mississippian who prides himself on his individuality, in reality lives in a climate where nonconformity is forbidden, where the white man is not free, where he does not dare to express a deviating opinion without looking over his shoulder."[22]

A history professor's speech to a group of colleagues does not normally make news. But the reporter Claude Sitton had gone over the speech with Silver beforehand, and Silver had been quoted in the *New York Times* during the Ole Miss crisis.[23] So his words wound up on the front page of the *Times* the next morning, under the headline "Mississippi Professor Declares That His State Is 'Totalitarian.'"

The speech marked the beginning of Silver's lionization as a lone, courageous dissenter. It was this image, as much as the professor's idea, that helped shape the picture Americans were forming of Mississippi. The day following the speech, the *New York Times* carried an adulatory profile under the headline "Southern Dissenter." "With a disregard for his personal safety and professional future bordering on the cavalier," the anonymous profiler wrote, "he has engaged the fervent segregationists at crossroads after crossroads. He has flouted their customs, laughed at their arguments, ridiculed their philosophy and denounced their tactics," all because he was "compelled by deeply felt humanism to oppose anyone who would deny an individual the opportunity to do what he is capable of doing."[24]

Silver himself was considerably more modest. "I was just lucky as hell," he told an interviewer in 1981. "Most people teach until they die, they're not involved in anything. . . . I was just lucky as hell that Barnett became governor. No, I feel that way. It is the greatest, most spectacular part of my life."[25] He did, in fact, fade back into obscurity after leaving Mississippi for good in the summer of 1965.

But in the weeks and months that followed his speech at Asheville, the abuse coming the professor's way amplified his heroic status. Before the speech Silver had played golf with the lonely new student James Meredith and had sat with him in the cafeteria, which had provoked postcard writers to call him an "honorary nigger." After the speech, Governor Barnett commented: "He ought to have been kicked out a long time ago."[26] In Jackson, the *Clarion-Ledger* reported that Silver had "abused the state of Mississippi, its people, officials and newspapers."[27] Applause and cheers greeted a legislator in the state house of representatives whose bill sought Silver's removal from the faculty: the legislator pronounced himself "ready to join any move—short of violence—to oust" Silver.[28] In Oxford, old friends crossed the street to avoid him. The governing board of the state's universities hounded him for "contumacious conduct."[29]

In June 1964, Silver's book *Mississippi: The Closed Society,* based on the speech, appeared. Published the day after three civil rights workers (James Chaney, Andrew Goodman, and Michael Schwerner) disappeared in Philadelphia, Mississippi, when national interest in the state was at its most intense, Silver's book—a historical essay that ranged back and forth in time from antebellum days to the murder of Medgar Evers, a work of intellectual history—quickly became a best-seller. It was one of those rare works that, appearing at the very moment of historic upheaval, actually helped to define that moment, and its conclusions have remained solid for almost thirty years. Most arrestingly, Silver documented in *The Closed Society* the enforced absence of dissent from Mississippi's reigning ideology, white supremacy. It is a polemical work, filled with blunt rage. That Silver himself was very much part of the story was evident from the form of the book: almost half is made up of his letters on the Ole Miss riot, in a section headed "Some Letters From the Closed Society."

He journeyed to New York the week the book was published, and he was interviewed to the point of wearisomeness.[30] Flattering profiles appeared in *Newsweek* and *Life*, which ran a story under the headline, "Campus Scourge at Ole Miss." The magazine ran a full-page spread of pictures: Silver relaxing on a bench in front of the Lyceum building, his dog at his feet; Silver swimming in the river; Silver sitting back in his office. His book, the brief story said, was an "explosive attack" on Mississippi. None of this increased his already shaky popularity back home.

When Silver left Mississippi to take a teaching offer at Notre Dame, the received wisdom was that he had been forced out of the state. But Silver himself, in a memoir published in 1984, four years before his death, is considerably more circumspect, mentioning only a conversation with an Ole Miss provost, an old friend. This man "suggested that the university administration would find it easier to deal with the legislature if I were not on campus." But Silver also writes: "It seems to me that I was too stubborn to have allowed myself to be driven away," adding that a powerful inducement to leave was that the Notre Dame job "more than doubled my income."[31]

No matter. Silver as martyred political exile sealed the picture of him as a renegade dissenter. And it contributed to the emerging picture of Mississippi as not-America, the place the writers wanted. Silver was a white Evers, according to the writer Robert Penn Warren: "For some years Dr. Silver took his chances on being shot in the back—by some hero, from the dark, of course. But now he is not at Ole Miss. After twenty-eight years, he has gone North."[32]

No other place in the nation had political dissidents, much less exiles. But what made the place especially haunting to the writers were the submerged hints of normality they kept finding. In fact, they found a human and urban landscape hauntingly reminiscent of America.

Warren went to Jackson to interview student activists and others in the civil rights movement for his 1965 book *Who Speaks for the Negro?* He expected that Jackson would be very far from homogenized America, and he clearly conveyed that in the book by repeating the words *Jackson, Mississippi,* a number of times in the text, to emphasize a place apart from mainstream U.S.A., a defiantly self-sufficient entity. He says: "Even Mississippians slip, now and then, into that rarefied atmosphere of that fourth dimension called America." The airport disappointed him because it had the "promise" of anonymous universality, a promise that "will make you free." He continued: "But I do not want to be free. I want to know what it feels like to be in Jackson." He was not disappointed long; as soon he entered a cab, manned by the stereotypical burly country boy, so full of menace and now so familiar from the news photographs and newsreels, he felt that he was in Jackson. The driver was an earnest supporter of the newly liberated Byron de la Beckwith.[33]

Nicholas Von Hoffman's Mississippi was a sort of Evelyn Waugh-meets-the-Deep South. Covering Freedom Summer for the *Chicago Daily News*, he played sarcastically with the stereotypes of the mythical Southland without denying that they were abundantly evident: "It does seem to be a land where all the Southern stereotypes come to life and form a monolithic society." Jackson is isolated and remote, he continued, a place that "normally attracts few visitors, so its jet age airport has the spacious lifelessness of an underused railroad station."[34] In case the reader felt inclined to visit, Von Hoffman gave a mock tourist itinerary in this strange land of burning crosses, dumb beauty queens, redneck sheriffs, and wandering G-men. "Now, if you are an American citizen and you get into trouble, just call up 'the Embassy,' as the FBI office is called, and they'll do their best to extricate you," Von Hoffman explained.[35]

Calvin Trillin, in the *New Yorker*, had to reach outside of American history to find a suitable parallel for the Council of Federated Organizations (COFO), the ephemeral civil rights coalition that had set up its headquarters in Jackson in the midsummer of 1964; it was as if the Republican Loyalists in the Spanish Civil War had set up their headquarters in Madrid. Mississippi was some strange twilight zone: the radio community bulletin board announced meetings of Americans for the Preservation of the White Race; the Mississippi Numismatic Exchange sold Kennedy half dollars for twenty-five cents ("That's all we think they're worth," said exchange members); and people could get the latest word from the Citizens' Council by calling Dial-for-Truth.[36]

The writers dug with a horrified relish into this locale's promise of strangeness. Then, faced with mounting hostility from all sides—Warren found even the hotel clerks, once they realized his mission, increasingly cool to him—they gratefully got on the next plane and left.

Once home, they often speculated about a possible "return to sanity" in the state, as did Claude Sitton of the *New York Times* in the spring of 1963.[37] But invoking "sanity" or its absence only roughly approximated the relationship in those years between Mississippi and its leaders, and the rest of the country. Mississippi did not think of itself as insane. Appeals to some commonly accepted standard would thus have little meaning. The state existed in an altogether different dimension, one in which the rules governing behavior in other parts did not seem to apply. This was evident in the thousands of encounters that were now taking place, for the first time, between outsiders and Mississippians.

Here and there, the precise texture of these encounters has been preserved, independent of the participants' fading memories, in sources such as the transcripts of hearings held by the U.S. Commission on Civil Rights in Jackson in February 1965. The commission's purpose was to collect evidence of civil rights abuses committed by Mississippi officials in the preceding several years. A superabundance of examples existed: dozens of beatings of civil rights workers, arson of black churches, and instances of harassment of blacks who had sought to vote or had simply sat at lunch counters. In all such cases the perpetrators had gone unpunished, and in many cases they had been actively encouraged by the authorities.

The commission heard from black would-be voters who had doggedly submitted themselves to the humiliations of Mississippi's registration tests. Blacks were asked to "interpret" an abstruse section of the Mississippi constitution to the satisfaction of the barely literate white registrars; invariably these would-be voters supposedly failed.

Often, even after a black person managed to pass this test, brute intimidation kept him or her from voting. On February 17, 1965, an elderly black farmer told the civil rights commissioners that when he had left the Tallahatchie County courthouse after voting in a 1963 election, a cursing, stick-wielding man had declared, "I'll make sure that you won't vote no more." Why bother voting under these circumstances? "Because I am a citizen in Tallahatchie

County," James Henry Rayburn testified. "I was born at the place I am in now and have been there for 63 years."[38] At the time the Civil Rights Commission held its hearings, less than 7 percent of Mississippi's blacks were registered to vote.[39]

But even more revealing than this catalogue of iniquities are the testy exchanges between commission members and the subpoenaed Mississippi officials. Here is an unedited record of the collision between rationality, as represented by the U.S. Constitution, and the strange rules governing white supremacy. On one side are the civil rights commissioners, impatient and incredulous; on the other, the Mississippi officials, obfuscatory and evasive. Finally, the rules have been thrown back in the faces of these men. The net result is, necessarily, a kind of tense silence: if the Mississippians admit the logic of the outsiders, their world must crumble.

"I didn't ask you to read it, Mr. Hood. I asked you to interpret it," Erwin Griswold, the dean of the Harvard Law School, says sharply to registrar Guthrie Hayes Hood of Humphreys County, where no blacks had registered or voted since 1955, partly because of the very test Griswold is now imposing on the registrar. Hood proves incapable of "interpreting" a section of the Mississippi constitution and sullenly retreats. "I will not," he tells Griswold.

The sheriff of Humphreys, John D. Purvis, next on the witness stand, liked to snap photographs of blacks as they left the registrar's office. The commissioners charge that he was trying to intimidate them. "But I wanted to show just how peaceful that it was up there, for one thing," Purvis blandly tells the commissioners. "And another thing, I wanted them for my own use. I take a lot of pictures." Bemused, one of the commissioners can only think to ask: "As a hobby?"[40]

Two days later, the police chief of Laurel, Mississippi, is on the witness stand, and Dean Griswold asks: "Have you heard of the Civil Rights Act?" Chief L. C. Nix had arrested a black man for entering a white-owned coffee shop, and Nix thereby had violated the Civil Rights Act of 1964. "I have no civil authorities—criminal—until it becomes criminal," is the chief's enigmatic reply to the Harvard dean.[41]

It was hard to know how to respond to such a statement. The outsiders—in this case, the civil rights commissioners—could muster all the moral earnestness they were capable of. But at a certain point, they would run up against an impenetrable wall, and they would be baffled. The transcript of the 1965 hearings reflects this puzzlement. Laughter greeted the police chief of Natchez when he said, about a Ku Klux Klan rally: "I couldn't see anything that night that would make you think they were anything but upstanding people"; Dean Griswold found the recalcitrant registrar of Humphreys County "rather surprising." With those words Griswold was simply giving expression, albeit mild-mannered, to what most of the world was thinking about Mississippi as a whole.

Ironically, Jackson did not want to be thought of as odd, as different from the rest of America. The dream of its city fathers was simple: the world would consider it just as devoted to commerce as any bland Midwestern city. A promotional film about Jackson, made in the mid-1950s by the Chamber of Commerce and later distributed by the Citizens' Council, could not be more explicit. This Jackson is an All-American city, with bustling downtown streets, construction sites, well-manicured parks, country clubs, busy highways, even tourists. The traditional Southern siren calls to Northern industry—cheap, docile, "American" labor—are all sounded.

The film's audience is implicitly asked not to think about the past—the Southern heritage of racist violence and poverty that would have been close to the forefront of every Northern investor's consciousness. So Jackson is said to be "in the vanguard of growing Southern cities. . . . Today Jackson symbolizes a new and aggressive South." The narrator even has a neutral accent, not one that is regionally identifiable. But the makers of this film knew that race and segregation would be on the minds of the Northern industrialists at whom it was aimed.

The question is addressed obliquely. On the one hand, there are hints that the era of Jim Crow oppression is past; thus, a shot of blacks picking cotton unfolds into a scene of mechanical harvesters. On the other, the explicit message is that segregation, Jackson-style, is just another modern mode of living. The film seamlessly incorporates a section on "Negroes" and their happy life in the city.

"At College Park is the only exclusive auditorium for Negroes in the country. College Park offers complete facilities for Negroes." So "Negroes," 40 percent of the city's population, peacefully dwell in their own sphere in this bustling city of commerce.

"In 1900, this town was located on Highway 51 between two Burma-Shave signs! Population: 7,000. Today . . . 170-thousand!" exclaimed Paul Harvey ("Hello, Americans") in a February 1960 radio broadcast from Jackson, gratefully reprinted in that month's issue of the *Citizens' Council.* "And a skyline that looks like something out of tomorrowland! . . . You're carrying a picture of Mississippi around in your mind. Tear it up . . . throw it away . . . It doesn't fit anymore!"

The idea of Jackson as a Southern boomtown was not completely far-fetched. Devastated by the Civil War, it had begun the century as a rough frontier village, with dirt streets, wooden sidewalks, and three hotels of varying degrees of luxury where the politicians put up according to their means. A photograph of downtown Jackson in a 1915 flood shows horse-drawn carriages, men lounging at the side of the wide dirt road, and insubstantial two-story frame-and-brick houses built haphazardly along the sidewalk. White high society was rough-and-ready: at a stag dinner in the Governor's Mansion in 1912, one of the guests reached for his finger bowl, squeezed a slice of lemon into it, added a spoonful of sugar, and happily drank the liquid. All the other guests, perceiving that a gaffe had been committed but not wanting to embarrass the man, followed suit.[42] These unpolished politicos, the men who then dominated Jackson, were just as rough-hewn when out practicing their craft. Ethelbert Barksdale, a Mississippi candidate for the U.S. Senate in 1891, became so enraged at a political rival, he pitched a law book at him during a rally. Drawn guns on all sides and fisticuffs preceded a fraught restoration of calm.[43]

By 1910, Jackson's population had tripled in ten years to twenty-one thousand people, and thirty years later the population had tripled again. A small genteel Jackson had developed, where whites of cultural pretension and some resources, the families of businessmen like Eudora Welty's insurance-man father, attended traveling theatrical performances and took music lessons. But the city grew during those decades because of the poor whites who flooded into town from the hardscrabble countryside. They were a rough lot, depicted in all their harshness in Richard Wright's autobiographical *Black Boy*. One white family that employs him comes to the breakfast table cursing and snarling at each other, for no reason. "As they hurled invectives, they barely looked at each other." In another family, the woman begins her interview with the young black boy by asking him if he steals, then serves him moldy molasses and stale bread, and reacts indignantly when Wright tells her he wants to be a writer.[44]

So, for all the growth in population, Jackson did not have a proportionate increase in sophistication. Photographs that the young Eudora Welty, working for the Works Progress Administration (WPA), took of her hometown in the late 1930s show a town as empty and rural as the other small Mississippi towns she captured, only a little bigger. The focus of life was Capitol Street, where Jackson's bustle and vigor were concentrated. By 1950, Jackson still had only one bookstore, given over entirely to religious material.[45] "Jackson is a curious town," John Gunther wrote in *Inside USA* in 1947. "Its population was only 62,107 in 1940, but it has steeply grown since; it possesses a handful of impeccably shining skyscrapers rising straight out of a muck of Negro hovels and poor white slums. The pictorial impact is very striking."[46]

Yet Jackson badly wanted to be thought of as normal, and in the pre–race conscious years immediately after the war, it had some success in selling this self-image. When the Southern journalist Harold H. Martin came through for the *Saturday Evening Post* in 1948, he found the same city the Chamber of Commerce was pitching. Martin described a bustling All-American town, no different from any another, "a busy metropolis in miniature, a city most spacious and most clean, engrossed in a myriad of affairs. Buildings of startling height look down on teeming streets where artisans toil with aluminum and blue glass to modernize the fronts of existing buildings." Hovering in the unspoken background of this rosy account is the reader's presumed mental image of Jackson, and Mississippi: backward, Southern, perhaps menacing. In fact, Jackson will leave one "surprised," the writer suggested: one could be as optimistic about it as about any other American community caught up in the postwar boom. "The new Jackson is a manifestation of Mississippi on the march."

What few Southern peculiarities are to be found here—such as a cantankerous old newspaper editor or businessmen who "still go home to dinner in the middle of the day"—are more than counterbalanced by its mainstream Americanism ("Jackson's spirit was one of getting ahead. . . . She faces the future with great confidence"). There is not much room for racial disharmony in this account: just enough to note a certain disagreement between Jackson and "its" 37,600 blacks about how they are treated. The writer quickly moves on to more important matters, like the city's twenty new millionaires, its "unostentatious" social life, and a handful of cheeky dancers at the country club.[47]

This uncritical view was an ephemeral one, possible only in the warm buoyancy of the postwar era. When James Silver looked at the same town fifteen years later, he saw a city that had ballooned to over 150,000, a place of "new men," smug entrepreneurs and Rotarians, where "there was little time devoted to thinking about the inevitable social and political changes bound to accompany economic progress."[48] Jackson's, and Mississippi's, richest man was Robert Hearin, a banker and oil-and-gas merchant worth $200 million by 1981. Hearin was the "closest advisor" and "chief campaign bankroller" to Sen. James O. Eastland, the man who liked to boast that he had personally killed 127 civil rights bills as chairman of the Senate Judiciary Committee.[49] Characterizing his good friend, Hearin told a reporter in the mid-1960s that Eastland was "solid, you know what I mean, really solid."[50]

The 1950s Chamber of Commerce film about Jackson ended contentedly: "A good place to live, a good place to work." The irony was that the city's relative prosperity was not bringing it any closer to mainstream America. Politicians talked about how crime-free Jackson was, and the Chamber of Commerce vaunted its perfect climate for making money. "Ours is a dynamic business community of which you gentlemen are part and parcel, and the essence of its success," a Chamber of Commerce man told the Kiwanis Club in the spring of 1962.[51] But this smugness insulated the white elite from what was happening in the streets and in the minds of blacks. Challenges to the established way were simply outside the white worldview. One prominent white businessman, who in the fall of 1962 had decried the violence at Ole Miss, was anxiously telling a reporter by May 1963: "I'm no moderate."[52]

The pages of the *Clarion-Ledger* and the Jackson *Daily News* are the mirror of white Jackson's never-never land. Even in those days, the Hederman family papers—run by brothers Bob, Henry, and Zach Hederman, and their cousin Tom—were considered a benchmark of racial extremism, so racist that *The Citizens Council* sometimes reprinted verbatim their articles and columns. In 1955, the Citizens' Council gave the papers an award for "fair stories" about the organization.[53] The Hedermans were teetotaling, hard-shell Baptists, sons of two Hederman brothers who had arrived in Jackson in 1894 from rural Scott County. The two brothers had had no money and had made their journey partly in an ox-drawn wagon. By sheer parsimoniousness, they saved up enough to buy the struggling *Clarion-Ledger* in 1920, meanwhile rising in the ranks of the First Baptist Church.[54] For decades, the papers reflected the viewpoint of the most insular, unyielding portion of the city's establishment: the Baptists.

"Washington Is Clean Again with Negro Trash Removed," was the headline on the *Clarion-Ledger* story about the August 1963 March on Washington. One of the paper's columnists once joked that scientists had found the cause of sickle-cell anemia—licking food stamps.[55] When Medgar Evers was killed, a *Ledger* columnist speculated: "It is barely possible that desperately ruthless forces may have used him as a sacrificial offering, to rekindle the flames of unrest here and spur their drive for 'victory' everywhere." And, in its most notorious flight of fancy, the paper greeted the arrest of Beckwith—the archetype of decayed Delta aristocracy—with the headline "Californian Is Charged with Murder of Evers," because he happened to have been born in California (see chapter 4).[56]

For these papers the world of the 1960s was full of troubling subversive forces—"agitators," "communists," "troublemakers," and "beatniks." And yet to acknowledge being troubled by them is to admit their seriousness. Attempts at sarcasm and belittlement became the papers' only possible weapons for thwarting such forces.

"Agitators who chant the 'freedom song' reminds [*sic*] us of the story about a chap who had just graduated, rushed out of the school shouting, 'I'm free, I'm free.' A little girl standing nearby said, 'So what? I'm four.'" So wrote Jimmy Ward, the voice of the column called "Covering the Crossroads," in the Jackson *Daily News* on June 2, 1963, during the height of the civil rights demonstrations in Jackson. Ward's paper ran what it called an "agitation box score" during the demonstrations. On May 5 it read: "pavement packers 518, sign toters 66, stool sitters 19, curb squatters 14, sluggers, chunkers 11, knee benders 14, arrested 618, in jail 31, on bond 469, in fairgrounds motel 117."

Dick Gregory, who planned to join the demonstrations in early June, was going to "parade up Capitol Street barefooted," Ward wrote. "Throw him peanuts and he catches them between his toes." The newspapers tried to pretend that the demonstrations were not really happening by treating them as a childish game: blacks were just unruly children, inspired by greed. "A Jackson Negro reports he is disappointed," Ward wrote on May 30. "He said he stayed up all night last night hating white people, and the NAACP ain't sent him his check yet."

But this was a difficult, lonely stance to maintain. True, the major television station in Jackson, WLBT, censored NBC's civil rights reports. Once, when Thurgood Marshall was interviewed on the "Today" show, the station broadcast a blank screen and claimed "cable trouble." (A civil rights group in Jackson challenged the station's license at the Federal Communications Commission, and it was revoked in 1969.)[57] But outside viewpoints could not be entirely blocked in Jackson. There were, for instance, the reports of the courageous New Orleans *Times-Picayune* correspondent Bill Minor, who had been the dogged bureau chief in Jackson for the New Orleans paper since the summer of 1947. For years, Minor and his friend Kenneth Toler of the Memphis *Commercial Appeal* provided the only objective accounts for those not blinded by the prevailing orthodoxy.[58]

So the *Clarion-Ledger*'s editors knew what the rest of the world was saying about them. And, ill at ease, they tried painfully to turn others' censure into a virtue. "Times have changed to the extent that most folks down South consider it an honor to be termed a bigot, a reactionary, and a race-baiter," wrote Charles Hills in his "Affairs of State" column on June 1, 1963. "These are terms invented by the mentally depressed Yankee who thinks his skin ought to be black . . . a situation in which he is unwanted either by the true white people or the true Negro."

Sometimes during the hot days of May and June 1963, the *Clarion-Ledger* columnists just wished all the turmoil would go away. "The novelty of the same silly-looking characters getting arrested day after day while squatting disgracefully in public places has already worn off," Ward wrote on May 31. "More important things are taking place in the world."

In the Jackson papers' view of the world, that was the literal truth. And so what is most striking about these newspapers are not the racist attempts at sarcasm but how removed from history their pages seem. Day after day the *Clarion-Ledger*'s readers were treated to stories and photos of beauty pageants, of "high-steppin' beauties," Maids of Cotton, Miss Jacksons, or Miss Homemakers. Such lovelies—draped around old railroad cars, in group photos, or in agricultural exposition get-up—often appeared on the front pages or on section fronts. Inside pages were dominated by notices of sorority reunions, of speeches by John Birchers, or of the latest addition to the staff of the Citizens' Council.

The dreams of the city fathers notwithstanding, Jackson was the nerve center of a peculiar kind of polity, the likes of which did not exist anywhere else on American soil. It was not a coincidence that Mississippi's capital was home to the national headquarters of the premiere white supremacist organization, the Citizens' Council.

Jackson was the heart of a racial state, run by ideologues for the purpose of maintaining white supremacy. The voting citizens of Mississippi—the white citizens—went along without open dissent. "I love Mississippi! I love and I respect her heritage!" Ross Barnett thundered, brandishing his fist, at the Ole Miss–Kentucky football game rally on the September weekend in 1962 before James Meredith was admitted to Ole Miss. The capacity crowd cheered, the band played "Dixie," and every other hand waved a rebel flag.[59] It was controlled pandemonium that night, a rare mass fervor which the old newsreels have captured for history. "Just the way Nuremberg must have been," a student said later—though he was not being critical; he approved.[60] The next day, after Bob Pritchard had turned in disgust to go home, two thousand people, many waving rebel flags, massed five deep around the Governor's Mansion in downtown Jackson. Some had brought their rifles, because they had heard that the federal marshals were coming to get their governor.[61] The bond between leaders and the led was complete.

There was precedent for scenes like this. One could go back fifty years, for instance, to a day in July 1911, when a crowd of thousands had welcomed the "White Chief," James K. Vardaman (Mississippi's governor from 1904 to 1908 and a U.S. Senator in the following decade), to Meridian for a rally in his U.S. Senate campaign. The crowd's cheers had drowned out the ambient renditions of "Dixie," and Vardaman, resplendent from head to toe in a suit of white, had fired their enthusiasm even more with his warnings about "the big, black buck" at loose in the Mississippi countryside.[62]

The state's racial militancy, though it had changed in character and degree by the 1950s, had existed embryonically for decades before. There had always been one principal issue in Mississippi; what was true in 1960 had been true in 1860, during the years of slavery before, and in every decade in between: "This is strictly a white man's country," Gov. Theodore "The Man" Bilbo had said in 1919.[63] This was a continuity that struck the 1960s integrationists with depressing force. "The all-pervading doctrine then and now has been white supremacy, whether achieved through slavery or segregation," Silver told the Southern Historical Association in 1963.[64]

There was, in fact, insubstantial precedent for the revolution being proposed in the 1960s. For a tenuous period of seven years during Reconstruction, between 1868 and 1875, Mississippi had been forced to experiment with integration. Blacks had voted and had held high state offices—lieutenant governor, secretary of state, speaker of the house. They even, under penalty of law, had had "full and equal rights" to use of railroads, steamboats, inns, hotels, and theaters. An ex–Confederate officer in Jackson in 1870 saw blacks and whites "arm-in-arm or side by side," a sight that struck him as exceedingly strange.[65]

But these experiments did not take hold, and Reconstruction in Mississippi turned into a bloody rout of blacks. By 1874, whites in Vicksburg had formed armed gangs to intimidate blacks and keep them from voting. They organized terror attacks in the surrounding countryside in which three hundred black people were killed. In September of the following year whites attacked the people attending a Republican barbecue in Clinton. Afterward the marauders went on a murderous rampage, and intimidation and mayhem ensued statewide. On election day in 1875, ballot boxes were stuffed, a cannon was aimed at a polling station in one place, and Democratic "redeemers" were swept into office.[66]

The brief attempt at black and white equality was over. But the methods used in this campaign grated on the consciences of respectable white Mississippians. A formal, codified means had to be found to disenfranchise the black. That was the all-but-explicit purpose of the Constitutional Convention of 1890: "All understood and desired," one delegate said years later, "that some scheme would be evolved which would effectually remove from the sphere of politics the ignorant and unpatriotic Negro."[67] The frock-coated men devised a number of such schemes, with the most effective proving to be the "understanding" clause, under which every voter would have to prove an ability to "understand" any section of the state constitution. The 1890 constitution, still in use today in modified form, served the cause of white supremacy in the state for over half a century. By 1892, only 8,600 black men out of 147,000 eligible were on the voting rolls.

Blacks were now effectively out of politics, but not out of politicians' minds. When the politicians were not using buffoonery to distract Mississippi voters from their destitution ("Caviar ain't a thing in the world but Russian catfish eggs," was Senator Bilbo's cheerful rejoinder in 1936 to critics who complained he was living the high life up in Washington, D.C.), they could always use blacks to stir up voters.[68] No one did this more effectively than Vardaman. After a black man was burned to death by a mob in Corinth, Mississippi, in 1902, Vardaman wrote:

I think they did right to kill the brute, but it would have been better had the crowd been denied admission. It does not help a man morally to look upon a thing of that kind. It is rather hardening. But I sometimes think that one could look upon a scene of that kind and suffer no more moral deterioration than he would by looking upon the burning of an orangoutang [*sic*] that had stolen a baby or a viper that had stung an unsuspecting child to death.[69]

Vardaman built a fine career out of such phrases. But as his opponents wearily pointed out, all the White Chief's rhetorical flaying of the black man was unnecessary. The politicians did not dispute the necessity for keeping blacks down, and the existing laws ensured that this would happen: the Constitution of 1890; Jim Crow legislation and ordinances, beginning in the 1880s, which kept blacks rigidly separated from whites in streetcars, restaurants, and virtually every other setting; and the perpetual underfunding of schools for blacks. (By 1940, Mississippi was spending $41.71 per year per white student and $7.24 per black student.) And even more effective than the laws was the infinite network of entrenched customs by which blacks were meant to know their place and stay in it.

Until the last several decades the keystone of the system was lynching. That Mississippi long led the nation in lynchings and was also white supremacy's firmest stronghold was not a coincidence. Unpunished, sanctioned, and sometimes headed by the community's leaders, the lynch mob was the system's ultimate guarantor. Every black man knew this, as journalists and sociologists who came to Mississippi throughout the 1920s and 1930s found. The sight of a lynch victim's bloody clothes made a profound impression on the young Medgar Evers, one mentioned in both his wife's and his brother's memoirs. Lynching had an accepted place in the social order that was demonstrated by more than the unwillingness of authorities to punish the mob or their connivance with it. "Many a white who deplores lynching yet feels it may serve a beneficent purpose," wrote Hortense Powdermaker, the Yale sociologist who spent a year in Indianola, Mississippi, in the early 1930s. "There are good and kind Christians who will explain that lynchings are terrible, but must happen once in a while in order to keep the Negro in his place."[70]

As ritual reaffirmations of the prevailing orthodoxy, lynchings were necessarily public events, because they were carried out for the benefit of collective morality. This explains why, year after year in the first half of this century, Mississippi's congressmen bitterly, and successfully, fought proposed federal antilynching laws. So well accepted was this popular adjunct to law book justice that in June 1919, the newspapers in Jackson and New Orleans actually announced an impending Mississippi lynching: "3000 Will Burn Negro" and "John Hartfield Will be Lynched by Ellisville Mob at 5 O'Clock this afternoon," the headlines read. Spectators carrying picnic meals poured in to see the black man "kicked unconscious, hanged from an ancient sycamore tree, and riddled with bullets before his body was engulfed by flames."[71]

Yet the Mississippi system was a fragile one, appearance to the contrary, and whites were not entirely secure in it. There was anxiety over "the American Dilemma"—Gunnar Myrdal's phrase for the contradiction between American beliefs, as expressed in the Constitution, and American racial practices, as expressed in the segregation system.

In the elaborate web of what he called "defensive beliefs," Dollard found considerable evidence for this anxiety in Indianola in the 1930s. At the heart of these "defensive beliefs" was the idea that blacks were not fully human beings—that they were children, or brutes; that they demanded constant vigilance, or paternal benevolence; that they were shiftless, immoral, and smelly, and were really quite happy in their lowly stations, if only the meddling Northerner would leave them be. Among the most remarkable of these beliefs was one enunciated to Dollard by a white planter: that the black sharecroppers who worked for him liked to be cheated, and even expected it, at settle-up time. Dollard, a rationalist, did not accept that the white Mississippian actually believed these notions. Rather, they were simply useful excuses for his treatment of blacks.[72]

If it was true, then, that "southern people [were] much more exercised over the contradictions in their lives than northern people," as Dollard wrote in *Caste and Class in a Southern Town*, any attempt to point out these contradictions was going to both stir the nascent anxiety and provoke defensive reaction. Twenty years after his book *Caste and Class* was published, Dollard sadly reported that it had cost him all his friends in the place he called "Southern-town." And if the critical analysis was combined with a dictate to change, then the reaction in white Mississippi was going to be qualitatively different. The insecurity could no longer be palliated with collective broadsides against meddling Yankees.

The Supreme Court's *Brown v. Board of Education* decision in 1954 transformed Mississippi's racial state. In the wake of what the segregationists called "Black Monday," it was obvious that the net-work of traditional customs could not sustain white supremacy and that racial custom would have to be made law and state policy more formally than ever before. The upholders of racial custom, ordinary citizens, would have to mobilize on a mass basis and take over the reins of power.

It was on the level of custom that the response was formulated in 1950s Mississippi. The instrument was the Citizens' Council—"the greatest force we have in this battle to save the white race from amalgamation, mongrelization, and destruction," Walter Sillers, the speaker of the Mississippi House of Representatives, was already calling it in 1956, barely two years after the council's birth.[73]

In the wake of the *Brown* decision, thirteen citizens of India-nola had met on July 11, 1954, in the home of the manager of the cotton compress. These ordinary citizens—the town banker, the dentist, the pharmacist, the mayor, the city attorney—had had a plan: form a grassroots organization to defend segregation. The name they chose reveals the group's reach and its focus—an orga-nization of and for *citizens*. The *Brown* decision had frightened these citizens because of its threat to the network of customs that held life in place. Preservation of custom—not political power in Mis-sissippi, which the Citizens' Council ultimately achieved—had been the initial focus.

Byron de la Beckwith was a charter member of the organiza-tion, and he understood this ordering of priorities perfectly. From his home in Greenwood in the spring of 1957, he wrote a blustery letter to the council's monthly newspaper to explain his view of the organization:

There are those who ask, "What is the Citizens' Council?" Well I'll tell them.

The Citizens' Council is the catalyst which set off the chain reaction which can save this Nation from mongrelization, totalitarianism and judicial dictatorship.

The Citizens' Council was the first effective vehicle created by people to express their sentiment so that our politicians would know which side to fight for. Politicians don't lead. They follow. They find out which way the people are going and then they run get in front of them and lead them there. The Citizens' Council showed them which way the people were going.[74]

The council grew from seeds of fear, the most potent of which was that a sacred custom would now be violated: the prohibition against exposing white women to black men. Robert Patterson, the Indianola plantation manager whose inspiration it was, gave a revealing interview to the journalist Howell Raines twenty-odd years after the founding of the council: "I got to thinking about it. And I had a little daughter who would start school immediately. . . . I remember I was lying awake at night."[75]

These were the fears of respectable men who were anxious to present an acceptable face to the world, anxious to proclaim they did not need the Ku Klux Klan's sheets and hoods. "It is not a secret organization," Beckwith wrote in his letter, "and its members are proud to stand up and be counted." The *Citizens' Council*, the organization's monthly broadsheet newspaper, never looked liked a crude hate-sheet on the order of Klan publications like the *Thunderbolt*. William J. Simmons, the editor of the *Citizens' Council*, was a man of some polish and literacy, the son of a prominent Jackson banker who had studied French literature at the Sorbonne before the war. No ranter, Simmons spoke in measured tones. "Well-schooled, calm, and friendly," is how a *New York Times* reporter found him in the fall of 1962, adding for caution that "even by Mississippi standards he has been ranked as an extremist."[76] This reasonable-sounding man had taken charge of the organization itself by the end of the 1950s.

A primary mission of his paper was to bolster the council's respectable self-image. The layout and the writing style helped: both were indistinguishable from those in ordinary daily newspapers. The contents were another matter. Dollard would have found his "defensive beliefs" evident here: a front-page Simmons editorial in the July 1960 issue entitled "Lesson From the Congo" expounds on the theme of black power, the "lesson" being that it inevitably means barbarism:

> Black Supremacy has come to full flower in the heart of darkest Africa. Congo natives celebrated their recently acquired independence from the faltering control of Belgium by going on a spree of unbridled savagery. . . . Not in modern times has there been an outburst of such unrestrained and purposeless barbarism.

In case the point is missed, a cartoon on the following page depicts a thick-lipped Sambo in a grass skirt and top hat, beating a drum labeled "The Congo."

This uncompromising perspective had helped the Citizens' Council recruit sixty-five thousand members in Mississippi by 1956.[77] But in its first years, it had relatively little influence in the highest circles of power. Although legislators were signing on, Gov. J. P. Coleman, a relative moderate, was neither a member nor an enthusiast. Its hold on policy making not entirely secured, the council engaged in organized grassroots vigilantism in the mid-1950s. For instance, it published the names of black petitioners in Yazoo City who demanded integrated schools; all faced economic ruin as a result.[78]

By the end of the decade, the Council had more than eighty thousand members in the state. Membership in the Citizens' Council was "akin to membership in the Rotary or Lions Club," Hodding Carter III wrote at the time, and in restaurants all over Mississippi patrons could pick up its literature "with the toothpicks at the cashier's counter."[79] The council's influence, inevitably, was percolating up to the top reaches of power in the state.

"Barnett Praises Council Activity" was the banner headline in the *Citizens' Council* of September 1959, a month after the amiable damage-suit lawyer was elected governor. Barnett had chosen a Citizens' Council dinner as the forum for his first postelection speech. "I am proud that I have been a Citizens' Council member since the Council's early days," the new governor said. "I hope that every white Mississippian will join with me in becoming a member of this fine organization. The Citizens' Councils are fighting your fight—they deserve your support."

The council became virtually an arm of government and received state funds through the Sovereignty Commission, the Mississippi agency that since 1956 had organized official efforts to maintain segregation. It had developed into a quasi–political party along the lines of those in totalitarian states, with ordinary citizens and public officials uniting to enforce a common ideology, white supremacy, through fear and intimidation. "They're a formidable force," Evers told a reporter two weeks before his murder. "They have infiltrated government here from the governor's chair down to the policeman on the beat."[80]

At the turn of the decade, in a sign of the organization's growing respectability, the council offices moved from their dusty headquarters in provincial Greenwood, Beckwith's hometown, to a modern office building in downtown Jackson. They were right across from the Governor's Mansion, an opportune siting. By 1962, Hodding Carter III, writing in the *Nation*, was calling Governor Barnett the council's "unabashed front man."[81] Its staff helped him with speeches, traveled with him, and served as all-purpose advisers on racial affairs.[82]

The dissimilarity of their educational backgrounds notwithstanding, Simmons and Barnett now passed considerable time in each other's company. If the tall, mustachioed "prime minister of racial integrity"[83] was not in the governor's office, he might be in the South Gallery of the house of representatives, where Joe Wroten remembers seeing Simmons giving orders to the troops on the floor below. Back in those days, legislators sometimes listed council membership in their official biographies, though that detail rarely turns up these days in their obituaries.

Outside on the street, Simmons would also have been among friends. By the early 1960s Jackson had some six thousand council members.[84] Thousands more would at least have professed sympathy—the council made sure of that. In 1958 it had gone block by block through the city to recruit new members. At the same time, it undertook to survey the "expected conduct" of every white resident of Jackson.[85] Several years later, when some of these new members had been tardy in paying their dues, the council sent out a form letter that gave them a choice to sign on again or to check a box that said: "Please drop my name from your membership rolls. I am not interested in maintaining segregation." Claude Sitton noted that "such an admission here would be considered little short of treason."[86]

In the face of such nearly unanimous opinion, Jackson's tiny band of white liberals was powerless. Jane Schutt, a plain-talking, earnest housewife who had the nerve to become the chairwoman of the Mississippi Advisory Comittee to the U.S. Commission on Civil Rights, was forced off that body by Sovereignty Commission pressure on her husband's company. A Yankee with no family ties in Mississippi, she had been able to accept the post in the first place because of those very traits, she told interviewers almost twenty years later. Her very ordinariness underscored the tenuousness of the white liberal position: no person of any prominence could have dared to take the stance Schutt did without facing total ruin.[87]

On October 26, 1961, the marriage of white supremacist ideology, in the form of the Citizens' Council and Mississippi officialdom, and the civic elite of Jackson was consummated. That day, five hundred people turned out for a twenty-five-dollar-a-plate dinner sponsored by the Citizens' Council at the fancy King Edward Hotel downtown. The attraction was Carleton Putnam, the author of "Race and Reason," a tract purporting to demonstrate the biological inferiority of blacks. But the author was what made this volume stand out. Because of his background, Putnam—a New England Brahmin, a Princeton graduate, a Delta Airlines executive, and the author of a biography of Theodore Roosevelt—had become a high priest of respectable white supremacy.

Governor Barnett declared October 26 "Race and Reason Day" in Jackson, and the governor himself introduced the tall, balding, dark-suited speaker. All of Jackson's leading industrialists had served on the "Carleton Putnam Dinner Committee," and most attended the festive occasion. (Many of these people's names are still prominent in Jackson today.) There were the newspaper-owning Hederman brothers; Stuart Irby, a leading electrical contractor; Nicholas Dennery, a leading restaurateur; and George W. Godwin, the head of a large advertising agency. Putnam stood behind an enormous American flag and lectured his attentive audience in waspish tones on the follies of integration. But he never raised his voice. His grammar was flawless, he did not say "nigger," and he was able to freely pull quotations out of the air. He chided Northern newspapers, Northern editors, and Northern society. Here at last was a Yankee who was not scolding. "You have a completely indoctrinated society in the North," he told his audience. "On that indoctrination, the integration movement rests."

The nicely dressed crowd, seated at banquet tables, felt at home with him. These were people of "education, culture, and high position," as U.S. Congressman John Bell Williams put it in a glowing review of the occasion for the *Citizen*, the newly rechristened publication of the Citizens' Council. Settling back into their seats, the audience applauded Putnam warmly. Putnam, too, felt at home. "The racial integrity issue," he told the crowd, "you have made your own in Mississippi more than in any other state."

It was "A Night We'll Remember," in Congressman Williams' account, a night in which the speaker had "enunciated an ideology around which the entire movement for racial integrity [could] become consolidated."[88] And Putnam concluded that he was standing in "the heartland of the struggle for racial integrity."[89] Putnam could not have known how true his words were, could not have known just how seriously the state of Mississippi was taking that struggle.

Beneath the surface, the state was waging war through the Sovereignty Commission, which conducted some of its activities overtly and many others covertly. As the activities of the commission have become known in recent years (see chapter 8), it is clear that they offer the truest insight into the practical application of the paranoid worldview. If the Mississippi of the late 1950s to the mid-1960s deserved to be called a police state, it would in large measure be because of the commission. Through this agency, the state actively intervened in the daily lives of ordinary citizens to further the goal of "racial integrity."

The commission was created for precisely that purpose. By 1956 there was increasing clamor from the Citizens' Council and other segregationist forces for a state agency dedicated wholly to the war against integration. That year the legislature voted overwhelmingly to establish just such an agency, through a bill proposed by the council. Throughout its seventeen-year life, the Sovereignty Commission always maintained a public face, even employing a publicity director to go outside the state and spread the Mississippi gospel. Everybody knew the commission employed investigators, informants, and stool pigeons in the civil rights community. No secret was made of its financial support for the Citizens' Council, and documents leaked in the 1960s showed that it forced the firing of Tougaloo College's liberal president in 1964.

But for more than thirty years—from the Sovereignty Commission's closing by Bill Waller in 1973 through the legislature's 1977 sealing of the commission's records and a subsequent half-century of enforced secrecy—the commission's day-to-day work remained largely a mystery, the subject of intense speculation. By mid-1989, some of the records had come to light (see chapter 9).

These documents offered an unprecedented picture of the paranoid, dirty war against suspicious outsiders, civil rights workers, blacks seeking their rights, and men and women suspected of carrying on interracial liaisons. "Medgar Evers, Race Agitator," a 1958 Sovereignty Commission memo obtained by the Jackson *Clarion-Ledger*, contained a suggestion by Gov. J. P. Coleman that "spot checks be made of the activities of Medgar Evers, both day and night, to determine whether he [was] violating any laws."[90]

The commission counseled police officers on how to evade the law successfully, and it waged guerilla war against civil rights workers. The commission's head, Erle Johnston, knew he was breaking the law: one directive from February 1965 charges investigators to remove from agency files documents that could be "construed to mean that the Sovereignty Commission has interfered in any way with voter registration drives." Beyond revealing the commission's secret work, the files also mirror the darker fears and obsessions of the Mississippi populace itself, because the commission investigators often had pursued their tasks at the behest of the citizenry.

These documents make strange reading today. On the one hand, they give an almost comical picture of bumbling investigators obsessed with reporting trivia to the home office. Nothing was too small to escape their notice, and these diligent men could not distinguish between what was important and unimportant, even in the context of their own misguided missions. If Mississippi was a police state, it was a hopelessly provincial, Keystone Kops one: the commission's director proudly reported to Gov. Paul Johnson in September 1964 that he had subscribed to "publications of communist front organizations" and had arranged to have them sent to a compliant Jackson man with a "Russianish" name, to preserve the commission's cover; a confidential informant spying on the COFO office in Jackson in May 1964 reported from the febrile organizing site that "the novelty of mixed sex [had] worn off"; in July 1964, when the sheriff of Jackson County told a commission investigator that "the Kirschenbaum boy said that he did not believe in Jesus Christ and . . . he did not believe in God," the investigator offered without comment the sheriff's analysis that "he struck him as being a young Communist convert."

On the other hand, this obsession with the meaningless is exactly why the documents are so chilling. Things that seem trivial to us, innocuous things, personal things, were threatening to the paranoid worldview. They had to be investigated, and if possible, stomped out.

Most threatening of all were interracial liaisons and "mongrelization"—the greatest fears in the paranoid worldview's extensive catalogue of fears.

Mrs. Mabel W. of Grenada, Mississippi, comes from a "fairly good family," the Sovereignty Commission investigator Tom Scarborough noted with his customary precision, in a report of April 3, 1964.[91] Scarborough's methodical, patient investigation of Mabel W.'s private life, undertaken on behalf of the state of Mississippi, would lead to the firing of a black man from his job and the departure of Mrs. W., who was white, from her hometown.

Her family background made the stories about Mrs. W. all the more troubling. In truth, people in the little northern Mississippi town were "very much disturbed" about the whole lurid affair, Scarborough wrote at the beginning of the report to his bosses in Jackson. Sheriff Ingram's phone had been ringing off the hook for two weeks. And no wonder.

The facts of the case were simple. Mrs. W., the thirty-eight-year-old ex-wife of Lee W. (himself of a "prominent family," Scarborough noted) and the mother of two young boys, had had a baby. Nobody had seen this baby since its birth three months earlier. The sheriff had heard it crying from a back room, but Mabel W. had locked the door behind her before the sheriff could get a look at it. At the very least she had had her baby out of wedlock. What had the "whole town of Grenada . . . very much stirred up" was the rumor that the father was a black man, so the baby might have been "part-Negro."

The story made its way down to Jackson. Sovereignty Commission Director Johnston immediately dispatched Scarborough to Grenada to investigate, and Scarborough went to see Sheriff Ingram. The investigator put it to the lawman in straightforward terms: Talk to the woman. "It would be to her advantage to let him look at the child," the sheriff should say, "and be in a position to clear her of the charge of having had a part Negro baby." If she refused that request, Scarborough told Sheriff Ingram, only one conclusion was possible: "We must conclude that child is part Negro."

Mrs. W. denied having had an affair with Harvey Lee H., a black man who worked at the Monte Cristo Motel in town. She agreed to let the Sovereignty Commission man and Sheriff Ingram inspect her baby, but only after H. had been interrogated.

The two men proceeded to Room 71 of the Monte Cristo, and Harvey Lee H., an "indispensable" employee of the motel, the man who did all the buying and all the weighing of food, was brought. After several dozen sharp questions, the investigator turned to H. and accused him of "not levelling." H. was forced to admit that he had arranged trysts for Mrs. W. with a white man, but he denied being the father of her child.

The investigator was not satisfied. "Harvey Lee," he began, addressing him, as was the custom, by his first name, "do you realize, as much talk as has been done about the child being a Negro, that you would stand guilty as being the father, whether you were or not—if the child did show Negro features?"

"Yes, sir."

"You would be guilty by public implication," the investigator concluded. There was no point in further discussion with Harvey Lee, so he was dismissed from the room.

The next day, Ingram and Scarborough went to inspect Mrs. Mabel W.'s new baby. "I know what you're thinking," Mrs. W. said anxiously, as Scarborough looked closely at the baby's fingernails and fingertips. "That baby is no part Negro," she insisted. "Its father is an Italian."

But Scarborough was not going to be swayed from his purpose by this possible red herring or by any false sentimentality. Mrs. W. asked plaintively whether he did not think the baby cute. There was no polite assent from Scarborough.

As for the baby's racial purity, Scarborough was unconvinced. "After viewing the child, I had a weak feeling in the pit of my stomach and the sheriff expressed himself likewise. We both agreed we were not qualified to say it was a part Negro child, but we could say it was not 100 percent Caucasian."

And so there the matter rested. H.'s boss said he was going to fire him. Once that was accomplished, Scarborough added, "What disposition will be made of H. is yet to be seen." Mrs. W. said she was going to leave town. And the investigator ended his report with a surreptitious pat on the back for himself by recording that a local notable had "expressed deep appreciation for the manner in which the sheriff and [Scarborough] handled the investigation."

There are other such reports in the Sovereignty Commission files from those years, other cool accounts of lives damaged, destroyed, or threatened because black men were suspected of consorting with white women.

There is the May 1964 report on the V. E. family of Raymond, Mississippi: "Earl C. stated that he 'knew his neck could be broke for messing with a white woman but that he was not guilty and wanted a blood test to prove it.'" The Sovereignty Commission members duly arranged blood tests, but they could not prove conclusively that little Bessie Marie V. E. had none of Earl C.'s blood. "Mrs. V. E. (Bessie's mother) was extremely emotionally upset while awaiting the reults of the blood tests and wept when she had the report read to her (she cannot read)."

There is the poignant case of Edgar and Randy W., two young boys of Jasper County, Mississippi. They were "white males, sons of white parents, but possessing an amount of Negro blood believed to be between 1/16 and 1/32." So the local school board would not allow them to attend white schools; but, being white, they could not attend black schools. Either situation would have meant breaking Mississippi law. "They are now eight and nine years old respectively and have never attended school one day," Johnston, the Sovereignty Commission director, noted in a February memo to Gov. Paul Johnson himself. Johnston said he had tried, unsuccessfully, to persuade the school board to let them in; his greatest worry was that the usually compliant Mississippi press would break their agreement with him and write about the case. "This story would make national headlines and we have attempted to avoid it," he wrote. Attached to his report is a photograph of the two boys—tow-headed young country lads wearing overalls and staring innocently at the camera.

"Race-mixing" was the greatest fear, made even greater when, as in the foregoing cases, it was not induced by the hated outside agitator but was voluntarily engaged in by Mississippians. Still, all by itself, the figure of the outsider was deeply menacing. As the aggressive agent of race-mixing, the outsider represented the potential for the worst of all calamities, mongrelization. So the outsider—the agitator—had to be quickly identified and quickly brought to heel. Much of the focus of the Sovereignty Commission papers was on identifying outsiders and dealing with them.

The paranoia reached its peak during and immediately after Freedom Summer, when the state was flooded with hundreds of Northern college students. They looked, smelled, and acted different, and their avowed purpose was subversive. But many others besides unkempt Freedom Summer volunteers fell under suspicion. Dr. Robert Eugene B., a white chiropractor from Ohio, could testify to that much. The Sovereignty Commission's investigation of Dr. B. is eloquent testimony to the agency's paranoia.

Dr. B.'s greatest offense was that he had moved from somewhere else to Indianola to set up his practice. Nobody in Indianola knew him, and chattering around town began immediately.

The intrepid Scarborough was dispatched from Jackson at the request of the head of the local health department: "Many people were concerned with his [B.'s] activities," noted Scarborough. And he suspiciously found that B. "had no business except Negro customers and that he was not known to associate with any white people." And his secretary was an unmarried mother and also someone new in town. Scarborough made inquiries of the young doctor, who turned out to be an agreeable young man of twenty-four. They had a "congenial" conversation.

But the doubts were not allayed. Scarborough asked. "What possessed him to ever come from where he came?" The doctor could have absolved himself of suspicion, but the burden was on him. There is a "mystery" to Dr. B.'s appearance in Indianola solely because he had shown up in town. Of course, it did not help that the young doctor's arrival had coincided with that of some COFO workers.

Unlike Dr. B., these COFO workers were not innocent until proven guilty. Their very appearance immediately proclaimed their guilt. Everywhere in the Sovereignty Commission documents, great care is given to describing the civil rights workers' appearance—the first, most important thing to be noted about them. Here the obsession with the trivial becomes substantive. It is as if, unable to fully back up the frequently proclaimed certainty that all the civil rights workers are Communists, the commission members latched onto the demonizing effect of the outsiders' weird appearance as alternate, if substantial, proof of political subversiveness. Thus, Investigator Scarborough commented on Charles S., twenty-four, of Arlington, Virginia, and newly arrived in Indianola: "S. had on an old turned up, frazzled straw hat, was wearing filthy clothing and a pair of tennis shoes with the heels out of the back of them . . . He has every earmark and has the background and activity of being a young communist."

In the files, *beatnik* and *agitator* are interchangeable terms to describe the white civil rights workers. Thus, their nonconformism is what had disturbed the Mississippi authorities most deeply. The beatnik's defining characteristics were physical, in the mind of Scarborough: "A beatnik is a person who has not had a haircut for months and has let his whiskers grow out, with dirty, filthy, nasty clothes on, and in many instances wearing a pair of shoes which normally you would expect to retrieve from a garbage dump, and having body odor which stinks."[92]

The way they look turned out to be ample justification for their arrest, as Scarborough wrote from Aberdeen in September 1964: "I advised the officers[,] since most of them looked like tramps anyway and were broke they could pick them up for investigation to determine whether or not they were vagrants and at least find out who they are."

In direct contrast to the hairy, smelly civil rights workers, Mississippi blacks, in the few glimpses available from the commission papers, existed in a state of childlike innocence. These were the people the civil rights workers were supposed to be organizing, but the blacks clearly would have been contented if only the outside agitators had left them alone. "There is nothing more satisfying to a Negro than being sick and having some white man rub him," Scarborough wrote in his investigation of Dr. B., explaining why he believed at least some of the doctor's story. "Negroes as a race are very religious and anything Communist sounds like Godless atheism," Director Johnston wrote authoritatively to Governor Johnson. When black cotton choppers in Bolivar County grew restive in June 1965, there was a simple explanation: a young civil rights worker, "Mary Susan G., white female, from Portland, Oregon, . . . has promised all of the Negroes who will strike food, money and housing."

Attempting to guide the innocent but easily corruptible native blacks was the hand of the great white Mississippi father, seen in all its paternalism in these documents. "Providing the Negro community with facilities of their own not only perpetuates local harmony and respect, but also creates something that might be taken away if a local situation gets out of hand," Johnston wrote to the governor. "We believe that decent treatment can be an effective deterrent to outsiders."

The Sovereignty Commission papers are in fact full of hints about the instability of the system itself. There is the anguished memorandum from Director Johnston to the head of the Jackson Music Association in October 1964: Should it stay all-white, and continue losing dates with artists? Or should it admit blacks who have begun to apply, in which case "the problem will continue"? There is the phone call from the head of the local Princeton alumni association: Should contact be made with a Princeton graduate doing civil rights work in Jackson?

Although the paranoid worldview demanded control over all facets of life, this could have been effected only through a true police state. Mississippi was not equipped for this, despite the best wishes of some of its leaders. And so, even during the height of the Sovereignty Commission's activities, in the summer that followed Byron de la Beckwith's mistrials, the white supremacist edifice was beginning to break down. In the inaugural speech of Paul Johnson on January 21, 1964, there had been hints of the coming breakdown. The governor's remarks were astonishing enough to wind up on the front page of the *New York Times*: "Mississippi is a part of this world, whether we like it or not. . . . We are Americans as well as Mississippians."

A critical moment in the breakdown of the old order came when the Jackson Chamber of Commerce, in the summer of 1964, urged its members to go along with the newly passed Civil Rights Act, which opened up public accommodations. Hovering in the background of that decision were the nightmare stories the Jackson businessmen were repeating to each other, like the one about how Sears Roebuck was shipping out $175 million worth of Mississippi products a year in boxes marked "Tennessee" to avoid any stigma.[93] And so, just hours after passage of the public accommodations bill, "Negroes were eating and sleeping in the city's better restaurants and hotels."[94] But on the Dial-for-Truth line listeners could hear the Citizens' Council's Richard Morphew fulminating against this "surrender to the vicious and tyrannical Civil Rights Act."[95] The anxious tone, however, betrayed what many already knew: the game was just about up. Or, as a furious state senator put it, the choice had been made "for the dollar mark rather than principle."[96]

The agents of the white supremacist state's destruction were, in part, of its own making, and the forces of violence created by that state ultimately discredited it. The Citizens' Council's ideal man, for instance, was not supposed to tote a gun openly, but he was expected to make his militant views known.

"We hoped this would be a cold war," said Louis Hollis, the executive director of the council, the day Medgar Evers was shot. "But if it isn't it's still a war, and we don't intend to surrender."[97]

One of the members of his organization, Byron de la Beckwith, had been listening to Citizens' Council pronouncements like this since becoming a charter member.

Perhaps he understood why men like Hollis felt bound to express publicly the hope for a "cold war." But personally, he had never wished for any such thing.

CHAPTER FOUR

BYRON DE LA BECKWITH

E
arly in his trial in 1964, Byron de la Beckwith played a little
trick on Bill Waller which gave Beckwith great satisfaction.
Quick as a sprite, he edged up to the stout man prosecuting him
for murder and tapped him lightly on the shoulder. Reaching fast
into an inside pocket of his smart blue suit, Beckwith pulled out a
couple of fine cigars and then shoved them quickly into Waller's
lapel pocket.[1] This act was both a mocking gesture to show his
contempt for the proceedings and a demonstration of the solidarity
of all white men.

Outside the courtroom, white Jackson was tense. How would
blacks react to the certain acquittal? The gray, leafless February days
added to a sense of foreboding. But inside the Hinds County Courthouse, Beckwith was enjoying himself. In truth, the trial was the
high point of his life, a heaven-sent chance for him to confirm all

his most cherished notions about himself: he was the epitome of the Southern aristocrat, a pure defender of Southern values; he balanced courtly manners with a manly devotion to guns; he had high-bred disdain rather than lowdown, visceral hatred for "Negroes."

But Beckwith was not just living out some private fantasy for his own reassurance. Those weeks in the courtroom were a perfect vehicle for delivering his message: they were all white men in this together, for God's sake. The ostensible issue—whether he had shot Medgar Evers—was trivial, and he displayed his annoyance with that question in an impatient performance on the witness stand. The real point was to demonstrate white unity in the face of the massed enemies.

Waller would not go along with Beckwith's game. He turned down the cigars, and he sharply asked the judge to order Beckwith to stop. But the Beckwith role encompassed a whole range of evocative postures, all calculated to play on the sympathies of the watching populace.

There was his carriage in the courtroom, for a start. It was so pronounced that virtually everybody who wrote about the trial remarked on it. He seemed like "a monarch approaching his coronation," one writer said in the *Nation*, or "a man come to receive the homage, not the judgement, of his peers," as the *Saturday Evening Post* writer concluded.[2] At the table of his defense attorneys, Beckwith sat back with grand insouciance. His spot in the courtroom combined throne with stage. "He sat upon his throne of glory," Waller's assistant, John Fox, told the jury at the end.[3] After giving Waller the cigars, he would "immediately glide over to [the defenses's] table as though waltzing across a polished floor to sounds of a big band's opening notes."[4] To Beckwith, the trial could well have been an episode in what he himself considered a pinnacle of social aspiration—the Saturday night dance at the country club.

Then there were his clothes and the way he wore them: just the hint of a white handkerchief sticking out of his breastpocket, the carefully revealed French cuffs on his monogrammed shirt, the crisp pleat of his trousers. He had combined the salesman's punctilious attention to detail with a kind of romantic Southern archetype. "He favors suits of white linen, Confederate gray or Marine green, and Delta planter khaki of the whipcord variety," according to Beckwith's queer, self-published 1991 "biography," much of which he wrote or dictated himself.[5]

Lest his audience think all this less than manly, there was plenty of talk on the witness stand about guns, about "getting the business,"—about his having been wounded as a marine during World War II. Beckwith, always self-conscious about his unimposing frame, had procured a mail-order muscle builder while in jail. He was as susceptible as the next man to modern advertising campaigns. "I decided to give it a try, having no desire to appear at my trial looking like a pale type willing to swallow sand kicked in his face."[6]

He had the common touch, too, as he moved around the courtroom smiling and talking, even patting Waller on the back during a recess. At one point, "a planter whose crop had been serviced by Beckwith stood at the dividing rail, and the two talked casually about cotton prices," the biography says.[7]

Like Waller, the Northern journalists covering the trial were more than a little bemused by this performance. But the outsider journalists did not count. To many Mississippians, Beckwith had in fact become an archetype; with the audience that counted, he was a success. "My goodness," the reporter for the Memphis *Commercial-Appeal* overheard a lady in the courtroom saying, "he could charm the birds off the trees."[8]

Even before the trial, while still in his cell, he had obviously been admired. "Glad to see you," the jailer in Hinds County had said to Beckwith when he was brought in. "Mighty glad to be here," had been the natural reply.

There were reports that housewives in the suburb of Brandon had taken turns bringing Beckwith meals so he would not have to eat the jailhouse food, even that he had been allowed to keep his precious gun collection.[9] His old employer at the New Deal Tobacco Company had sent him boxes of candy and cigars. Contributions from well-wishers had poured into his legal defense fund. Beckwith himself claims that the Rankin County sheriff had received him as an "honored guest" and had allowed him to "go shopping, visit a barber shop, [and] see a dentist."[10] He furiously wrote letters, sometimes twenty a day. There would always be one for his wife, to whom he boasted of the special treatment he was getting.[11]

At that juncture, he could have been regarded as a leading citizen. His imprisonment was a detail that simply added to his heroism. Fourteen of Greenwood's most prominent businessmen had formed a White Citizen's Legal Fund especially for Beckwith's defense, moved by the "awesome spectacle of one man standing alone against the preponderous [*sic*] power, authority, wealth and ingenuity of the Federal Government."[12] A few months later, after President Kennedy was assassinated, Beckwith offered measured, statesmanlike condolences from his jail cell: "It was a fearful thing, I say. I express my sympathy to his wife and family and parents." He could have been any high-ranking state official. Privately, in the letters to his wife, he was expressing joy over the president's death.[13]

"A gentleman and a law abiding citizen" was the description of Beckwith in 1964 by Robert Patterson, the president of the Associated Citizens' Councils of Mississippi.[14] Large numbers of right-thinking Mississippians would only have echoed this view. So Eudora Welty's story "Where Is the Voice Coming From" represented wishful thinking by a member of Mississippi's tiny enlightened class. The story, written in the ten days between the killing of Evers and the arrest of Beckwith, attempts to get inside the mind of the then-unknown killer. The man in Welty's tale is a redneck, full of poor-white talk, class resentments, and Snopes-like motivations. But it was not necessary to harness the anger of the redneck Mississippian to kill Evers; the genteel classes had plenty of motivation. Beckwith's kin could have rubbed shoulders with Welty's. The young Bob Dylan's song on the killing of Evers, written that summer, reflects similar misconceptions. "Only a Pawn in Their Game" depicts Beckwith as a poor white manipulated by the ruling elite. But Beckwith was a member of that elite.

At the trial, spectators were outraged at white witnesses who implicated Beckwith: the sturdy young Delta farmer who had traded him what was identified as the murder weapon, the cab drivers who said they had encountered him looking for Evers three days before the murder, the young drive-in carhops who had spotted him that night. "Damn if I thought I'd ever hear a white woman in Mississippi testify against a white man in a case like this," Harold Martin of the *Saturday Evening Post* overheard someone say.

The high point in Beckwith's validation was when Ross Barnett strode into the courtroom, on the last day of the February trial.

The genial ex-governor smiled, shook Beckwith's hand firmly, and chatted with him for five minutes in full view of everyone in the courtroom, *jury included.*

At long last, all of Beckwith's humiliations—his marginal life as a traveling salesman, as the mean-living scion of an old family gone to seed, as the husband of a scandalous alcoholic—could now be forgotten: he was the ultimate defender of the white man, a hero to many people, as he wrote proudly to his wife from jail.

From the instant that Barnett let go of Beckwith's hand, though, the course would be downhill. Nothing would ever again match that moment, not even his triumphal ride under the big plastic Welcome Home banner in Greenwood early in June. His supporters had stretched it across the Highway 49 viaduct just outside of town, and later they were on hand at the LeFlore County Courthouse to greet the tearful Beckwith. "Sheriff Speeds Dela Home to Freedom," the front-page headline in the *Greenwood Commonwealth* read the next day, the friendly use of the familiar nickname only adding to the sense of fond reunion.

But by then, first six, then five white Mississippi men on two successive juries hearing the Beckwith case had declared that racial solidarity was not the ultimate value. They had not believed Beckwith's story and had not been willing to go along with his pretensions to eminence. There was to be no acquittal, only unsatisfying hung juries. The illusions would prove difficult to maintain after that. "We're disappointed," Hardy Lott, Beckwith's principal lawyer, had said immediately after the second mistrial, with good reason.

From then on, Beckwith was condemned to a life that he had always half-dreaded—a life on the fringes. Those eleven jurors had inflicted an unshakable stigma on him. True, he wore his new identity as a badge of honor among the white supremacists who by necessity replaced his uptown dreams. But it excluded him from the respectable society that, tantalizingly, had seemed to lionize him for a moment.

Almost thirty years later, in the same Hinds County Courthouse out of which Beckwith had walked a free man in 1964, the thought of the stigma aroused him to passionate anger.

In the summer of 1992, he was called to the witness stand by his lawyers. They were trying to show that the old man's memory was so poor, he had not been able to help in preparing his own defense. He looked frail enough—thin, bent-over, and wall-eyed behind thick spectacles. But the lawyers' strategy did not work. His pitiful physical appearance notwithstanding, Beckwith had a sharpness of mind that was immediately apparent. In a confident, booming voice he was able to recount much about his past, particularly the details that would not have helped his lawyers. There was surprising rhetorical skill in the long, rolling periods of his sentences, reminding one of his early training in Latin and his immersion in the Bible. "I presume it was in the summer because I recall being like a dog sitting on the concrete floor and the floor was cool, so it must have been summertime," he said of his stay in the state lunatic asylum, where he had been sent for psychiatric evaluation by Waller in 1963.[15]

On the witness stand, he careened jaggedly from a kind of genial expansiveness to vehement indignation over his own plight. At times he seemed bemused by all that was happening to him. "People do dream up things," he said gently, responding to inquiries about the trail of boastful confessions he had apparently left over the years. But his jokey demeanor could change instantaneously. When the prosecutor asked him whether or not he had been "embarrassed" by his arrest for the murder of Evers, the mask fell away. From the witness stand came an eruption: "I resent all the damnation and condamnation [*sic*] that has come down on me and my family and the whole state of Mississippi, because this thing has been blown out of such proportion. It is ridiculous." He was not denying the crime; he was simply denying its importance. And there was a biblical warning for his enemies: "I will not look with kindness upon those that attack me."

He had remained consistent for twenty-eight years. The death of Evers was such a trivial thing, it was indecent that he, Beckwith, the distinguished citizen, had been tarnished by it. And in his suffering, Mississippi had been made to suffer too. Because he was still what he had been before those eleven white men on two juries had voted against him: a Shriner, a Mason, the Mississippi state treasurer of the Sons of the American Revolution, a charter member of the Citizens' Council, and a Sunday School teacher at the Episcopal Church—in short, an exemplar on behalf of his state.

The ease with which he was able to maintain this posture in the courtroom seemed to surprise him. He was back on the same stage he had been on in 1964, and he was enjoying it thoroughly. True, his band of fans had shrunk precipitously. But he could still be jaunty and charming, as when a friend asked him that day in 1992 about the jail food and Beckwith smacked his lips and exclaimed *"C'est si bon!"* The important thing was that he occupied the center of attention, and so—involuntary eruptions aside—he could be a Mississippi statesman, circa the Ross Barnett era.

But back in his tiny cell on the ground floor of the Hinds County Detention Center, with no audience, it was harder. There, alone with his copy of the *Protocols of the Elders of Zion*, his anti-Semitic leaflets from the Liberty Lobby, and his David Duke stickers, the world of the Jewish conspiracy and the savage Negro closed in on him.

In the Greenwood of the 1950s and early 1960s, most people thought of "Delay" Beckwith—to the extent that they thought of him at all—benevolently. He was the talkative little fellow people saw making his salesman's rounds, taking a break on Sundays to hand out anti-integrationist literature outside the Episcopal Church, bustling into the pool halls or the cafés with his buddies and walking his funny wide-gait walk. Sometimes, they noticed, he was carrying a .45. Other times, a Bible was under his arm. There was a certain jokiness about his extremism: he would, for instance, grin and call himself "rabid" about race. It was hard to know whether to take him seriously.

Beckwith moved away from this area for good in the early 1980s. But Greenwood is a small town, with twenty thousand people, plenty of whom remember him well. The person they recall is not an extremist with a hair-trigger temper, bursting with elaborate invective against blacks and Jews. He may have talked too much, but in other respects he was perfectly representative of his time and place. "He wasn't any different from a whole lot of people in that area who talked a lot," says Betty McPherson, who remembers a middle-aged Beckwith from her own adolescence in Greenwood. "He wasn't all that way-out," insists a high school classmate of Beckwith's. "I don't think he's any different from any of the other old boys around here," says one of his former employers.

In his moment of crisis he had been warmly embraced by the city that had nurtured him. Greenwood's establishment had staunchly stood by him. After all, when he was arrested, "there was genuine shock," according to Thatcher Walt, the editor of the *Greenwood Commonwealth* at the time. Beckwith's lawyer, Hardy Lott, was the city attorney and the president of the Citizens' Council. One of two Greenwood police officers who provided him with his crucial alibi, James Holley was the vice-president of the city council into the 1990s. Some of these elderly warriors from the heady days of all-out war against integration still meet once a week at the downtown bank building to reminisce about good old times.

But in public, at least, the pleasant old cotton town drowsing on the banks of the Yazoo River appears reluctant to acknowledge its past affection for Delay. Few here wanted to be quoted by name on the subject. Says the high school classmate, one of the town's liberals, "He may be peculiar"—a judgment whose unnecessary timidity underscores Greenwood's hesitation on the subject. A local judge, Harvard educated and a lifelong acquaintance of Delay's, has nothing to say about him. Talk about Beckwith is not welcome. "He's asking too many questions," growls a heavyset, tatooed man at the Cotton Row Club, a joint in back of Greenwood's famous riverfront row of cotton brokers, in response to some inquiries about Beckwith.

Even Lott, once a segregationist power in these parts, is skittish about being publicly associated with Delay, though he still defends him. After all, Lott's current law partner and son-in-law is a public figure, a former U.S. congressman, Webb Franklin. But those who insist Beckwith's only distinguishing feature was a relative lack of inhibition ("He Is Friendly but Outspoken" was the headline in the *Greenwood Commonwealth* on June 24, 1963, two days after his arrest) have to acknowledge that Beckwith's background alone set him apart.

His mother was a Yerger, a family with deep roots in the upper reaches of Delta plantation aristocracy. The Delta, like nowhere else in Mississippi, has always been besotted with the romantic ideal of a leisured, aristocratic planter class. There has been more illusion than reality in the claims of individual aspirants to this notion: the region was a rough wilderness in the years before the

Civil War, with more wildcats than people, let alone planters. The few fortunes were mostly made in the cotton boom around the turn of the century. Often, the money disappeared as soon as the price of cotton dropped, though this usually did not put a damper on the notorious Delta inclination to lavish spending and all-night revelry. The hours-long journey to a party has been proverbial in the Delta for over a hundred years.

Beckwith's pretensions are exceptional in one important sense: the Yergers had had money before the Civil War. By the time he came along, the family was almost broke, although it had not by any means given up its aspirations to distinguished roots. A curious volume devoted to the Yerger family tree, in the state archives in Jackson, traces the clan all the way back to Adam, taking in Charlemagne and Boudicca on the way. The verifiable history is more modest. A founding member of the Mississippi branch, J. Shall Yerger, had come from Maryland to settle in the Delta, and by 1850 he owned 101 slaves and twenty thousand dollars in real property. As a man of means, he opposed secession and voted against it at 1861 Mississippi's convention on that issue.[16]

But that kind of moderation apparently was not the rule in the family, and early intimations of hotheadedness appeared. Beckwith's grandfather Lemuel Yerger signed on with Nathan Bedford Forrest's cavalry at sixteen. After the war, the violent exploit of another Yerger rocked the state in 1869, brought condemnation even from Bourbon Redeemers, and made it into the pages of the *New York Times*. On June 8 that year, Edward M. Yerger, a turbulent newspaperman described by one historian as "mentally unsound," pulled out a long knife on the steps of the state capitol in Jackson and stabbed to death the well-respected provisional mayor of the city, Union Army Maj. Joseph G. Crane.

It seems that "Prince Edward"—even family members acknowledged he was unbalanced—had been agitated because Crane had put his piano on the auction block to satisfy back taxes. Edward Yerger's earlier distinctions had included expulsion from college for whipping an insubordinate slave, and passionate praise for John Wilkes Booth in the pages of an obscure Jackson newspaper. He was jailed for Crane's murder, but he managed to escape a trial thanks to the skillful exertions of his lawyer-uncle William Yerger, who in the 1850s had served on the state supreme court.[17] In 1913, one Lawrence Yerger became the secretary of the state prison board and was promptly indicted for embezzling thirty thousand dollars of the board's funds.[18] Around the time of Delay's arrest, a distant cousin, Wirt Yerger, Jr., was achieving notoriety as the chairman of Mississippi's ultraconservative Republican party. He drove remaining blacks out of the party, led the Southern movement for Goldwater, and planned a "white conservative voter registration campaign."[19]

For Beckwith, the most important Yerger connections stretched back to his grandmother Susan Southworth Yerger, who had been friendly with Jefferson Davis. Beckwith was proud of a thank-you note from Jefferson Davis to the family and of some Davis family china that the Yergers had inherited. In 1963, the *Commonwealth* published a neighborly picture of Beckwith displaying these pieces for the camera—for all the world the harmless local antiquarian.

Wirt Yerger is now a businessman who lives in Jackson, as do numerous other Yergers. They have not been much in evidence at Beckwith's court hearings in the Hinds County Courthouse there. An estrangement between this respectable wing of the Yerger family and Beckwith would explain why, in Beckwith's strange "biography" more room is given to exploring his father's California antecedents (in fact, he manages to trace this branch of the family all the way back to William the Conqueror and 1066) than to describing the Yergers.

This, even though the state where he was born played no part in his later life, except for the *Clarion-Ledger* imputing the murder of Evers to an out-of-stater ("Californian Arrested in Murder of Evers"): Beckwith was defined as only partly of the Delta, partly of Mississippi. Yet all his life, from his lonely, punishment-filled childhood to his blustering old age, he has identified obsessively with Southern plantation aristocracy ("Delay lived in a style common among Southern gentlemen of good family," his "biographer" wrote), perhaps because he felt his birth gave him only partial claim on it.[20]

Beckwith's paternal grandfather had arrived in California in 1860, a none-too-wealthy twenty-one-year-old immigrant from

Ohio with a taste for adventure. He achieved modest success, becoming the town druggist, postmaster, and telegraph operator in the town of Lodi. At some point late in the last century, he became friendly with a businessman in San Francisco whose wife, Sally Yerger, was from Mississippi. This couple helped raise Beckwith's son, grandly identified as Byron V in the biography, the father being absent much of the time because of illness. In 1912, Byron V married their niece Susie Yerger, an emotionally disturbed spinster who was visiting from Mississippi on a rest cure.[21] The ceremony was held in Greenwood, and it was "notable for the number of Confederate veterans in uniform" who attended—invited, no doubt, by Lemuel Yerger, the old, crippled colonel who was Susie's father.[22] The young couple settled in the farming town of Colusa, California, near Sacramento, where Beckwith V went on to own a title deed firm and to dabble unsuccessfully in orange and grape growing.

Their only child, Byron de la Beckwith VI, was born on November 9, 1920, in Sacramento. Guns were an early and prominent part of the young boy's life. Both his parents were gun aficionados ("Her son certainly inherited genes from two gun loving parents!" he writes), and the two blurry childhood snapshots Beckwith reproduces in his book both show him with guns. When Beckwith was five, his father, ravaged by alcoholism and pneumonia, died in a sanatorium and was a quarter of a million dollars in debt.[23] A prominent memory in the biography is of "Captain" Beckwith, the father, inflicting discipline on him with a razor strop.[24] Widowed, the lonely Susie Yerger Beckwith moved back to Greenwood and the embraces of the Yerger clan. Mother and son settled in the rambling old three-story house on George Street built by his Confederate grandfather Lemuel at the turn of the century, which had become a nesting place for Yergers in varying stages of impecuniousness. When the child realized that this was to be his home, he threw a violent temper tantrum, whereupon his Uncle Will marched him to a broom closet, took off his own belt, and beat him soundly.[25]

Susie Beckwith's health was fragile, and when her son was eleven, she succumbed to cancer. The young orphan was thrown onto the none-too-tender mercies of Uncle Will and his mother's cousin, a dry, buttoned-down young lawyer named Yerger Moorehead. A sometime occupant of the old George Street house was

Holmes Southworth, another cousin of his mother's. The three men looked on the raising of their young cousin as an unpleasant duty. "He told me those three old bachelor uncles didn't really want him," says Burris Dunn, an old friend.

Yerger Moorehead had already demonstrated a fondness for mocking Delay. The first memory the young boy records of Moorehead is of being tricked into swallowing beer, and then having to spit it out. His childhood became a succession of humiliations at the hands of Moorehead, now his legal guardian. He was the favorite butt of Moorehead's jokes; Beckwith "bitterly resented" the older man and "never became inured to pointless gibes," although he admired Moorehead's education and polish. Shaky at school, he sometimes turned out of desperation to his cousin for help. These approaches were not well received: "His face generally revealed gloom at my approaches and satisfaction at my departures."[26] Beckwith himself records with satisfaction that he got back at Moorehead, much later in life, by emptying a bucket full of soapy water and dirty undergarments on his head as he slept.[27]

To the young man's great relief, Moorehead sent him off to a prep school favored by the local gentry, the Webb School in Bell Buckle, Tennessee. But the relief was short-lived: Beckwith was not a good student, and the school was demanding. "For a while I thought myself in hell," he wrote.[28] He transferred to a less difficult military academy, where the uniforms delighted him, but he wound up back at Greenwood High School. Alone with Yerger and Uncle Will in the old house, Delay deeply felt the loneliness of his adolescence. The two aging bachelor uncles were not proud of this awkward young man. True, he attended the school dances and laughed along with everyone else. But "he was always needing to be the center of attention," remembers a contemporary, Virginia Alford. "There was something about him that made him an outsider. Everybody sort of made fun of him." A teenage memory stands out: once, Beckwith got so excited during a conversation, "he literally jumped up on the coffee table."

To his own surprise, he passed the entrance exams for Mississippi State College; he lasted three months. But if books did not interest him, acquaintances remember that guns did. He hunted in the woods around Greenwood, talked animatedly about guns, and collected and traded them. Guns were to be a lifelong passion. So it was not surprising that he was an early volunteer for the U.S. Marine Corps and enlisted less than a month after Pearl Harbor. He was in the first wave of what would prove to be a bloody assault on Tarawa Atoll in November 1943, the primary U.S. thrust at Japanese dominance in the Pacific after Guadalcanal.

He carried a Bible, a copy of the *Rubáiyát of Omar Khayyám*, and a straight razor in his uniform, as a last resort to use on any Japanese who might venture too close. The twenty-one-year-old corporal's job was to provide cover fire for landing troops. Even after his machine gun was knocked out of commission, Beckwith stood erect behind the weapon, "giving his comrades at least the hope of some covering fire in the last moments of the approach," according to a history of the Tarawa campaign.[29]

With comrades falling all around him, he caught a bullet in the thigh and spent the next four months in the hospital. In September 1945, he married Mary Louise Williams, a member of the WAVES he met at a base in Memphis where he was sent to recuperate.[30] As a direct descendant of Roger Williams of Rhode Island, she fancied herself something of an aristocrat, like Delay.

Back in Greenwood, bolstered by a new self-confidence from his war days, Beckwith began his thirty-five-dollar-a-week job as a clerk with Chicago and Southern Airlines, a position his Uncle Will had gotten him. It was a living, but a meager one: married, the father of a newborn son, he was still forced to live in the old house on George Street, with its large communal bathroom, its increasingly sagging porch, and a lock that could be opened with a ten-cent key from the hardware store. The door was never kept locked anyway. So when his tormenting cousin Moorehead breezed in one day, home from the war, he was surprised to find the young couple camping out upstairs.[31]

Beckwith took a succession of jobs that brought him into wide contact with people throughout that country where the flat Delta land meets the hills of North Mississippi. He became a salesman for some of the Italian immigrants in town, first for the DeCanale Produce Company, then for the New Deal Tobacco Company, a tobacco and candy distributor in Greenwood owned by the Cascio family.

The company was a fixture in Greenwood for years: its 1930s-era sign stood out prominently on a downtown block until, early in 1991, the business closed for good. A few days before the end, the last Cascios stood around in a storage room crammed with the company's remaining goods. One remembered Beckwith well from those years in the 1950s, a man who tirelessly made the rounds selling New Deal's wares to country stores. An "excellent salesman," one of the Cascios called him, "someone who could talk to people. He could talk to anybody, sell anybody anything." Beckwith liked to talk more than sell, and he always remembered the names of the store owner's mother, or brother-in-law.

Race hatred does not figure prominently in these memories of him, nor in David Jordan's. For years, Jordan has been the leading civil rights figure in Greenwood, a combative city councilman and, since 1992, state legislator who founded his own homegrown voters' organization in the town. As a boy, he worked at one of the crossroads stores on Beckwith's route. He remembers "the little old freewalking guy" sidling in, amiably playing cards on the counter with the proprietor. "He never did say anything to us," Jordan remembered. "Most of my employees were colored," says DeWitt Walcott, for whose Delta Liquid Plant Food Company Beckwith sold fertilizer in the early to mid-1960s. "None of them were afraid of him. He was good to them."

But for those who wanted to see it, there was a darker side. Sometimes, there were eruptions against blacks—"a mention of Negroes would send him into a rage," Vincent Cascio told a reporter in 1963—and these quickened as the 1950s progressed.[32] The 1954 Supreme Court decision on school desegregation was a turning point for Delay. In May, Tom Brady, the Mississippi circuit court judge who was to provide respectable cover for the extremists, gave his famous "Black Monday" speech, in which he likened blacks to chimpanzees, to the Greenwood chapter of the Sons of the American Revolution. Delay, the organization's state treasurer, was sitting in the audience. "From my aunt's perspective, that's when he lost it," says Mary Louise's nephew Reed Massengill. Suddenly, his life was filled with purpose: here was escape from the demeaning salesman's life. "He talked Black Monday breakfast, lunch and dinner," Mary Louise told her nephew.

"That speech changed Delay overnight. He became rabid on

the race question. I do not say that lightly," a relative told the *Saturday Evening Post* in 1964.[33]

Rabid was the word Delay began using to describe himself, to nurture his identity as the white Greenwood citizen most fervent on the race issue. He threw himself into the activities of the Citizens' Council. "RABID ON THE SUBJECT OF SEGREGATION," he wrote Gov. J. P. Coleman in May 1956, pleading for a spot on the new Sovereignty Commission. The coming race war was consuming more and more of his mental energy, and he was chafing in his trivial saleman's duties. "It is sinful for me to waist [*sic*] my talents and energies as a tobacco salesman when I could, by the stroke of your pen, be placed in a position of great usefulness to our state and nation," he wrote in his letter to Coleman.

Where was the army that could use his energies in the great cause? Clearly, the nascent Citizens' Council, to which he had signed on immediately, would not be enough. He would, if only the good governor saw fit, become a foot soldier for Mississippi: "I therefore request that you select me, among many as one who will tear the mask from the face of the NAACP and forever rid this fair land of the DISEASE OF INTEGRATION with which it is plagued with." As for the weapons in this war, something stronger than words, or the law, was obviously called for: "expert with a pistol, good with a rifle and fair with a shot gun," he assured the governor.[34]

But Governor Coleman did not see fit; Beckwith would be forced to channel his fervors elsewhere. He began writing letters to the newspapers in Jackson and Memphis. "I believe in segregation like I believe in God," he wrote to the Jackson *Daily News* in 1957. "I shall combat the evils of integration and shall bend every effort to rid the USA of the integrationist, whoever and wherever he may be." The word *segregated* is written in block capital letters, shouted through the text. "And furthermore, when I die I'll be buried in a SEGREGATED cemetery. When you get to Heaven you'll find me in the part of Heaven that has a sign saying 'FOR WHITE ONLY!' and, if I go to Hades—I'm going to raise Hell all over Hades 'til I get in the WHITE SECTION OF HADES!"[35] It was all just joking, in a way. But it was obsessive joking, in which the theme—segregation—permeates every twist and turn of Beckwith's thinking.

Frank Smith, the liberal Delta congressman who miraculously kept his seat until 1962, remembers being pestered by Beckwith in the late 1950s to send his fevered denunciations of President Dwight Eisenhower on to the White House. Usually, he put up with Delay as "one of those unpleasant things you had to endure when you were in public office." But one letter, an attack on Eisenhower, was "so crude in expression and grammar" Smith told him flatly he was too embarrassed to send it.

But in the circles where it mattered—circles themselves filling up with the more prominent men in the community—Delay was noticed. His outspokenness "afforded him status," Smith wrote in his 1964 memoir, *Congressman from Mississippi*. "Among the people that thought like he did, he was quite admired," remembers Thatcher Walt, the former editor of the *Greenwood Commonwealth*. On Greenwood's street corners, Beckwith sold copies of Judge Brady's "Black Monday" speech and spent considerable sums of his own money on anti-integration handbills. When the "Colored" sign was removed from the Jim Crow waiting room at the Greenwood bus station after the Interstate Commerce Commission banned segregated interstate bus travel in the spring of 1961, he stood in a doorway to block blacks from entering the white room. One Sunday at church, congregants were startled by the sound of a pistol falling out of his pocket. He deluged the church hierarchy with letters attacking its moderate stand on race.

There was no moderating influence at home. His wife, Mary Louise (or "Willie," as Beckwith called her), was even more radical on the race issue than Beckwith. "She was tough and mean," remembers Walcott. She stayed drunk much of the time, and the pair were constantly fighting. She was as ready to pick up a gun as was her husband. Gordon Lackey, a close friend who, according to congressional investigators, recruited Beckwith into the Ku Klux Klan in 1965,[36] remembers Mary Louise taking shots at Delay. "I said, 'Delay, why don't you kill that woman?' She was just a damn drunk." In fact, "she had every kind of problem God ever created in this world," says Walcott. On the day of Beckwith's arrest, she was "undergoing treatment for a nervous disorder" in the local hospital, as the *Greenwood Commonwealth* delicately put it.

But she had borne Beckwith a son, as he explained to Lackey, and that alone was reason to try to stick by her. Of course, Beckwith himself, consumed by the race issue, was hardly the easiest person to live with. A year before his arrest, and probably before, he had been treated by a University of Mississippi psychiatrist.[37] By 1963, he and Mary Louise had divorced, remarried, divorced, and married for the third time.

Beckwith's personal life was disastrous. And it was at this juncture, the beginning of the 1960s, that the world around him seemed to be collapsing, too. As much as any other place in the Delta, the Greenwood redoubt had seemed secure from what Beckwith called "the evils of integration." Why else would the Citizens' Council have established its headquarters there? There was no local NAACP representation to speak of. Less than 2 percent of the blacks in Greenwood and surrounding Leflore County were registered to vote, though blacks outnumbered whites three to two.[38]

So the specter of race-mixing mainly haunted relatively advanced Jackson. Up in Leflore, in the heart of the Delta, where civil rights workers hardly dared venture, it seemed a distant menace. But on Saturday, August 11, 1962, the integration movement came to Greenwood. On that day, a lonely parade of twenty-five blacks, led by two Student Non-Violent Coordinating Committee (SNCC) leaders, marched to the neoclassical courthouse in downtown Greenwood (Beckwith's grandmother had modeled for the monument to Confederate mothers that was by the courthouse steps) to register to vote. Nothing like this had ever happened before, and so it took the stunned whites a few days to react. When they did, the response was brutal. On the following Monday, one of the young SNCC men, twenty-five-year-old Sam Block, was pulled from his car downtown by three white men and severely beaten.[39]

The world of Greenwood, with its slow rhythms tied to the cotton harvest, its shady streets of frame houses on the white side of the tracks and its sorry shotgun shacks on the other, would be turned upside down for the next two years. Far more isolated and provincial than Jackson, it was a place where only the stationery store sold books, and most of these were on cooking and religion.[40] The main currents of American popular culture in the early 1960s might just as well have been flowing in a foreign country, as far as white Greenwood was concerned: "Nobody had ever heard of him," Lackey says dismissively of the black performer Dick Gregory, who played a notable role in the demonstrations of 1963. The day Evers was killed, the *Greenwood Commonwealth* almost blamed him for his own murder: "Of course it is wrong to indict Mississippi's people for the act of murder," the paper said in an editorial. "Of course Negro leadership have invited just such action as this. But the snuffing out of a life cannot be rationalized. Killing is wrong."

Much of this was to change. From Block's lonely registration campaign in the fall of 1962, to SNCC's defiant food distribution effort in the winter of 1963, to the mass rallies and registration marches that spring, through the Freedom Summer of 1964, when SNCC brazenly established its national headquarters in the old cotton town, Greenwood lived an upheaval that was the entire civil rights era in microcosm.

The whites of Greenwood responded with a rearguard action as brutal as any other of the civil rights era.[41] They shot repeatedly at the civil rights workers, loosed police dogs on them in the streets, beat them in the jails and in the alleys and as they were coming out of movie theaters. There was no protection, for the police department was closely allied with the roving band of thugs, some of them "respectable" citizens. For instance, William Greenlee, a petroleum products wholesaler, and Wesley Kersey, the service manager for an industrial company (and later a Ku Klux Klan officer),[42] were eventually arrested by the sheriff, under pressure from the FBI, in the shooting of Jimmy Travis, a civil rights worker.[43] The local judges and lawyers, Lott prominent among them, did everything they could to put the civil rights workers in jail and keep them there. Greenwood's city fathers asserted that the attacks were staged hoaxes or Communist plots, or both. The handful of enlightened whites stayed silent. "Greenwood isn't run by the city government, but by a bunch of thugs," Hodding Carter III, the managing editor of the liberal *Delta Democrat Times,* told a SNCC worker, Sally Belfrage, in 1964.[44]

The climax of the campaign had come a year earlier, in the spring of 1963. Two months before Evers's murder, to show it would not be cowed by the shooting of Travis, SNCC targeted the city for intensive voter registration efforts. Ultimately, they were a failure, for the U.S. Justice Department struck a deal with the city officials that left the civil rights workers hanging: eight SNCC workers would be released from Greenwood's jail, in return for which a federal lawsuit asking the city to stop harassing—indeed, start protecting—those seeking to vote, would be dropped.[45] But before, for over a week, at the end of March and the beginning of April, there were mass meetings and marches to the courthouse to register, all in full view of the national media. During one confrontation, massed police loosed a dog on a line of marchers. As it tore into one of them, the white mob shouted, "Sic 'em, Sic 'em." From March 29 through 31, with the story of Greenwood firmly implanted on newspaper front pages across the country, civil rights celebrities poured into Greenwood—James Farmer of the Congress of Racial Equality (CORE), Dick Gregory, Dave Dennis, and Medgar Evers. "You've given us inspiration in Jackson," Evers told a mass meeting at the Wesley Chapel church.[46]

For certain whites, "the thing to do was to go down to the courthouse to watch the blacks picketing," Betty McPherson remembers. But respectable people stayed away from downtown, and white high school students were warned by their teachers to steer clear. David Jordan remembers seeing Beckwith at the edge of some of these crowds, hanging back, watching. Beckwith could not have missed the protests, as his dilapidated old house was just up the street from the courthouse. One or more of his friends was usually present downtown. Once, one of them found amusement in draping a protest placard around a monkey and setting it loose by the courthouse.

If Beckwith had turned "rabid" on the race question as early as the mid-1950s, the effect of all this turmoil was only to intensify the urgency of his feelings. Already, during the Ole Miss crisis in the fall of 1962, he had loaded his pickup truck full of weapons and driven toward the campus, only to be turned back by friendly police warning him to stay away.[47] In January 1963, he wrote to the National Rifle Association: "Gentlemen, for the next 15 years we here in Mississippi are going to have to do a lot of shooting to protect our wives, children and ourselves from bad niggers."[48] The letter went on to ask for advice about how to set up a shooting range in Greenwood where white people could learn to shoot guns.

By the next month, he had taken a new job selling fertilizer for a company based in Greenville, the Delta Liquid Plant Food Company. That late winter and early spring of 1963, he roamed all over the Delta in the company's white Plymouth Valiant, its long radio antenna for two-way communication trailing in back. He called on farmers and plantation managers, and he regularly broke the car's speedometer over the rutted gravel roads. The car did not belong to him, but at least he had the privilege of keeping it on weekends. And Beckwith had given it some homey touches: a Masonic shield attached to a chain, swinging from the rearview mirror, and, above all, his guns. He liked to travel with his shotguns and rifles on the front seat so he could feel them there. "I carry as high as thirty or forty with me at one time," Beckwith testified later. "That seems impossible, but you can take several suitcases and put forty pistols in them."[49]

Dewitt Walcott did not mind; he did not see his new salesman that much because he was out in the field advising customers about their crops. Besides, Beckwith seemed "thorough" and "aggressive." Certainly, there was nothing to complain of in his work.

But he was strange, too—a loner, Walcott remembers, "a real weirdo." There were times, in the discussions they had that spring, when Beckwith went way beyond the standard Mississippi conservatism Walcott was used to. Walcott knew the kind of people Beckwith was talking to all day, the agriculturalists of the upper Delta, and he knew it would be hard to find a more hard-core bunch. It was not difficult to imagine the sort of conversations Beckwith had with them.

In Greenville, the company's home base, Carter was writing liberal editorials in the *Delta Democrat-Times* and consequently infuriating Beckwith. One day that spring, Walcott heard Beckwith say: "If I get my chance, I'll kill him." The businessman felt obliged to take his threat seriously; there was something determined, persistent about him, Walcott remembers. Besides, he knew what a good shot this queer employee was. "I said, 'I don't want any of that stuff around here.'"

By mid-April, the Greenwood movement had been stifled. The focus of the action shifted to Jackson, and to Medgar Evers. To Beckwith, Evers was the "big nigger," the "head nigger," and Beckwith would launch into a tirade against Evers every time he read of some new demonstration Evers was leading.[50]

Beckwith has been careful since those days to say little publicly about the NAACP leader, beyond referring to him as "Mississippi's mightiest nigger." But his friend Lackey, once the Grand Kleagle of the White Knights of the Ku Klux Klan,[51] feels no constraints and still can rouse himself to a fury on the subject of Medgar Evers. Normally genial and expansive, Lackey can get very mad, very fast, like Beckwith. And about Evers, he gets very mad. His opinons are all the more striking in that, even among the diehards, it is rare to find white Mississippians now who still get exercised on the subject. Who was Medgar Evers' inspiration, Lackey asks? Kenyatta and the Mau-Maus. And what did they do? There follows, in a rising voice, a graphic description of Mau-Mau eviscerations of whites, particularly white women. That was what Evers wanted to do.

On the continuum of fury that Evers was arousing in white Mississippians in 1963, from the hate mail to the abusive phone calls to the complaints that poured into WLBT-TV after his May speech, the feelings of Beckwith's friend Lackey, assuming they have not changed, are somewhere near the outer edge. And Beckwith's own feelings are probably not much different.

The fertilizer salesman was going about his job, generally making a good impression on his boss. "Everywhere Mr. Beckwith went, even when he was going with the young boys or with the older salesmen that had been doing that work, he did a good job," Walcott testified later. His ramrod-straight bearing, learned in the marines, marked him obviously as an ex-military man. This did not hurt with customers: "He left a favorable impression with the people," Walcott said later.[52]

In 1963 he and Mary Louise were separated again, and he was living alone in the old Yerger house. It was a wreck, in "a fearful state of repair," he said at the trial, so much so that he felt no compunction about keeping his company equipment out in the barren yard. In fact, the old house had not been painted in years. The interior was described as "dismal" by people who had penetrated inside, with wallpaper sagging from the ceiling and most of the old furniture sent off to relatives.[53] It was hardly the life of a country squire.

But there were other, more important irritations gnawing at Beckwith. He felt lingering bitterness over what Greenwood had recently been through. It had made Delay "mad as hell," Lackey says, "frustrated," just like the rest of his crowd.

Eddie Cochran, who runs a decrepit liquor store in the remnants of what was once the city's black hotel, has a disquieting memory of the salesman from a few weeks before the shooting of Evers. Cochran had been the local NAACP man in the 1950s, before any overt association with the group had become too dangerous. Late one night, he was behind the bar in the old Plaza Hotel, when he saw Beckwith's familiar face emerge from the shadows of the darkened room. Looking back now, Cochran remembers feeling a vague fear. When he came from behind the bar to find out what Beckwith wanted, Cochran had his pistol in his hand. "I don't know if he had something in mind or not," Cochran says.

At about four o'clock on the afternoon of Saturday, June 8, 1963, Herbert Richard Speight was sitting in his White-Top cab in front of the old Trailways bus station in downtown Jackson, waiting for a fare. He was chatting about this and that with his fellow cabbie Lee Swilley, who was sitting beside him.

A white man came up to the cab. Leaning down, he asked Speight "Do know where the Negro NAACP leader Medgar Evers lives?"

The veteran cabbie said no.

The man seemed calm enough. He went into the bus station and came back with a map, apparently torn out of the phone book. Could this Negro live on Lexington Street? Clearly, the man was an out-of-towner. Lexington Street was in a white neighborhood, as the cabbie explained. "I got to find where he lives in a couple of days," the man said. Back into the station he went, and the cabbies saw him checking the phone book. Buena Vista Street? No, another white neighborhood. Again, he went in, and came out with another address. But this time too, he was wrong. Just then, Speight got a fare, and he drove off. He thought no more of it.

The following Wednesday, Swilley saw in the papers where the Negro leader that the man had asked about had been shot. He called the police station, passed on the details of his recent encounter, and left his name. Ten days later, the police called Swilley back: a man had been arrested. So he and Speight went down to the station to look at a lineup. Speight had been in "public life," as he called it, all his life, and he never forgot a face once he saw it. It was the man in the shirt monogrammed BDB, the one with the darkish hair: he was the one who had been at the bus station on Saturday, June 8, two weeks before.[54]

Later that Saturday evening, the family of B. L. Pittman was assembled in Mr. Pittman's modest grocery store on Delta Drive, barely 350 yards through a parking lot from Medgar Evers's house on Guynes Street. A car pulled up by the side. In the fading light, young Bob Pittman, the grocer's seventeen-year-old son, could see that it was a late-model white Plymouth Valiant, with a long antenna trailing in back. Young Pittman could see what looked like a Shriners emblem hanging on a chain from the rearview mirror. A man got out of the car. It was strange: the man was wearing white shoes, a hat, and sunglasses, even though it was dark. He walked up and down in an adjoining field for a while, then left.[55]

On Sunday, June 9, Byron de la Beckwith was relaxing at home in Greenwood. The company's white Plymouth Valiant was parked in the driveway. As was his custom, he decided to do a little target-practice shooting. He took out a vintage, 1918 .30/06 Enfield rifle he had gotten a few years earlier in a trade with a local farmer. Although not the best gun in his collection, it was a serviceable weapon. Besides, Beckwith was not all that discriminating: "Anything that shoots, I like," as he said later; or, "I like guns, and I like people that like guns." On this occasion, he brought along a few of Walcott's young summer employees, high school kids, to show off a bit. The next day, they brought their boss the target Beckwith had used. "They were just dumbfounded he could shoot that good," says Walcott. Beckwith, his "boys" told him, had set the sight on his rifle so it was "deadly accurate."

On that Monday, June 10, Beckwith drove over to the company offices in Greenville early in the morning to discuss the field testing the young employees were doing, and to get some pointers on spotting problems in the coming cotton crops. His boss noticed a scar on Beckwith's forehead, between his eyes: evidently the gun he had used the day before had kicked back and cut him. Beckwith did not stay in the office long. The crops were well along in the southern Delta, and the salesman needed to get back on the road.[56]

The evening of Tuesday, June 11, was warm and dry in Jackson. At about nine o'clock, Bob Pittman was playing outside his father's grocery store when he noticed that same white Valiant he had seen on Saturday. It was driving slowly, up and down a vacant lot on Missouri Street, five or six times. It was odd: there was nothing special about the street. Across the lot was Guynes Street, where colored folk, including Medgar Evers, lived.

Business was slow that night at Joe's Drive-In on nearby Delta Drive. The drive-in, one of a strip of businesses along this road leading out of town, was a familiar landmark for the young Evers family who lived within easy walking distance on Guynes Street. Martha Jean O'Brien, a seventeen-year-old carhop, was standing around that night talking to her friend and ex-colleague Barbara Ann Holder. The two girls saw a white Plymouth Valiant pull up behind the building. They thought it was a police car because it had a long radio antenna in back. The car was quite dirty: obviously, it had been on some rough roads recently.

There were other strange things about this customer. He did not blink the car lights for service, as was the custom. When the driver emerged, he was wearing sunglasses, even though it was dark out. He walked to the drive-in's toilet, and Holder thought his carriage was unusual: "Well, he walked straight, because most of those people out there don't walk straight, and he did, he walked erect and straight."[57] Just like an ex-military man might have walked, an ex-Marine, say. When she left her friend at 11:30 that night, she noticed that the car was still there.

A few hundred yards away, in the Evers house, the lights were still on. They would, of course, stay on all that night.

In Greenwood, police officers James Holley and Hollis Creswell, both old acquaintances of Beckwith, were on the night shift, patroling in the city's black neighborhoods. Beckwith used the same shooting range as the Greenwood policemen, and he was familiar to many of them. On this night, the two officers were listening to the country music station out of Nashville, Tennessee, as they usually did, when the news came in that Medgar Evers had been shot.

Back in Jackson, Evers was dying in University Hospital. As if following the script Medgar himself had established in the event of an atrocity, Myrlie had called the UP reporter Cliff Sessions, who was at a nightclub drinking illegal whiskey; he sobered up quickly. Police began to descend on the scene in increasing numbers. Myrlie screamed at them: his blood was on their hands; they were the same police who had been following her husband for months. She had an urge to mow them down with a machine gun.[58] By the time Detective John Chamblee arrived, twenty-five neighbors had gathered on the lawn of the Evers house, and Myrlie "was incoherent and almost in a state of shock."[59]

What followed could not have been predicted by anyone who had observed the Jackson Police Department over the years. It was a department riddled with violence-prone racists, for whom harassing Evers and others in the Jackson movement came as second nature. After the Ku Klux Klan had reestablished itself in Mississippi in February of 1964, close relations between the Klan and many Jackson policemen had developed. But in the early morning hours of June 12 and on through the day, the immediate impact of Evers' killing was such that a few members of the department, notably Chamblee and Capt. Ralph Hargrove, conducted a thorough investigation.

The first break came when Chamblee shined his flashlight from the spot where Evers had been shot, to retrace the trajectory of the bullet. For six hours, all night, the officers searched the path of the bullet. The beam had illuminated a clump of bushes two hundred feet away, across Guynes Street from the Evers house, which was directly visible through a ten-inch hole someone had torn in the foliage. It was a dense area of sweetgum trees and honeysuckle bushes, perfect for concealment. Some of the vines had been trampled, and a tree branch had been broken off. This was the place.[60]

The immediate area was searched intensively. At around 11:00 A.M., 150 feet away from the bushes, the detectives found, hidden in some of the honeysuckle vines, a perfectly clean, well-cared-for, vintage 1918 .30/06 Enfield rifle. This gun was identical to the one Beckwith had traded for in 1960 with a young Delta farmer, Ines Thornton McIntyre. Attached to the gun was a steel-blue Japanese telescopic sight, a Goldenhawk; this standard-issue, six-power sight would prove critical in cracking the case. From it,

Captain Hargrove was able to lift a good fingerprint three hours later—a fresh fingerprint, as it turned out, one that contained moisture along the ridges.[61]

U.S. Senators were orating on this murder, and the president himself had now, finally, made the case for civil rights in personal, moral terms. The FBI was called in, and that night, an agent left Jackson for Washington with a bundle: a photograph of the fingerprint, the gun and scope, the bullet, an empty cartridge case, and six live rounds found in the rifle. As black Jackson's emotions erupted in riot immediately after Evers's painful, grief-filled funeral, the pieces of the FBI's case began to fall in place. The Goldenhawk's importer was in Chicago; the FBI found it had sold fifteen thousand of the sights to over two hundred dealers across the country. Sixty of them had been sold in the Mississippi area, and FBI agents working day and night from Memphis and Jackson checked thirty-five of the sights. It turned out that five had been sold to a gun dealer in the northern Mississippi town of Grenada. The agents traced all but one to their respective purchasers—a Goldenhawk sold to one Byron de la Beckwith of Greenwood.[62]

It was now Friday, June 21, nine days after the murder of Evers. That morning, the FBI agent Sam H. Allen, Jr., arrived in Greenwood. First, he called on Walser Prospere, the FBI's resident agent in town. It took no more than a glance through the telephone book to find that Byron de la Beckwith lived at 308 George Street, right downtown. The agents drove to the old Yerger house, but found nobody home. The two men sat in the car until 7:45 that night, and finally someone in a white Valiant with a long radio antenna drove up. In the twilight, Beckwith spotted the agents sitting in their car. He walked over to Allen's side.

"Are you looking for me?" he asked cordially.

"Are you Byron de la Beckwith?" was the reply.

"Yes."

Allen identified himself and introduced Prospere.

"We want to talk to you about a rather serious crime that has been committed," Allen said. "Would you mind having a seat in the car with us?"

Immediately, Beckwith's tone changed. "I have no comment," he said abruptly.

The agent tried to question him about the scope. "I have no comment," Beckwith said again sharply. He turned and walked into the house.[63]

The two agents sat in their car, discussing strategy. Evidently, it did not include keeping Beckwith under surveillance, because the next day, they were obliged to roam around Greenwood looking for him.

But time was running out for Beckwith. At the FBI lab in Washington, the fingerprint from the scope was being compared against the fingerprint record that Beckwith, like all other servicemen, had left in his military records. By midday Saturday, the word came back to the Memphis and Jackson offices: in fourteen points of comparison the print in the photograph matched the print of Beckwith's right index finger.

As Prospere and Allen searched that Saturday, teams of agents watched the Yerger house. Beckwith was at work in the company office in Greenville. The phone rang.

It was the neighbor, and she was anxious. "The yard is full of FBI agents," she said. "They are running all over the block, and they are up and down the street and they are worrying us to death."

Beckwith called his lawyer and old Citizens' Council associate, Lott. Walcott was advising Beckwith to give up. Late on the night of June 23, in Lott's office in downtown Greenwood, Beckwith turned himself in.

Driven through darkness the ninety miles down the narrow old two-lane highway to Jackson, Beckwith was a model of jaunty self-possession. He was wearing a dark brown suit, a dark green tie, and white buck loafers, and in his breast pocket was his carefully folded handkerchief. "Certainly glad to meet you," he drawled to the federal commissioner on hand to meet him at 2:00 A.M. for the preliminary hearing.

Over the next few days, Beckwith would talk amiably with the detectives about hunting and fishing and sundry other manly topics. But for questions about the crime he had only a steely "no comment." He especially had nothing to say about a scar, so new it was bright pink, on his forehead. It was the kind of scar a rifle makes when it recoils sharply.

All through his imprisonment, his examinations by a psychiatrist, and his first trial, Beckwith maintained his insouciance. The old newsreels show a confident, relaxed Beckwith: breezing out of Waller's office, chatting with Lott and the sheriff, he smiles for the camera, laughs and jokes. His hair slicked back, immaculately dressed, he is the man in control, a corporate CEO conferring with members of his team. Delay felt so confident that he wrote the editors of *Outdoor Life* magazine a teasing letter, just two days before the trial: "Sir, I have just finished an article on garfish hunting at night, which is sure to be of interest to the reader, along with several ideas I have on shooting at night in the summertime for varmints."[64]

True, some bad moments occurred during the trial. For example, there was the testimony about his gun being the murder weapon. And there were those witnesses in Jackson who kept spotting him and his white Valiant, like the simpering, slant-eyed carhop and her chubby blonde friend, as well as those two backstabbing cab drivers ("The boss kicked their asses out," Robert Penn Warren's cab driver told him two days after the trial's end. "'Said, 'Git yore asses out and don't ever set them asses back in no Yellow, even if you're payen for it.'")[65] In fact, Waller had presented an exceptionally strong murder case, as all the commentators agreed.

But on the whole, Beckwith had every reason to feel relaxed. The jury was all white, and no white man had ever been convicted for killing a black person. So Lott's team offered only a desultory defense. They hardly bothered to refute the substantial evidence Waller and the FBI had accumulated. Lott produced Greenwood policemen Holley and Creswell, who swore to having seen Delay at a filling station around 1:00 A.M. the morning of June 12, 1963. But these alibi men sounded tentative, particularly Holley, whom Waller launched into sharply. Why had he kept the information about Beckwith's whereabouts a secret for eight long months, while his old acquaintance languished in jail? There was no good answer.

All of the defense statements were no more than preliminaries. The clencher would have to be Beckwith himself, delivering the word of one white man to twelve others. He strode to the witness box to deliver it, tugged at his cuffs, and smiled at the jury.[66] He was in his most respectable getup, a dark suit with a Masonic emblem in the lapel. For Hardy Lott he was all respectful "yes sirs" and "no sirs," with plenty of the latter for the questions about whether he had shot Medgar Evers. Given the rifle to examine, he practiced aiming it over the jury box and suggested that it had been stolen from his bathroom closet the day of the murder.

All the physical evidence in the world was not going to convict Beckwith. Getting up slowly for the cross-examination, Waller knew he would have to establish a motive. But here was the ultimate dilemma of Waller's case: establishing Beckwith's motive for killing Evers might only serve to make the defendant even more sympathetic to the jury; there were, after all, thousands of white Mississippians who would have had the same motive. Waller would have to try anyway.

Beckwith was calm. The prosecutor read him his 1957 letter to the Jackson newspaper, the one about how he would "bend every effort to rid the U.S.A. of the integrationists." Did he still feel that way?

The defendant was indignant. Every white man should know the answer to that. "Of course I feel that way, sir."

It was an appeal which was, finally, irresistible. Back in the jury room, the twelve men argued, politely, for seven hours that night, and four hours the next morning. But in the back of all the jurors' minds would have been Beckwith's words to Waller: "It *is* a cause, sir—the cause of white supremacy." Beckwith was obviously its staunch champion. How, then, could he be guilty of anything? And then there was the powerful statement that the defense lawyer Stanny Sanders had sent the jurors off with: "I do not believe you will return a verdict of guilty to satisfy the Attorney General of the United States and the liberal national media."

On the morning of February 7, on the trial's twelfth day, the jury reported that it was hopelessly deadlocked, at seven for acquittal and five for conviction. That day, the mayor of Jackson sent three hundred policemen to block off the roads leading to the Jackson State College campus, as well as the famous hybrid "tank," a fearsome-looking armored paddy wagon devised to quell black rioting. "I've seen a Marine outfit storm a fortified hill in Korea with fewer men and less fire power than the mayor sent out to prevent this anticipated riot," Harold Martin wrote in the *Atlanta Constitution*.[67] No riot occurred, but the jumpy police shot into the crowd of students and wounded five of them.

White Jackson had been nervously expecting black rage over the outcome. There was none. The reaction was not anger but astonishment. Myrlie, at a loss for words, could say only that the hung jury signified "something." No one was in any doubt: the mistrial signified a rebuke for Beckwith, his lawyers, and the Citizens' Council. "The whole state, including the prisoner, was stunned by the mistrial," Silver wrote not long after. "Everyone had expected acquittal."[68]

Beckwith was to remain in jail two more months, through a second arduous rehearing of all the evidence against him. He looked bored and glum this time, but he need not have. A second set of jurors was again split, this time reportedly with eight for acquittal and four for conviction. "There was disagreement, but there wasn't any fighting," remembered one juror, John T. Hester, an analyst with the state highway department. He says he found the evidence "contradictory." Beckwith had picked up significant new support since the first trial, and it was much in evidence in the courtroom that April (see page 136). Another mistrial was declared, Waller sounded unenthusiastic about seeking a third trial, and Beckwith was on his way home.

On April 17, 1964, Jane Biggars, the veteran reporter for the *Greenwood Commonwealth* whose 1963 profile of Beckwith was the basis for every one written thereafter, came running into the paper's newsroom. "They've let Delay out, and he's coming back to town," she shouted. He was arriving home in grand style. His chauffeur was the sympathetic sheriff of Hinds County, Fred Pickett, leading a sizable motorcade. Balloons, honking of horns, and people waving from the street greeted the favorite son. It was, remembers Thatcher Walt, "a real circus."

In fact, the greetings had begun soon after the car had entered the Delta, with a Welcome Home sign posted in the village of Tchula. When he reached the courthouse in Greenwood, "well wishers rushed up to him and greeted him," the *Commonwealth* reported on the front page the next day. All this "brought tears to my eyes," Beckwith told the reporter. That night, he was treated to a steak dinner at one of the best restaurants in town, and he and his wife, helped out by sympathizers, moved into the Hotel LeFlore.

His friends were going to take care of him. Flat broke and "starving to death" when he got out of jail, Beckwith went back to his old job selling fertilizer. The city's police department made him an auxiliary policeman. He was allowed to ride up front, with his own gun and club, in police cars during trips through the black neighborhoods.[69]

When Beckwith was out of a job later in the decade, a prominent right-wing Greenwood businessman, Tom Barrentine, hired him to sell farm equipment in five states across the South. Barrentine was someone Beckwith could always go to for cash. He kept Beckwith on the road almost continuously—with a "deliberate intention," Beckwith later said, of keeping him out of Mississippi. He added: "I just was barely able to keep myself in clothes and . . . I ate on the company. And I was glad to have a job."[70]

In spite of the friends, money was scarce in those years. The federal government had bought the old Yerger property from him for twenty-five thousand dollars to build a new post office. Beckwith and his wife moved into a trailer in a loop in the highway on the edge of town. The ruinous state of his marriage became more public. Betty McPherson remembers seeing the couple stumble out of a restaurant one night; they had obviously been drinking. One of McPherson's teenage friends recalls a commotion at the Beckwith place. Police were called. When the teenager rode down on his bike to see what was happening, Delay was chasing his wife around the trailer. On several occasions, he beat her, and she filed charges against him. Once, he tied her up and left her all night. After these outbursts, she would flee their trailer in terror.[71]

Mary Louise was drinking more and more heavily. Their marriage had become "unbearable," Delay wrote in his third and last divorce filing, in August 1965. "She stays in a drunken state for prolonged periods," Delay wrote in the suit. When drunk, "she gets profane and obscene and curses complainant in front of their son and others." Mary Louise would become violent, firing a gun at Delay. He complained that he often had to "confine her in jail." The divorce went through quickly. She fled Mississippi for good and changed her name.[72]

Beckwith's eccentricity was growing. The seat covers of his car in those days were covered in Confederate flags. Virginia Alford remembers running into Beckwith in the grocery store and being embarrassed by the sweeping gesture to the floor that he made in greeting. At the same time, his respectability was diminishing. The writer William Bradford Huie described the process, repeated several times during the civil rights era, whereby the Southern race killer gradually lost the support and esteem of hometown champions.[73] As the 1960s wore on, Beckwith "was very much ridiculed," Alford remembered. "He really thought everybody supported him."

Beckwith's only sheltering direction was toward greater extremism. During the turbulent Freedom Summer of 1964, Beckwith divided his time between the bar of the Travel Inn motel, where the SNCC worker Sally Belfrage spotted him, and the roving band of white men who terrorized blacks and civil rights workers. The recently integrated movie theater was a particular target, and one night Beckwith went with the tough crowd and shined a flashlight into the faces of whites emerging from it. He was spotted at a gun show in Jackson later that summer. "There he was, smiling and talking about guns and how they could shoot, without any embarrassment at all," someone who saw him there said.[74]

Even during the second trial, there had been hints of this new, second existence. That April, as Beckwith returned to the courtroom, burning crosses lit up the night sky around Jackson in a gesture of solidarity, and seventy-five hard-eyed Klansmen filled the benches of the Hinds County courthouse.[75] Only two months before, the Ku Klux Klan had reestablished itself in Mississippi.

Groups calling themselves the Klan had always existed in one form or another elsewhere in the South; in Mississippi, there had been no need for a Klan because white supremacy had been enforced so effectively. Beckwith was a founding hero to the nascent group, which was born of the same frustrations he had been feeling—

frustrations that sprang from the Citizens' Council's obvious inadequacy in containing the tide of integration.

In February 1964, Sam Bowers—a Laurel, Mississippi, businessman and a fanatic whom FBI agents would laughingly call an "unasylumned lunatic"—organized the White Knights of the Ku Klux Klan at a meeting in Brookhaven, Mississippi.[76] Bowers, who liked to give stiff-arm Nazi salutes to his old dog, created a bizarre paramilitary structure for his new organization. Besides clinging to the notion that a worldwide Communist-Jewish conspiracy existed, this effete grandson of a congressman from New Orleans believed the United States was going to be invaded by African troops who would land at Biloxi, Mississippi.[77] In his five years as Imperial Wizard of the White Knights, he was suspected of ordering at least nine murders; almost seventy-five bombings of black churches; and three hundred assaults, bombings, and beatings.[78] Beckwith was to play a small but significant role in the group's murderous activities.

Beckwith's old friend Lackey, in 1964 a small-time motorcycle repairman, had been a charter member of the White Knights and had helped Bowers draft a constitution for the new organization. During the Freedom Summer, he had proposed blowing up the SNCC headquarters in Greenwood, a plan that was later dropped because of FBI presence around the office. In August 1965, he recruited Beckwith into the Klan, and by the end of the first week of that month, Beckwith had attended a state "Klonvocation" near Jackson.[79]

Following the Klan's elaborate secrecy dictates, Beckwith has never admitted nor denied being a Klan member. But he has expressed only admiration for Ku Kluxers: "The only men I ever heard of being associated with Klans were upright citizens concerned for welfare of our people," Beckwith told his biographer.[80] From the congressional investigation it appears that he and Lackey engaged in small-scale acts of terrorism together in the mid-1960s. They were questioned about having harassed a white Greenwood man who had unwittingly hired the relative of a black student at Ole Miss, and about tossing beer bottles filled with gasoline and rags into the house of a black woman whose family had been active in Freedom Summer.[81]

It was around this time that Lackey initiated Beckwith into

Bowers's worldview. "You're too carried away with being upset about these black people," Lackey told him. "They're not your enemy."

"Well, who is?" Beckwith answered incredulously. "They're the ones who are going to go to school with your son, and rape your daughter and mutilate your son."

"True," Lackey replied. "But they're not your enemy. These blacks didn't create the civil rights movement, and they are not driving it. Not only are they not driving the train, they ain't even blowing the damn whistle. It's a Jewish conspiracy."

The point was hard for Beckwith to swallow. He had grown up with Jews and had dealt with them as a salesman.

"I'm not gonna have you talking ugly about my Jewish brethren," Beckwith answered his friend hotly.

"He got angry with me," Lackey remembered. But Beckwith soon began to see the wisdom of Bowers's analysis. Blacks, after all, were not capable of complicated thought. In recent years, his hatred of Jews has far eclipsed his dislike of blacks. Much of the "biography" is a fevered anti-Semitic diatribe in which Jews are referred to as "sectists."

Beckwith was not an ordinary Klansman. Like Bowers, he was educated enough to have read materials supporting his views, which only made his racial convictions more passionate. In fact, Beckwith's extremism shocked and on occasion frightened the rank-and-file Ku Kluxers, according to people who had extensive dealings with the Klan in the late 1960s. "A lot of people in the Klan are afraid of Beckwith," one man said. There was "no credibility gap with Beckwith." Unlike many of his big-talking colleagues, he seemed fully able and willing to act on his extreme beliefs.

But if some of his Klan colleagues feared him, others in the hierarchy merely ridiculed his grand airs. Beckwith entered the 1967 lieutenant governor's race because "he was conned into it," one Klan associate says. "I was given a large sum of money to finance his campaign. They were using him. I guess it was just a big joke." Beckwith did not realize the joke was on him. Nevertheless, during a campaign that no one seemed to take seriously, he was able to muster a kind of darkly playful style. He would introduce himself at rallies as "the man they say shot Medgar Evers" and would coyly tell crowds about his love of guns. In a year when Barnett could manage only a fourth-place finish, Beckwith's platform of "absolute white supremacy under white Christian rule" was going nowhere. He got 5 percent of the vote.

That year, in accordance with Bowers's theories about Jewish string pulling in the civil rights movement, the Mississippi Klan's terror campaign shifted from blacks to the state's tiny community of Jews; Jackson had numbered no more than 140 Jewish families. In September 1967 the synagogue in Jackson was bombed; two months later the Klan bombed the home of Jackson's outspoken, pro–civil rights rabbi; and in May 1968 the synagogue in Meridian was hit by an explosion. Mississippi Jews were in a panic. They began paying informants inside the Klan and in 1968 even bankrolled the setup of two Ku Kluxers, who then attempted to bomb a Jewish businessman's house in Meridian. A total of about $100,000 was paid, and one of those who helped raise the money was the Anti-Defamation League's (ADL) representative in New Orleans, A. I. Botnick.[82] A vigorous FBI campaign, and the fiasco of the Meridian setup, in which one Klan bomber was killed and another captured, crushed the terror attacks.

But Beckwith had not forgotten. In the late 1960s he was spending much of his time as a salesman for Barrentine in Florida. On one of these trips, he went to an extreme-right convocation in Winter Park.[83] He was seen at a national Klan convention in New Orleans in the mid-1970s. And early in September 1973 he was spotted at a Citizens' Council rally in Jackson. George Wallace was the featured speaker; and Beckwith, dapper as always, arrived in a well-tailored suit. Reporters heard the avuncular Beckwith utter anti-Semitic statements.[84]

Three weeks later, Al Binder, a Jewish lawyer who had been active in the anti-Klan campaign, was in his office in Jackson when a Klan informant came to him with important information: Botnick was to be the recipient of a Klan bomb, and Beckwith was to deliver it. So thoroughly had the Klan been penetrated that both Binder and the FBI were told exactly when Beckwith was to pick up the bomb, where, and when he would be arriving in New Orleans. On September 26, 1973, Binder and an FBI agent sat in the old Mayflower Cafe in downtown Jackson. Two tables away sat Beckwith and a man known to the FBI as the Klan's chief bomb maker, L. E. Matthews. Binder saw Matthews pass a brown paper bag to Beckwith. He saw Beckwith reach inside the bag, and then the "damn fool turned it on."[85]

The New Orleans police were waiting for Beckwith when he came down Interstate 10 early the next morning. He had just crossed over Lake Pontchartrain when police ordered him out of his car at a roadblock. Beckwith was wearing a fully-loaded .45-caliber automatic pistol. In the car, they found three rifles, a machine gun barrel, and the makings of a powerful bomb on the floor: a black box containing seven sticks of dynamite, a clock, a battery, wires, and a blasting cap. On the seat beside him was part of a map of New Orleans, with the route to Botnick's home traced in red.

Jaunty and garrulous as always, Beckwith teasingly insisted he had no idea why the bomb was in his car. He was on his way to New Orleans, he said, to sell some inherited china that had once belonged to Jefferson Davis. He wrote a letter to the *Greenwood Commonwealth* pleading for bond money, and in court he offered to display for all the precious wares he had come to sell. But he had been caught, as one of the federal prosecutors put it later, redhanded. Surprisingly, the federal court jury of eleven whites and one black failed to convict him early the next year, apparently because the government lawyers made a weak showing.[86] "You are a very lucky man," the astonished judge told him.

But the state had filed identical charges against him, and he was not so lucky in the Louisiana court in May 1975. Convicted of carrying a bomb, he was sentenced to five years at the infamous Louisiana State Penitentiary. He arrived there in the spring of 1977, and his presence created a small uproar among the black prisoners. The guards kept him in the maximum security unit, and he was moved every few weeks for his own protection.[87] Beckwith wrote to *Attack*, a white supremacist hate-sheet:

> I'm being kept in solitary confinement here, but after being a traveling salesman and a Sunday school teacher for thirty years, I don't mind the privacy. At 57, a lot of things annoy me that used to amuse me. Still, there is work to be done by

those of us who aren't too liberal to survive, and I can't do what needs doing while I'm in here. Any help your readers can send will be appreciated indeed.[88]

The "work" Beckwith was referring to would likely have been on behalf of the Christian Identity Movement, a racist, anti-Semitic group in which he became increasingly active after 1975. Beckwith was particularly enthusiastic about its belief in the War of the Identity, which an FBI agent described as "the war of the white people to take back the U.S. from what they called the Zionist Occupied Government, which they called ZOG." Even from his jail cell, this shadowy world of white supremacist vigilantism, mostly bluster (though in the early 1980s Identity members were convicted of murders and robberies), was now Beckwith's own.

Beckwith was released in 1980, and three years later he was living in a trailer at the end of an isolated dirt road, in the hill country of north-central Mississippi near Greenwood. He had no telephone and, for a good while, no electricity. He was earning a meager living three days a week selling auto parts out of his van. "Posted" signs bordered his property, and Beckwith usually carried a gun; inquisitive visitors were not welcome.[89]

But he kept up his ties to the far-rightists, and it was through them that he met his second wife, Thelma Neff—like Delay, a stalwart of the anti-Semitic Liberty Lobby. She had a modest bungalow high up on Signal Mountain, Tennessee, outside Chattanooga. Beckwith moved in with her there after their marriage.

"He was such a gentleman, that's what I noticed at first," said Thelma, one sunlit afternoon in January 1991 at her Signal Mountain house. Amidst the comprehensive assortment of hate literature, she had made moderate efforts at gentility in their cramped little dwelling. Her Daughter of the American Revolution certificate hung in a frame, some unassuming antiques were shoved against the wall, and prints of neoclassical paintings were scattered about.

Ten years older than Beckwith, she had just come from seeing her husband in court, and her conversation was confused. She knew he was in a predicament, but the exact dimensions of it were not clear. "It's just the little things about him," Thelma observed, in the midst of an excursus on the iniquities of the ADL, the Trilateral Commission (the private East-West foreign policy group sponsored by Chase Manhattan Bank president David Rockefeller, which has become a bogeyman of far-rightists tremulous over "one-worldism"), and blacks and Jews. "When he says grace at the table, it's never the same twice."

They had been happy together, attending Klan rallies and cross burnings, taking part in their local town government, and corresponding with other white supremacists. Beckwith had his little study and worked fitfully at an always-in-progress memoir.

In the fall of 1989, the grand jury in Jackson again began looking into the events of twenty-six years before. Reporters trooped up to Signal Mountain to record Delay Beckwith's thoughts. He was happy to oblige, glad for the attention after so many years. "God hates mongrels," he told one reporter. "My people came here to take this country from the red man by force and violence, and that's the way were going to keep it—by force and violence," he said to another.

When they came to arrest him a year later, he was jocular. "I'm ready to go, boys," he said. "I'm not guilty. Do you want to search me for a bomb?" But it had not yet dawned on him that this was not just a big joke. When the Mississippi officers came for him, several months later, to take him back to his ancestral land, he was shocked, and Thelma was distraught. "What the hell is wrong with Mississippi?"

He would fight anybody who tried to fingerprint him. Leaving the jail in Chattanooga, he told the Hinds County deputies they would hit a roadblock, they would never make it over the state line, the good people of Tennessee would never allow such a thing. That night Delay Beckwith was back in the Hinds County Detention Center.

Less than four years before, he had had a most unlikely encounter. In the summer of 1987, Delay showed up with Thelma at the last surviving Citizens' Council rally in Mississippi, at a hamlet near Greenwood called Black Hawk. This was his kind of crowd. The barbecue and that year's crop of gubernatorial candidates only provided an excuse for like-minded whites to get together and reaffirm some eternal Mississippi verities. Bill Waller, who was at the end of his career, was making one last lunge at the governor's mansion. He too came to Black Hawk that day, along with most of the other candidates.

So here Beckwith was, face-to-face with the man who had persecuted him in that unthinkably distant era. Waller chuckled, half-embarrassed. Beckwith was jovial. "Mr. Waller tried to put me in the gas chamber twice," he joked. "I told Mr. Waller back then I had a sinus condition and that smelly gas would upset my sinuses." It was all so long ago. It was history. He could afford to joke about it now. He was safe. There was nothing wrong, really, with Mississippi.

There was, in fact, much that Beckwith would have had to adjudge wrong with Mississippi, had he ventured beyond the time-warp cocoon of the Black Hawk rally. Had he given the matter thought, he would have had to hold Bill Waller as responsible as any man for making his beloved state unrecognizable. Waller, in turn, could give Beckwith some of the credit for his own transformation, and the state's. For twenty-three years before the strange meeting at Black Hawk, Waller had had that other, more celebrated, encounter with Beckwith in a courtroom in Jackson. The jovial little white supremacist had forced the prosecutor to take a public stand back then—against Beckwith and what he stood for (see chapter 5). Once taken, this stand was one Waller had had to uphold, even after reaching the highest office in the state.

Byron de la Beckwith and his second wife Thelma appear at a bond hearing in Chattanooga, Tennessee, on December 18, 1990, shortly after his indictment for the murder of Medgar Evers. (AP Photos)

Medgar Evers
(© Black Star)

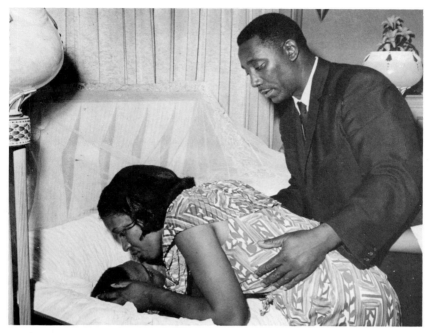

Medgar Evers's widow Myrlie, at the funeral home in Jackson, June 13, 1963. At her side is Charles Evers. (AP/Wide World Photos)

Mourners walking from Union Station in Washington, D.C., follow the hearse carrying Medgar Evers, June 17, 1963. (AP Photos)

From *The Citizens' Council* newspaper, February 1957. (The Political Ephemera Collection, Special Collections Division, Howard-Tilton Memorial Library, Tulane University)

Byron de la Beckwith marches toward the Hinds County jail, Jackson, carrying an extra suit of clothes, June 27, 1963. Behind him a Jackson policeman obligingly carries Beckwith's suitcase. (AP Wirephoto)

Bill Waller, District Attorney, arrives at the Hinds County Courthouse
to begin the prosecution of Byron de la Beckwith, January 27, 1964.
(AP Wirephoto)

A disappointed Bill Waller talks to reporters in Jackson, April 17, 1964, after his prosecution of Beckwith ends in a mistrial for the second time. Next to him is his assistant John Fox. (AP Wirephoto)

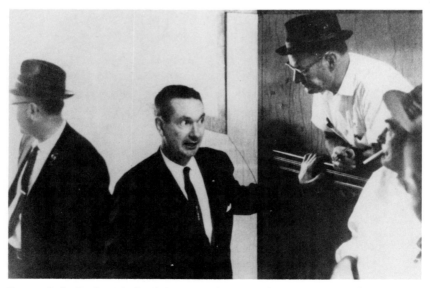

Byron de la Beckwith, back home and among friends at the Leflore County Courthouse in Greenwood after the second mistrial, April 17, 1964. (AP/Wide World Photos)

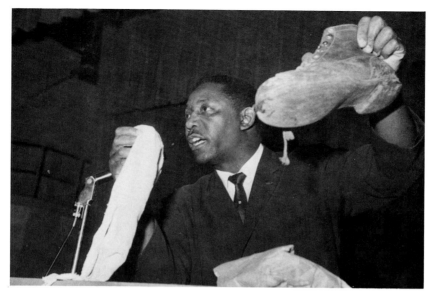

Charles Evers, installed in his brother's old job as Mississippi NAACP Field Secretary. At an NAACP meeting in Jackson, February 4, 1964, he holds a tattered shirt and shoe which he says were torn off a black man pulled through a briar bush by Jackson police. (AP/Wide World Photos)

On the road to empowerment: Charles Evers addresses supporters in Jackson, February 28, 1968. After a strong showing in the special election for Congress, he calls it the "beginning of the end for racism in Mississippi." (AP/Wide World Photos)

Evers, candidate for governor, in Drew, Mississippi, June 1971. The mood is angry: an eighteen-year-old black girl had been shot the month before by whites in a passing car. (AP Wirephoto)

Capitol Street, Jackson, August 25, 1971. Waller and family celebrating the triumph. (AP/Wide World Photos)

Anxious: Buddie Newman in the late 1980s, on the way down from his command of the Mississippi House of Representatives. (Scott Boyd, *The Clarion Ledger*)

Jubilant: Ray Mabus, Democratic governor-elect, and his wife Julie. Jackson, November 4, 1987. (AP ColorPhoto)

Before the fall: Beck-with outside his home in Chattanooga, Tennessee. (Scott Boyd, *The Clarion Ledger*)

Bobby DeLaughter outside the Hinds County Court-house, Jackson. (Brian Albert Broom)

Jackson, February 4, 1994: Beckwith and Thelma arrive at the Hinds County Courthouse for the last day of the new trial. (AP/Wide World Photos)

CHAPTER FIVE

BILL WALLER

I n the courtroom during those tense weeks in February 1964, there were a lot of things Bill Waller did not need to notice: the growing banks of reporters seated in the galleries, so many they seemed to be hanging over the rail; Beckwith, sitting back with ever-so-studied coolness in his starched cuffs and new cufflinks, his Southern gentleman pose infuriating to the tough-minded young prosecutor; Ross Barnett entering the courtroom to shake Beckwith's hand. But most of all, he did not need to notice the electric tension suffusing the air and making everybody a little jittery. He was one of the twin centers of a drama the whole nation was following, and it was a heady experience for the thirty-seven-year-old district attorney. With his hair slicked carefully back and his smiles for the press cameras at the end of the day, he obviously enjoyed the attention.

As it turned out, though, he did not get distracted easily. He saw the reporters who drifted in and out as being about as substantial as "morning fog." Certainly, he got agitated when he looked over at the smirking Beckwith, that "coward" and "ambusher." And it was hard when Beckwith patted him on the back as he left the courtroom (as if to say, We're all just white men here), or tried to offer him a cigar. Barnett's walk-on cameo was most definitely improper, and it too made Waller mad.

But then Waller reminded himself of his basic credo: "Here is a victim; it is a homicide." Despite all the petty distractions, Waller was going to plunge ahead—"single-mindedly moving along," as he puts it—until he had done his duty as he estimated it to be.

This did not include making a hero out of the "victim" in this particular murder case, Medgar Evers, whom Waller had not admired. Waller speaks respectfully enough of him now, but it is clear from his words that he has about as much appreciation for Evers's contributions as do most other white Mississippians of his generation—not very much. He chiefly appreciates what Evers was not: not an "insurrectionist," not a Malcolm X, not a hate monger. When Myrlie Evers was called in to be interviewed as a potential witness in 1964, Waller coolly told her that "he didn't agree with what Medgar had been doing."[1]

The district attorney had other motivations for "moving along" in the case. Those motivations are to be found somewhere in a mentality that could ask prospective jurors in 1964: "Do you believe it is a crime to kill a nigger in Mississippi?"

Waller, evidently, did. But he was not going to give up much to those who might recoil at the way he chose to find out who agreed with him.

Waller had never been a flaming partisan of the civil rights movement. His vision of the black insurgents who battled the police thirty years ago, right at his Jackson law practice doorstep, is not complicated by any notions of their heroism. The Freedom Riders who rolled into town in 1961 are the only civil rights workers who made a lasting impression on him—but not a positive one; the memory brings a deprecating smile. It was all just a staged event, like a football game, in which the riders were the derided out-of-town team. He lumps what happened subsequently—downtown boycotts and sit-ins and marches—with this first semiludicrous foray. People in Jackson did not take much of it seriously. "The sit-ins, the drive-ins, the ride-ins and all that were just kind of . . . Everybody in town was laughing about that. It was just kind of frivolous, the way they went about it," he says today.

Waller was not then, and is not now, a dedicated integration-ist. But this has less to do with his feelings about blacks than with his distrust of abstractions like "integration." In the world of his father's hardscrabble northern Mississippi farm, there wasn't much need for abstract thinking. Integration was something anonymous masses of people were engaged in, people Waller neither knew nor could see. He is still uncomfortable with mass movements and sus-picious of groups. Waller will call himself a "champion of the underdog," but then quickly add, "not that I've been crusading as a member of a group."

The symbolic triumphs of the civil rights movement are not significant to him. "A lot of crusading whites and blacks believe that one drinking fountain and one restroom and the front of the bus represented prosperity," he says. Waller believes only in a move-ment that means the possibility of individual self-improvement. "I mean, everybody wants to better themselves. What's left out of the whole deal is that this is an opportunity to work hard personally for our own betterment."

Waller gets testy when the talk turns to Jim Crow Mississippi. This is a historical generalization about relationships on a mass scale, and he distrusts it. Waller does not deny the iniquities of Jim Crow, but the realm of his own experience includes decent relation-ships with blacks. So his thoughts run, in a semipaternalistic way, to the good relations between individual blacks and individual whites. "Some states like the blacks as a race. We like the blacks as individuals," Waller says. "There's some real rapport and some real camaraderie between whites and blacks as a small group." There is no question about who is setting the dominant terms of the rela-tionship here: whites.

He has traveled some distance from his old-school Mississippi roots, but not all the way. His vision of the white–black dialogue has its roots in the old Mississippi folkway of kindly individual relations, based on definite caste distinctions. Those roots are clearly visible in the racial attitudes of his stolid brother, Don, the head of the deeply conservative Mississippi Farm Bureau Association. The family of Percy Waller treated its black tenant farmers with scrupulous fairness, Don Waller asserts today with some petulance. "I have not treated the blacks wrong. My father didn't treat the blacks bad," he says angrily. Like Bill, he generalizes from his experience, so harping on the systematic unfairness of Jim Crow is a mystery to him.

Bill Waller believes in the individual, not the group. In his worldview, individuals face large, anonymous forces and are therefore at a disadvantage. Waller does not like those forces. In a famous declaration two decades ago, he called himself a redneck, the first Mississippi politician in a generation to do so. Half the redneck tradition, in Mississippi at least, was not racist, but populist: it carried a festering resentment against the overprivileged, the bullies, and the powerful institutions. Waller comes from that tradition. He still inveighs against the large corporations that exploit Mississippi's natural resources and do not give back much except low wages.

Waller's identification with the underdog is personal, the natural outcome of his background and his distrust of groups. He looks like a well-fed Jackson lawyer now, and he lives in a comfortable house in the upper-middle-class northern end of town. But he came to maturity as an outsider from the hinterlands (his decidedly nonhomogenized, hill-country twang is a reminder), and he grew up milking his father's herd of Jersey cows, early in the morning before school and in the evening when he came home.

The high and mighty, the snooty and the bullying—thinking about them is "what really sets him on fire," says Don Waller. The philosophical groundwork for Bill Waller's prosecution of Byron de la Beckwith was laid well before the shot was fired. "I've always felt that a professional license such as being an attorney gave you a license to make the wheel move in a smooth circle, and take out any inequities," Waller says. He saw the Beckwith prosecution not as the righting of a racial wrong, but as part of his larger effort to make sure "that there's no favoritism shown because of a person's race or standing in the community or wealth." Waller equates the unfair judicial privileges of the rich man with those of the white man. When he says, "We tried long before Beckwith to enforce the law equally," he closes the thought not with an observation on race, but with one on class: "It's a standard rule that money and prominence gives you a lighter sentence."

Thus, he was able to establish a kind of posthumous "rapport" with Evers, according to his own vision of individual struggle and the terms of the white–black dialogue. Evers as the champion of a certain philosophy may not be a sympathetic figure to Waller, but Evers as the solitary, struggling individual is. They were almost exact contemporaries—Evers, thirty-seven when he was killed, and Waller thirty-seven when he prosecuted Beckwith. The prosecutor was compelled to do him justice. "I think he was an individualist," Waller says now. "I think he was driven to help the blacks." Further separating Evers from the mass, Waller adds, "But I'm not sure he had a large following before he was killed."

In 1964, the job at hand was to apply justice evenly. Waller was going to do that. He was not going to make out of the case a statement of sympathy for Evers, and he was not going to use it as a vehicle to reproach white supremacy. He was not even going to admit previous iniquities in the Mississippi judicial system. He was simply going to do his job. And the world would know that Mississippians were not wild and lawless, as was being said about them by so many. "I appreciated the opportunity," Waller says now. "It was a chance to prove that we are a law-abiding people, that we exact a penalty on anybody that commits a crime, equally." Waller was going to do that, without acknowledging collective guilt or trumpeting ideology. This was a posture made up of equal parts shrewd political calculation, genuine devotion to justice, and bluster.

Today in Jackson, Waller is frequently thought of as a blusterer, a man with firmly held, loudly expressed convictions but no very convincing platform from which to deliver them. He has always been verbose, circling around his point with a spray of words and sometimes not hitting the target. Even a simple biographical declaration can be painfully labored: "I had at that point a steady attitude of a law practice in the city of Jackson and had what was better defined as a personal, private practice. That is to say, I was self-employed and had myself and no one else to look to for a live-lihood or for professional existence," he told an interviewer twenty years ago.[2]

The blowhard judgment is a reminder that Waller's real ac-complishments are not much remembered anymore. But it captures a part of his persona.

As a young man, he liked to give vent to his opinions and to argue, but those predilections were not necessarily useful in the backwoods environment in which he grew up. So Waller was for-tunate that his father, Percy, was keenly interested in the affairs of the little northern Mississippi town near his farm. Percy took an interest in politics, maintained a friendship with his old schoolmate Ross Barnett, and had even run, unsuccessfully, for a few local of-fices. Barnett came to dinner at the Waller house in Clear Creek the night before he spoke at young Don Waller's high school gradua-tion in 1950.

Politics was a diversion from the hardening duties at hand during Waller's boyhood: farming the family's three hundred acres in the midst of the Great Depression. The three Waller children were thoroughly involved. There was not much money to spare, but the Wallers were better off than many of their neighbors and often produced enough to share with some of them. It was a classic hard-scrabble Mississippi farm childhood, and Waller was to make the most of it in his future campaign literature. He never had trouble establishing his common-man bona fides; his self-proclamation as a redneck came easily.

Waller has always had the capacity to bulldoze his way through difficulties. He looks on the period when he was establishing him-self as a lawyer as a struggle, a word that comes up frequently in his recollections of that era. He did night work in a Memphis fu-neral home to put himself through Memphis State University. Don stayed on the farm, but Bill was ambitious. In 1950, after law school at Ole Miss, he went to Jackson, borrowed $400, bought himself a $10 desk, and set up as a lawyer. He did not want to join a larger firm; $200 earned on your own, he thought to himself, was better than $2,000 working for somebody else. But it was a tough road. The big money for lawyers was in working for the Jackson banks, the utilities, and the insurance companies, all of whom had "a clubby fraternity approach to who they hire." They were not about to take a chance on a struggling young attorney.

He did not feel the lack keenly. Of course, he wanted to make money, particularly since he had a growing young family. But he was finding other satisfactions in the "human drama" of the law office. He was forced to take on cases that were not bringing in enormous amounts of money (a practice he continues, voluntarily, today) but that were giving him a growing insight into the peculiarities of Mississippi-style justice. In an early case, Waller represented a black sharecropper in the Delta who was being ruined by a bank's exorbitant interest rates. "The bank up there just wiped him out," Waller remembers. "It was what I call the Delta Common Law. If you've got it, you keep it; if you don't have it, you don't get it."

Most of the time, blacks and poor whites did not get it when they got caught up in the justice system. Prosecutors obviously did not care when a black was accused of killing another black, but they cared very much when a black was accused of killing a white; this bothered him. And defendants who had money and influence had a better chance of getting off. "The whole spectrum of law enforcement was kind of suspect as far as minorities and poor whites were concerned."

With memories of a spartan upbringing still fresh, and struggling to earn a living, Waller saw politics as a sideshow—"extracurricular," as he puts it. But he began to perceive holding office as a way not only of advertising his lawyerly skills but of acting on fundamental instincts. In 1959, after several unsuccessful attempts, he got himself elected district attorney. In Hinds County, that office had for years been a do-nothing position, a kind of super-honorific in the backslapping, good-old-boy world of the Jackson bar. So clubby a world was it that the district attorney worked only part-time and was allowed to keep his private practice going all the while.

Much was to change under Waller, who instituted a reform administration. Today, his public years before Beckwith are remembered chiefly for his efforts to clean up local syndicate-inspired corruption. But there was more to it than that.

There were sheriffs and police chiefs and some other prominent folk who quickly became disenchanted with Waller's way of
doing his job. A year before the Beckwith trial, he put a white man
in jail for twenty years for murdering his black fishing companion.
In one sensational case, a rich white lady went on trial for murdering her husband. The newspapers all said she was a cinch to get off
lightly; Waller went after her with a vengeance. This way of proceeding was unheard of, and Waller recalls the threats made against
him to cease and desist.

He did not. But there was no great harm done to his law
practice, which he expanded with a few partners after becoming the
district attorney. "I liked his ethics. I liked his integrity. I liked the
fact that he would work," says the ebullient Bob Pritchard, who
was courted by Waller for nine months before he joined the firm.
Waller's particular ability—brilliance, his ex–law partners would
say—is to see the big picture in the case, the ultimate result, and
convey it to the jury. Without much preparation, he can walk into
a courtroom and quickly win the jury over to his side. The detail
work he left to his conscientious assistant John Fox, and the chore
of drumming up clients, to the gregarious Pritchard. They were
good foils for Waller himself: Fox, stolid and crew-cutted, maintained a kind of military erectness reassuring to clients, while the
flamboyant, motor-cycle-riding Pritchard charmed them. Waller
riled the big folk from his perch as the chief county prosecutor, and
his law firm prospered.

Waller's distance from the ambient white extremism of the
times paralleled the suspicion he felt for the civil rights movement.
He would not have been found among the tiny gatherings of nervous white liberals in Jackson. But it is telling that he was drawn
to the quietly skeptical Bill Minor, whose dispatches to the New
Orleans *Times-Picayune* were among the few sources of objective
coverage to people in Jackson. Minor remembers being "adopted"
as a friend by District Attorney Waller in the early 1960s. He was
invited to dinner at the Waller house, where the journalist was dismayed to find that the abstemious Baptist couple served no wine.[3]

Minor found other compensations. Waller was not contribut-
ing his voice to the segregationist bluster at the center of political
discourse, and the journalist was attracted by that. Unlike virtually

all his political peers, Waller had no ties to the Citizens' Council. And Governor Barnett's handling of the Ole Miss crisis had offended the young district attorney's sense of the Constitution; as a matter of plain and simple ideology, he thought Barnett's actions had been wrong.

Mostly, though, he did his thinking in private in those years; it would have been political suicide to speak out on such matters. The explanation Waller gives now for his silence—that he had had no forum in which to break it—is partly disingenuous. For any politician with an eye on his own advancement, the risks in expressing the philosophy of dissent were great. They were so great that even in his own law firm, among the men he was closest to, "it would not have been expedient politically to articulate that philosophy," remembers Pritchard.

It certainly would not have done Waller any good to think openly along those lines during the trial of Beckwith; the simple fact of putting Beckwith on trial branded Waller as a liberal, and the young firm lost business.[4]

Still, in the memories of Waller and his associates, the prosecution of Beckwith was approached in about as carefully nonideological a manner as can be imagined. This was a murder case, plain and simple; their job was to prosecute murder. "As best I can recall, our discussion was, we were hired to do this job, let's do it," remembers Fox. In Waller's recollection, there was no political calculation, either immediate or future, in his handling of the case: "I really wasn't politically sensitive. I wasn't playing any political games with the case."

But these memories gloss over the dominating importance of the contemporary racial conflict. That much is clear from looking at the prosecutor's strategy. It was a calculating, subtle course of action that would both help him accomplish his immediate goal— convict Beckwith—and protect him in the future. The legend of Waller's prosecution is that it was unexpectedly vigorous—in memory, if not perhaps in fact, the first time a white man had ever been conscientiously prosecuted for killing a black man. The press certainly did not expect it; the early stories invariably refer to Waller as a "seventh-generation Mississippian," as if that sealed his likely complicity with Beckwith as a Mississippi white man.

It did not. The 1964 trials of Beckwith may have been the first time time race had ever been removed as an issue in a race killing. Waller's great achievement in the trials of Beckwith was to neutralize race.

The lesson of previous race-killing trials in Mississippi—Emmett Till in 1955, Mack Charles Parker in 1959—was clear and discouraging. The defense would always win, and the killers would always be sprung because race, not the crime itself, was always the issue. The jury would be left with the irreducible fact that the victim was black. And so the critical effort, from Waller's standpoint, would have to be accomplished before a single bit of evidence had been presented. Evidence had not mattered in previous race-killing trials; the key would be to make it matter in this one.

From the first day of jury questioning Waller took the case outside the realm of the dominant ideology of white supremacy. I'm one of you, he told the jurors over and over again. "I don't enjoy what I'm doing," he said early on. "But I think it's my duty." I may be prosecuting this sympathetic-seeming white man, but you and I agree on the important things. The visiting reporters were initially confounded by this approach. "Waller's skill and purpose were not immediately apparent, clouded as they were by his comments," the correspondent for the *Nation* wrote.

"The deceased worked in a way obnoxious and emotionally repulsive to you as a businessman and me as a lawyer—can you put that out of your mind and judge this case like any other case?" There were murmurs of anger and disappointment from the largely black audience in the courtroom; Waller did not care. "Evers was engaged in things that were contrary to what you and I both believe in." The spectators responded with more anger. "I'm a little upset right now with all these nigras in the courtroom—does that bother you?" he asked. "I like Mr. Beckwith. He has a pleasant way," Waller said. "He's a Mason, you're a Mason; he's a veteran, you're a veteran; you're a father, he's a father."[5] The message was clear: Beckwith is much more one of us than the victim. White jurors were always called "mister" by Waller; blacks were only entitled to a last name.[6]

Later, at the trial's opening, he was unconsciously condescending to the black witnesses. "Was that a rented home or were you all buying that, in the sense of owning a home?" he asked Myrlie Evers. "You all are not trigger-happy, are you, Houston?" he asked the Evers's neighbor, who had fired his pistol in the air on hearing the fatal shot.

Waller had a doubly difficult task: Medgar Evers had been not only a "nigra" but an agitator. He had to be divorced from both of these identities. The prosecutor's case rested on a single, slender appeal, enunciated early on: "In the sense of being killed, he *was* a human being." Once established, this principle made relevant all the careful, lumbering unfolding of evidence that followed. To observers at the time that evidence seemed overwhelming, both as to circumstance and as to motive.

"When he gets going on something, man, he works on Saturdays and Sundays, and everything. Man, he's got a driving force behind him," the head of the state highway patrol, Chet Dillard, said years later. Naturally a hard worker, Waller worked harder now than he had ever worked before. It was nine months of "intense concentration," Fox remembers. During the trials, Fox went for a month without seeing his children, because he got up before daylight and returned home after dark.

To Waller, the evidence did not seem overwhelming. He gave himself only a fifty–fifty chance of winning. It was not enough to demonstrate Beckwith's fanaticism on the race issue. Sentiments like those were so common that there was no necessary connection between them and an act of violence. He wanted a witness who could show "predisposition" on Beckwith's part, who had seen him commit violence against blacks. None was forthcoming.

Other frustrations were gnawing at Waller. Beckwith had almost certainly not acted by himself. He must have had help planning the murder. Waller suspected that a lookout was used, that the conspirators had staked out the Evers house. He thought the two alibi witnesses were part of the conspiracy, but there was no way to prove any of his suspicions—no way, in fact, to seal Beckwith's guilt in the Mississippi system of 1964.

He emerged from the trials exhausted and disappointed, but he put a brave face on the proceedings. After the first trial the television cameras caught him, all pudgy-cheeked and smiling, promising to go on Monday to another murder case in Yazoo City. But there were plenty who thought his future was in doubt. "He may have put his career on the block by his tireless prosecution of the case," the *New York Times* commented in February 1964, at the end of the first trial. He hardly seemed well positioned to look for higher political ground. If white people in the state knew his name at all, they would have associated it with something not exactly positive—the prosecution of Beckwith.

In fact, Waller could not have asked for a better outcome. Five white men had held out for conviction, and the outside world judged him a winner. He had earned the gratitude of blacks, soon to become a huge new group of voters. And by not obtaining the conviction of Beckwith, he had shielded himself from the permanent enmity of many whites.

Waller is an impatient man. He once left his third-floor governor's office in the state capitol building to browbeat a legislative committee on the floor below. Told firmly that he was not on the agenda that day, Waller charged angrily back upstairs, slammed the door, and kicked it hard enough to put a hole through it.

Abrupt, overbearing, and *brusque*: these three words come up often in discussions of Waller, a man who definitely does not sugarcoat his manner in the Southern fashion, who has no patience with people he considers foolish. "He's not a friendly guy. He turns a lot of people off," says Minor. "Oh yeah, he's hollering and screaming all the time," says Dillard.

By the mid-1960s, Waller was in an impatient, angry mood. He was disgusted with the dismal rearguard action Mississippi had been mounting for so long, "sick and tired" of the Ross Barnetts and their crazy, quixotic rhetoric. As the district attorney in Hinds County, he had a limited forum in which to express this disgust. So his decision to run for governor in 1967 did not surprise the people who knew him well. John Fox, a friend since teenage days, says Waller has been running for governor since his senior year in high school.

Waller had no money and no organization. But he was convinced he had a different appeal from the other players in this race, which was dominated by the reactionary old guard—men like Congressman John Bell Williams, the paranoid one-armed arch-segregationist whose railing against the federal government eventually put him over the top. "White Mississippi, Awake," a Williams campaign circular warned.[7] The specter of massive increases in black voter registration hovered—between 1964 and 1969 the percentage of eligible blacks registered to vote increased from 6.7 percent to 66.8 percent.[8] It was making everybody nervous. "I have never met Bobby Kennedy before. I have no connection with the Kennedy family," Williams's principal opponent, the moderate state treasurer William Winter, felt constrained to tell a press conference. Twenty-one blacks were elected to county offices in Mississippi that year, the first since Reconstruction. Robert Clark became the first black man elected to the legislature: looking shy but triumphant, he submitted to the nervous questions of a local television interviewer about the potential "militance" of his strategy.[9] Barnett, whose appeal was based on promises to outdefy anyone else in Mississippi, dragged himself out again, and so did the almost equally segregationist lieutenant governor, Carroll Gartin. Waller was the brash young upstart, several decades younger than the other contenders.

He was spoiling for a fight. Waller's memory of that race is dominated by a metaphoric physical assault on the other candidates—the youthful pugilist as deliverer of renewal. In memory he is "young, physically active, hardworking, aggressive," and he is "out there knocking and hitting on isolationism." He is the champion of the "new politics," the "fresh approach," free of what he called "emotionalism," campaigning without resort to blunderbuss attacks on the federal government.[10]

The reality was not quite as pure. The 1967 campaign carried tantalizing hints of what was to come. But out on the stump, Waller kept quiet much of his dissenting opinion, cautious though it appears today. Occasionally, it popped out of his makeshift campaign in fits and starts, as he traveled the length of the state in a large camper bus. But this was a race dominated by the past. The times were not right for a man who proclaimed himself, however fitfully, a champion of the new. It was the last old-style Mississippi governor's race, and repressing blacks was still the central issue. They were not yet registered in sufficient numbers to be removed from the rhetoric; Mississippi's rearguard action was not yet thoroughly spent.

An indication was that Beckwith's spirit hovered in the background, an evil shade with especial malediction for the Waller campaign. When Waller spoke to the Greenwood Elks Club one night in February, stink bombs were tossed into the building. There was no doubting the motivation: earlier that day anonymous leaflets had been distributed in town attacking him for persecuting the local hero. Don Waller, a reluctant recruit in the campaign, would stump for his brother in the dusty little country towns, and he was asked more than once: "'Is that that fellow that prosecuted that fellow for killing that nigger?'" Carroll Waller, the candidate's wife, remembers doors slammed in her face. At an auto repair shop, the wife of one of the mechanics "all but hissed at" her. Carroll Waller, a mild-mannered Southern lady, the epitome of careful gentility, "was just taken aback." She proceeded into a local coffee shop, "and there were two couples, and they all but spit on me." Don Waller has no doubt that the prosecution did not help his brother's campaign. "It had its effect," he remembers. "Sure did."

In the countryside emotions much stronger than Bill Waller's uncertain message were lurking. This was not helped by the haphazardness of the campaign, a "crazy" undertaking really, in Don Waller's memory. There was little money, campaigning was done on weekends, and sometimes the Waller forces would run out of material to distribute during rallies. George Wallace, next door in Alabama, was at the height of his popularity. Don Waller would go into the little towns and talk about his brother, and the old men sitting around the store would say, to the campaigner's embarrassment: 'Oh yeah, Wallace, I like Wallace."

The Waller pitch careened back and forth between past and future. In one bold action, Don was sent into the black sections of towns to gingerly recruit the recently registered black voters. This was new in Mississippi campaigns, "unheard of," Don Waller says, at least since Reconstruction. It was a job he did not like much at all. "It wasn't the easiest thing in the world. It was still that stigma out there. Lot of people out there didn't even think they should have the right to vote, let alone asking them to vote."

And then his brother made headlines in April when he bravely blasted the Ku Klux Klan in a speech in the tough piney woods town of Laurel, the first Mississippi gubernatorial candidate ever to do so. And he took a big chance in the same speech when he obliquely touched on a key element of Silver's closed society. "The KKK is not alone to blame," he told the Rotary Club audience. "The work of these secret groups is protected by our silence. Their success is magnified by our fear. They speak for Mississippi only because brave men have been pressured into silence."[11]

But in the same speech, he was careful to denounce civil rights activists—he named Stokely Carmichael—as well. A few weeks after denouncing the Klan in Laurel, he gave a speech to the Citizens' Council in Jackson that could only have warmed the hearts of the beleaguered segregationists: "I do endorse and support the ideals of state's rights and racial integrity as advocated by the Citizens' Council. I have been impressed by council literature in the past which emphasized peaceful means of resistance. I hope this will continue."[12]

The Jackson *Daily News* reporter who covered this speech noted: "[Waller's] criticism of the federal government's increasing interference in state affairs has been constant and loud. He has told campaign audiences that the federal government is building 'a conspiracy to force the liberal philosophy of government' upon Mississippians."

This was boilerplate segregationist stuff. There were older, better practitioners of the form delivering it that year, and the voting public did not take much notice of Waller. He was crushed in the first primary, receiving a mere 9 percent of the vote.[13] Things would be very different four years later.

"I am not ready to surrender," Judge Marshall Perry thundered, out on the campaign trail in the 1971 governor's race. "All this talk about getting back into the mainstream. We are already in the mainstream," he sneered. "It's the other people, the enemies of Mississippi, who have departed from the mainstream." Perry, an enthusiastic believer in the inferiority of blacks, was a fringe candidate in that strange political summer. It was a race full of such highways and byways.

In 1967, the decaying old order had triumphed. In the 1971 race it made a feeble last stand, but its decadence was plainly evident. The old rhetoric was trotted out one last time, and it reached a new pitch of rotting extravagance. Much of it was fantasyland stuff. After the furious registration campaigns of the late 1960s, there were 300,000 blacks on the rolls, out of an electorate of one million people. That news had not quite caught up yet with some of Mississippi's politicians.

So the campaign threw up candidates like Perry, fulminating about the iniquities of the outside world, and Jimmy Swan, a free-wheeling radio announcer, evangelist, and ardent segregationist who dressed in white suits in the great tradition of James K. Vardaman, the racist demagogue of an earlier era. "We must not allow our children to be sacrificed on the filthy atheistic altar of integration," Swan said over and over. He traveled around the state in a long silver bus with "Save Our Children" emblazoned in red on the side. "I say that Jimmy Swan and only Jimmy Swan can take the fat cats off the gravy train in Jackson!" he would tell his small but enthusiastic audiences.[14]

Swan kicked off his campaign holding up a copy of the late Sen. Theodore Bilbo's famous and outlandish racist tract, *Segregation or Mongrelization*. "Friends, we're at the last page," Swan said, pointing dramatically to the book. "Time has come that we have got to quit pussy-footing around." Bilbo, it turned out, had been right after all. "Every word he said has come true," the balding Swan told the cheering crowd in Raleigh, Mississippi. The inevitable country band had preceded Swan's appearance, and the reporter for the *Times-Picayune* heard one of the female singers cursing the motorcade of Charles Evers, who was making a quixotic run at the governorship.

Even the old racist judge Tom Brady—a personal friend of Barnett and the person who had delivered the "Black Monday" speech (see chapter 4)—got in on the act, becoming a candidate at the last moment to save the white race from the horror of Evers, who was running as an Independent.

Swan was a jokey sideshow. A decade earlier he might have had whites flocking to his rallies, and blacks running in the opposite direction. Not now. When he set up in front of the courthouse at Canton, outside Jackson, to deliver a segregationist tirade in the midsummer heat, the merchants stayed indoors. A jaunty crowd of thirty local black youths, led by an NAACP man, happened to be crossing the courthouse lawn. "Right on, Jimmy!" they cried, almost friendly in their derision.[15]

Even nostalgic whites knew Swan represented the past. Charles Evers, on the other hand, represented a strange new world, a frightening vision of the future for white Mississippi. He was a flamboyant ex-Chicago street hustler who had undergone a miraculous conversion to civil rights activist and politician. There had never been anything like Evers's inspirational campaign crusade before, and its like would not be seen again anywhere for over a decade, until the campaigns of Jesse Jackson. Charles Evers, so different from his brother, in many ways represented Waller's political foil. His mere presence was transforming the politics of the state, just as Waller's was (see chapter 6).

The eccentrics had had their day before, and they would again. There was, however, a startling new development in this race, and it captured the outside world's fascination. Maybe it was the presence of thousands of new black voters on the rolls. Maybe it was the specter of Evers himself, the ultimate expression of the white supremacist bad dream, a black man running as a serious candidate for governor. Maybe Waller and Lt. Gov. Charlie Sullivan, opponents in the Democratic runoff, were simply groping toward what they felt was the right course. But for the first time since Reconstruction, major candidates for governor in Mississippi did not use racial appeals.

That news found a prominent place in many of the dispatches filed from Mississippi that summer. When Waller won the Democratic runoff against Sullivan, the candidate of the Hedermans, it made the front page of the *New York Times*. And when he beat Evers that fall, Roy Reed wrote in the *Times:* "Mr. Waller set the tone statewide. He made little overt attempt to use the old politics of race against Mr. Evers. He campaigned, instead, as a moderate committed 'to every person in this state.'"[16]

Waller called himself a redneck. His posture was the country boy's equivalent of a delicate pirouette, an ongoing paradox which signaled the confused state Mississippi now found itself in. It was a masterly politician's job, at once exploiting that confusion and promising subtly to end it. He used a slick Memphis advertising man, Deloss Walker, itself an innovation in insular Mississippi campaigning. Walker had helped Dale Bumpurs get elected in Arkansas, and now he was to help Waller craft a neopopulist campaign, representing him as the outsider and attacking what they called the "Capitol Street Gang"—the bankers, the lawyers, and the newspapers centered on Capitol Street in downtown Jackson.

He chuckles over the patness of the phrase now, suggesting that it was only "accidentally" successful. Even today, old Wallerites will talk about having scourged the Capitol Street Gang. But the phrase took hold in people's minds, and there were good reasons, not at all accidental, for this. Waller was drawing on ancient instincts of resentment in Mississippi voters. Since Reconstruction days, these instincts had been channeled against blacks, with an undercurrent directed at what Swan picturesquely called "fat cats." Now the fat cats, not blacks, could become the prime focus. Besides which, it was gradually dawning on people that Capitol Street— the Hederman press, the establishment politicians—had failed the state miserably.

In fact, there were several establishments in Mississippi, and Waller was not nearly so divorced from them as his campaign slogan suggested. "I felt I was not the product of a political establishment, the political kingmakers, and the political machine," Waller told an interviewer, shortly after the Paul Johnson machine had helped carry him to victory.[17]

At that juncture, it was not possible to reject the political establishment completely. Many white voters, whatever their growing doubts, still identified with it. Waller was in a tricky position. He had to compete for black votes with Charlie Sullivan and at the same time not alienate whites wounded from a decade of defeats. He could not back away from his "new man" theme from four years before, but he also needed the force of the establishment political organizations—those of Johnson and Sen. James O. Eastland— behind him.

He wound up with a most curious list of friends and enemies in that race. Barnett said a public prayer for him, but those staunch Barnett backers the Hederman papers attacked Waller vigorously for campaigning on Sunday and allowing beer at a youth rally on the Gulf Coast. Charles Evers praised Waller's moderation, and he had the support of the Ku Klux Klan. He made speeches defending the "seg academies"—the private schools for whites, the cinderbox weeds sprouting across the state—yet promised an "administration without bigotry."

Waller's campaign rhetoric was pregnant with this dual stance. He looked forward and backward all at once, hinting at the repression that had proven so popular and yet promising things would be different under a Waller regime. "I will always champion and protect the right of peaceful dissent that is guaranteed by the Constitution," he said in a speech in August, a line Barnett would not have uttered. "But never for one moment will I tolerate the troublemakers who infiltrate our state solely to destroy lives and property and to interfere with the rights of others"—that line could easily have been Barnett's.[18]

Waller entered office a large, bluff man, bursting with energy and half-formed ideas for change. He consciously associated himself with the first wave of New South governors moving into office that year—Jimmy Carter in Georgia, Lawton Chiles in Florida, and Dale Bumpurs in Arkansas. At considerable political risk, he openly disassociated himself from the god of Southern political life, George Wallace.[19]

Unfortunately for Waller, it was a historical moment that could only partly accommodate enthusiasm such as his. He could not ignore a natural inclination to push forward. But whites, his constituency, were only reluctantly parting with old ways. He would have to handle them delicately, careful not to scatter salt on the fresh wounds. Waller seemed to understand this. He talked ever so tactfully, shortly after the election, of "incidents" (the "Meredith incident," the "Beckwith incident") that had "embarrassed" people like himself and motivated him to run.[20] But whether he could convert understanding into practice was another matter.

In January 1972, in one of those raw, gray January days in Jackson, Waller stood on the steps of the new capitol and swore to uphold the solemn duties of his office. The moment seemed emblematic. The oath was administered by the old segregationist Judge Tom Brady, the cultured Yale man who was the intellectual godfather of the Mississippi diehards. "It is my goal that Mississippi will be as popular and respected as any state at the end of these four years," Waller said earnestly in his inaugural speech—a goal for which the old judge must have found it hard to muster much sympathy.

Right away, Waller began making the sort of symbolic gestures toward modernity that were calculated to set diehards on edge. True to his campaign promise, he began appointing blacks—"the right thing to do, the just thing to do," Waller says now—and there was ineffectual sotto voce grumbling from the old guard. He removed the portraits of Mississippi's two Miss Americas from the state capitol, where they had sat for the last decade near rotating exhibits of the state's agricultural products. More grumbling. He tried, unsuccessfully, to get rid of the bronze bust of the crown prince of Mississippi demagogues, Senator Bilbo, from the capitol rotunda.

And Waller was going to work, hard. He came to the office each morning in his white Lincoln Continental, often staying until ten at night. Already well on his way to a substantial paunch, he often skipped lunch. Weekends frequently found him at his desk. After years of covering go-easy governors, even the reporters on the hostile Hederman papers were impressed. "In the first place, the man 'works,' just about as he said he would when he was running for office," the reporter for the Jackson *Daily News* wrote near the end of the first year.[21]

Working for Waller was sometimes a terrifying experience. "He would come in with that barreling voice of his," remembers Wayne Edwards, then a young press spokesman. "What did you do for the poor people today?" Waller would boom out. "He would walk into the Department of Education, and a bunch of people would be reading newspapers. And he would chew them out."

The temporal representative of the established order has always been the Mississippi legislature, and Waller was headed for a head-on collision with it. This roiling, cantankerous body of country lawyers, small businessmen and farmers had been for decades the real power in the state. The populist constitution of 1890, distrustful of strong governors, had limited them to one term. Legislators, on the other hand, could be elected year after year, gradually amassing immense powers if they occupied important positions in the hierarchy.

For much of the century, the most potent beneficiary of this system was Walter Sillers, "the Delta Dictator" as one Mississippi newspaper editor called him in 1959.[22] A tall, courtly plantation owner of exquisite manners, he was first elected to the house of representatives in 1916 from Bolivar County, and he served there until the day he died late in September 1966. For the last twenty-two years of his life, the deeply conservative Sillers was the Speaker of the House, a uniquely powerful man who established the legislature as the central force in the state, as no one before him had. His style of governance outlasted him.

The day after Sillers died, he lay in state in the capitol, and Mississippians filed by his bier for seven hours. The governor proclaimed all state offices closed, and flags were to fly at half staff for ten days.[23] "Governors came and went," Minor wrote on the front page of the New Orleans *Times-Picayune* that day, "but Sillers was unsinkable as Speaker of the House, the influence of the governors notwithstanding." A liberal legislator from the Mississippi Gulf Coast who opposed Sillers, Karl Wiesenberg, remembered years later: "No legislation could be enacted in that legislature unless Mr. Sillers wanted it enacted, not even if the governor put his full strength behind it. He was more important than the governor. He was more important than the legislature itself, because he was the legislature."[24]

He conducted much of the state's business from the grandiose Edwards House Hotel, later the King Edward, in downtown Jackson. He first moved in after coming down from the Delta in 1916, and he remained during all the years he was in the legislature. Sillers loved this genteel hulk, whose pigeon-dropping-covered ruin still anchors the west end of Capitol Street, and he took all his meals there for years. When he and his wife descended from the upper floors into the grand, vaulting lobby, everybody would "bow and scrape."[25]

The Edwards House was the "third house" of the legislature; here lobbyists brought women and booze for the legislators, the more rustic among them easily dazzled into compliance by these favors. Years later, Bill Minor remembered the sight which invariably greeted visitors to the upstairs rooms at the old hotel, where the more affluent legislators put up: a brown paper bag with a whiskey bottle in it, sitting on top of the bureau. Here the Dixiecrats met in 1948, and the Citizens' Council seven years later, and later still, the Mississippi Council on Human Relations, a rare early integrated gathering.[26] It was here that the Sillers forces met and marshaled themselves. Within its confines, "you would think you were in Austria in the days of the Hapsburgs rather than in an American system," Wiesenberg remembered, "because he ran as the emperor triumphant." The essence of Sillers's power as speaker was that he appointed all the chairmen of the committees, all of whom were his "henchmen, sworn to fealty." The most powerful of these men were called by their opponents Sillers's "inner guard." They would hold meetings before the legislature went into session, and they would decide which bills would be enacted and which would not. There was no deviation, and there were no mistakes. "It was an unbelievable system," Wiesenberg remembered.

Buttressing this feudal system, the legislative men were able to appoint themselves to executive boards and commissions, with decision-making power over everything from prison administration to budget making. The governor was reduced, at his most powerful, to being an ideological cheerleader like Barnett, or a ribbon-cutter. This aspect of the system would not be changed until it was ruled unconstitutional at the end of the 1970s. Barnett used to boast about the near-unanimous support he enjoyed in the legislature. But in truth, Barnett would have been in trouble if he had not simply been in tune with the legislature's collective mind.

In 1972, its mind was more than ever on blacks—obsessively. The principal obsession: how to keep them from making further inroads into power in general, and the legislature in particular. Hardly a single bill, a single proposal, came up in which the legislators did not see some racial overtone. "Race went into everything," remembers one of the lonely band of liberals, Gerald Blessey, who had come up from the Gulf Coast, traditionally more open-minded than the rest of the state. The going "paranoia" had it that reformism of any kind, whether aimed at schools or roads or consumers, really meant integration. In the wings, off the floor, the legislators still told their old racist jokes, albeit a trifle nervously now. Blessey, an idealistic twenty-nine-year-old in his first term, remembers "just being shocked." Robert Clark, the one black man elected to the house of representatives in 1967, was forced to sit alone for a time. Once, someone put a watermelon on his desk. Finally, the patrician gentleman who had succeeded Sillers, Johnny Junkin of Natchez, came and sat down beside him.

Delta men under Junkin's tutelage still ruled the roost. Waller, with his bull-headed idealism, was in for a tough fight. But he clung to the vague hope that "there's a certain amount of idealism in politics, and idealism would prevail." He was naïve. Six weeks into Waller's term, Speaker of the House Junkin came to the new governor and explained the facts of life to him: cut the ribbons, make the speeches, and we will run the state government.

It was war. Waller became the first governor in decades to take on the legislature. He was going to crack the unanimous governmental front that Mississippi had presented for decades. In that first session, Waller vetoed thirty-two of the legislature's bills, an unheard-of total.[27] A year later, Minor could write: "The legislature had finally come to the realization that it no longer had a governor with a rubber stamp."[28]

Just as infuriating, Waller had a reform agenda. In their paranoia, the older leaders saw him as a radical. He wanted to raise the oil and gas severance tax. The industry lobbyists were shocked. He wanted statewide kindergartens, a measure that did not pass until ten years later under Gov. William Winter. The legislators saw creeping integrationism and payoffs to undeserving blacks. He abolished the then-feeble State Sovereignty Commission. He wanted to reduce the pupil–teacher ratio. He wanted a compulsory school-attendance law. He vetoed a death penalty bill. He took on loan sharks, working for passage of a bill that would have capped interest rates from small loan operators. He tried to make it easier to obtain bank charters, to break the stranglehold of a few on credit in the state. He even testified before legislative committees, unheard of for a governor.

He dressed down legislators in the halls of the capitol if they disagreed with him, and he spent almost no time cultivating the legislative powerhouses. Instead, he would swoop down from a helicopter into the far reaches of the state, handing out Waller buttons and trying to cultivate the voters and the county supervisors. "He has a good bit of the ham, with a native instinct for showmanship about him the people out in the boondocks love," wrote Minor, still smitten with his first-ever progressive Mississippi governor.[29]

Whether or not the folks in the villages liked him, their representatives in Jackson were unequivocal: the rural legislators were stunned by this performance. "They thought the man was crazy," Minor remembers. Waller had the legislative beast where he needed it—wounded and bleeding. He should have moved in and organized his own team, but he did not have the political skill to capitalize on his triumph.[30]

He allowed the legislators to get back at him, and they were happy to do so. Waller resented any man who had at one time crossed him. That category came to include virtually the entire legislature, "almost to a man," remembers Ben Stone, a moderate. He was not careful about cultivating allegiances. Once, while a group of some of his small band of young Turk allies waited to speak to him, Waller ducked into his office for a phone call. He did not emerge after forty-five minutes; one of the young Turks made polite inquiries with the secretary, and it emerged that Waller had boarded a plane for a distant part of the state, without bothering to inform his now-angry visitors. For the first time in forty-four years, the legislators began to override a governor's vetoes, one after another. On one day in the spring of 1974, the legislature overrode three of his vetoes. Waller never recovered.

His victories were evanescent half-triumphs not readily apparent at the time, and this may be why they are so little remembered today. "We got killed at O.K. Corral . . . I mean, we got killed at O.K. Corral," said Waller, summing up the fate of two important initiatives. For Hodding Carter III, it was an "inconsequential" administration.

But as a racial healer, Waller made genuine achievements. Here was "the greatest value of the Waller years," Minor concluded early in 1976, as the governor was leaving office. "He brought harmony between blacks and whites in Mississippi's highly complex society which a few short years ago seemed impossible."[31] Since whites continued to dominate state politics, he had had to move cautiously, always with an eye to his white flank. Blacks were furious with him for releasing from prison on a work program one of the Klansmen convicted in the brutal 1967 firebombing murder of

Vernon Dahmer, the NAACP leader in Hattiesburg. The governor tried to cover his tracks by quietly letting it be known he would release a black man in the same way, and a few days later he put seven blacks on a state board.

The first black man in Mississippi state government was evidently selected with considerable regard for the feelings of the diehards. Jim Rundles, Waller's special assistant and a sort of liaison to Mississippi blacks, was a mild-mannered, easygoing sort who had endured a stint working for the *Clarion-Ledger* during its most viciously segregationist days. The paper's racism notwithstanding, he still speaks respectfully of editors there who compared blacks to monkeys and mocked the civil rights movement. When asked by Medgar Evers to take part in a sit-in, Rundles had declined. He remained a lifelong friend of Percy Greene, the much-vilified editor of the Jackson *Advocate*. Movement people suspected Greene—rightly, as it turned out—of being a spy for the Sovereignty Commission. As Waller's assistant, Rundles was not going to make waves.

Although blacks were in twenty-five departments of state government after Waller had been in office two years, there were still "dozens of departments" without a black person.[32] On the tenth anniversary of Evers's death, Waller startled a news conference by quietly proclaiming a statewide day of observance. But then he failed to show up at the ceremony in Jackson. He refused to intervene in the fight over *Mississippi: Conflict and Change* (see chapter 1). He backed off a pledge to reform Mississippi's regressive tax structure and sided with the old guard in the legislature.

Waller's tone was somewhat bitter when a historian interviewed him for the state archives in 1982, six years after he had left office. He had run a disastrous race for the U.S. Senate in 1978, only managing a fourth-place finish. His troubled daughter Joy had committed suicide the year before. An old political rival, William Winter, was successfully pushing through reforms Waller had failed with years earlier. Waller had settled down to a routine, if lucrative, law practice in Jackson, and his achievements were being forgotten.

To the interviewer he denied any bitterness. But he lashed out at the media, the legislature, even "the Mississippi citizen," the source of "the problem" in the state, in Waller's view.

Strangely, Waller himself had forgotten the extraordinary symbolic achievement of his time in public life. So much had happened in the decade since he took office that his administration's significance had become blurred, even to him. In 1976, immediately after stepping down, he had had a much clearer sense of what he had done.

Four months after he left office, Waller summed up his achievement. He talked clumsily of the "aesthetics or intangible accomplishments." Mississippi, he declared grandly, had shown itself to be a "progressive state and its people to be in the national mainstream."[33]

Both of these statements were untrue. Mississippi was still the poorest state in the nation. But Waller had circled close to the mark when he talked about "aesthetics." Nine public swimming pools had just opened in Jackson, the first time since the early 1960s the city's youth had had a place to swim. This time, the pools were integrated. Something in the life of the state had indeed changed, fundamentally.

On the face of it, Cliff Finch, Waller's successor, looked like a step backward, because he was a crude rural district attorney who had gone down the line for Barnett while serving in the legislature in the 1960s. But Finch's route to the Governor's Mansion in 1975 had even less to do with race than Waller's had four years earlier. "Finch was more afraid of being seen in company with the old-time segregationists than he was of having a black man escort him around the state," Minor wrote during the campaign.[34] He managed to build the elusive coalition of working-class whites and blacks that Democrats have only dreamed about since the advent of Reagan. By 1976, Finch was even seen at the Medgar Evers tribute in Fayette.

In the old days, a man running for governor (white, of course) would do everything he could to avoid having his picture taken with a black person. Waller, in 1971, "nearly flipped" when he found out that a picture of him talking to a black television reporter was going to be published. Now, in 1975, all the candidates had at least a few blacks in their television and newspaper ads. A year later the aging Senator Eastland himself was spotted breaking bread with blacks at a dinner for the newly unified state Democratic party. "One is bound to think of the millennium," Minor wrote.[35]

It was not the millennium, but it was a scene that would have been unimaginable in the not-so-distant past. Waller could take some of the credit. He had accomplished a feat very similar to the one he had pulled off in the trials of Beckwith in 1964. Waller, "the first governor [Mississippi] had who was not a racist,"[36] had presided over an administration that had not been about race at all. He had succeeded in refocusing the emphasis to what he called "the practical everyday transaction of state government." Race still permeates every level of politics in Mississippi, every day. But ever since the days of Waller, race has largely meant the division of spoils, not their denial to blacks. "Everybody had to feel like they belonged," Waller said in 1982.[37]

One day in March 1975, when Waller's governorship was winding down in frustration, Charles Evers boldly charged past the security guards in the Mississippi Senate and began speaking, uninvited, to the senators. The episode was significant for what did *not* happen next. Five years before, there would have been a riot, a "cordon of highway patrolmen and police officers."[38] On this day, the senators were not glad to see him, but Evers's intervention hardly jarred the proceedings. And it turned out to be a lunge, a quixotic shot in the dark, with little consequence for his chosen subject, reapportionment.

By the end of Waller's term, racial hysteria in the crucible of Mississippi politics, the legislature, had abated considerably. And Charles Evers, so recently the feared symbol of black takeover, was in danger of becoming a bore.

CHAPTER SIX

CHARLES EVERS

There was an awkward moment at the conclusion of the 1971 governor's race, when all the ambiguities of Charles Evers's career suddenly came into focus.

It was election night, and Evers was in a strangely mercurial mood. He insisted on shaking the hands of dumbfounded supporters of the victorious Waller at a seedy hotel in downtown Jackson, grinning as he did so. The victor himself was being interviewed at a local television station. To the chagrin of Waller's nervous aides, Evers managed to track him down there. Just as Waller's car was about to pull off into the night, Evers approached the new governor, who was in the back seat with his wife.

"I just wanted to congratulate you," Evers said into the darkness. At another time, Waller might have been phased. But now, he was too full of the moment. He bellowed back, "Whaddaya say,

Charlie!" Mrs. Waller was only able to manage a stiff smile for the black man.[1]

Evers and Waller had known each other for years, yet this was one of their only formal encounters during the campaign. What should have been a ritualized encounter—the loser congratulating the winner—instead had an almost supplicatory air about it. What was Evers? No more than the brother of Medgar, trading on the dead man's name? Was he a bona fide candidate, a real politician? Or was he just a sort of super-smart-alecky black man who had insanely forgotten his place? Clearly, there was some ambiguity in Evers's own mind, or he would not have subjected himself to such an encounter.

There was no ambiguity in the view of most whites: Evers was still a bogeyman, the "Great Nigra Peril." His candidacy in 1971 had angered and frightened them, and they had turned out in record numbers to beat him back. It was both the high point of Charles Evers's eight-year ascent to the pinnacle of bogeymanship and the beginning of his descent from that position. He had accomplished a singular feat in his audacious run, which was so daring that no Mississippi black man has attempted it since: he had not been killed. The whites had at least conceded him that much; they were not going to make him a martyr like his brother. Thus, this campaign was the beginning of the normalizing of Charles Evers, at least as far as whites were concerned.

As for blacks, that 1971 race had also marked a passage in their view of Charles Evers. Before, at the end of the 1960s, he had become "the focal point in the black community," as Robert Clark, the first black person in the Mississippi legislature, puts it. Evers's candidacy was the ultimate test of his stardom. He had wanted, as he says now, "to try to get the fear out of black folk that you can't run for office because white folk will kill you," and he had succeeded. But he had also been massively beaten. And so the limits of his power were revealed.

Like Waller, Evers has stayed on the Mississippi scene so long that the depth of his original impact has been obliterated. Now, much more than Waller, Evers is a figure of derision, scorned by blacks for the extreme turn of his politics—he publicly proclaims himself a born-again conservative Republican—and by whites for his long-exposed venality. Miming what is supposed to be a stereo-typical Evers gesture, someone will extend one hand for a shake while reaching into your pocket with the other. His name is likely to produce a snigger among whites and a scowl among blacks. Some in the first generations of black politicians retain influence; for example, Aaron Henry, Medgar's old colleague (see chapter 2), serves in the legislature and is still listened to by younger black leaders, albeit with increasing weariness. No one listens to Evers except the lonely Wednesday night stay-at-homes who tune in to his rambling radio talk show on the Jackson blues station he now owns.

Evers's marginality today would have been unthinkable in the decade after his brother's death. Personally galvanized by that death, he transformed himself into the embodiment of the white Mississippians' fears. He was the civil rights leader as successful politician, and he represented the sum of starry-eyed Yankee ideal-ism about Southern blacks: he was profiled in the *New York Times Magazine*, interviewed in *Playboy*, and invited on national television news programs. He was already very much a national figure by 1969, when he became the first black mayor of a Mississippi town with both blacks and whites—not an all-black town, like Mound Bayou—since Reconstruction.

Today, he frequently expresses contempt for liberals. But in 1969 some of the country's most prominent liberals—Ramsey Clark, Paul O'Dwyer, Theodore Sorensen, Whitney Young, Shirley MacLaine, and Julian Bond—traveled to Natchez to attend the ball inaugurating his tenure as the mayor of the tiny town of Fayette. Two years later, the National Committee to Elect Charles Evers Governor included Shirley Chisholm, George McGovern, and Ad-lai Stevenson. "No black leader in the United States has more white people pulling for him than Charles Evers of Mississippi," the vet-eran journalist William Bradford Huie wrote in May 1970.[2] Prac-tically alone among writers, Huie, the Southerner, was pessimistic about Evers. He turned out to be right.

To the whites of Fayette, Evers's coming was a biblical plague, the overturning of every relationship and hierarchy they had ever known. He has long since made a grudging peace with most of them, but they have not forgotten their bitterness. "Yes, they resented Charles Evers. Yes, they resented him deeply," said the late Marie Farr Walker, a onetime foe and the former editor of the Fayette *Chronicle*. She was perched in the high-ceilinged fastness of her crumbling antebellum mansion just outside town, a sanctuary worlds away from the dusty handful of streets that make up downtown Fayette.

Like his brother, Charles Evers had been a pioneer: the first black man to translate all the grudgingly conceded gains into political power over whites and blacks. But by the end of the 1970s he was just another soiled ex-politician—in whites' eyes, and more importantly, in blacks' as well. His was the passage from symbol to political has-been. Just as much as Waller's progressivism, the moment Evers achieved that status was critical to the political maturing of Mississippi. The moment this pioneer ceased to be menacing to whites and untouchably inspirational to blacks, an important stage in Mississippi's integration had been achieved.

Charles Evers's candor and bluntness are legendary, and even today his reputation for those seems well deserved. He'll tell you (in a rapid-fire, loosely constructed slur, freely dropping articles and prepositions) that he was the "son-of-a-bitch" of the Evers family, that he had problems with Medgar's wife and with the stuffy NAACP hierarchy, that during his "prostitution days" he did not mistreat women (throwing in for good measure that even now he does not "beat up on women"), and that he is running for chancery clerk this time around because there is more money in it. "I consider myself more as a hustler. A hustler is someone who does what it takes to get from here to somewhere else," he says proudly.

There is almost too much candor. He will repeat several times in an interview, "I have no secrets." The rush of self-revelation is blinding; it leads not to illumination but to mystification. His narrative encompasses such contradictory self-images—passionate believer in racial justice, venal politician, brothel keeper, and keeper of the sacred flame of his brother's memory—that one wonders whether to believe none, some, or all of it. "I live for women and money," he told a friend during the middle of his most important symbolic crusade, the 1971 governor's race.[3] Then, the same week, there could be bursts of the most passionate inspirational oratory: "We had no hope," he said at a rally in Greenville that summer. "We believed in the man upstairs, and we kept moving, moving in our hearts and our souls."

But the truth about Evers seems less important than what this uncongenial mix of images added up to for the outside world. During his heyday, there was a mystery about him. It only enhanced his aura: from the mid-1960s to the mid-1970s, Charles Evers became a kind of superfigure for anybody who looked at black–white relations, a larger-than-life civil rights leader cum politician cum wheeler-dealer. This was not just a matter of how the world perceived him. Evers himself, through his actions, created a swaggering, Lone Ranger image for himself.

Enraged by his brother's death, he wanted to kill as many white people in Mississippi as possible. "Some I'd shoot, others I'd stab, others I'd poison. I'd pick the leading racists in each county and knock 'em off one by one," he told an interviewer for *Playboy* in 1971.[4] His anger cooled into a curious sense of guilt. So he muscled his way into his brother's old job, to the muted dismay of Myrlie (she was said to have exclaimed, "Oh God, Medgar, not Charles") and the eventual distress of Roy Wilkins, who never got along with him and was not enthusiastic about his ascendancy.[5] That was just too bad, in the eyes of Charles. "They had no choice. What I told them, either you accept me, or I'll form my own movement, call it the Mississippi movement."[6]

It would have taken unusual forbearance, or naïveté, not to be suspicious of this man. True, his views on the need for black equality had always been as fierce as Medgar's. But his résumé—pimp, disc jockey, numbers runner, nightclub owner—did not make him the ideal choice to fill his brother's job. It would be another eight years, during the campaign of 1971, before all the details of his seedy past came spilling out. But there were suspicions, well-founded ones, even in 1963.

His first successful business had been a brothel in Quezon City in the Philippines during World War II. "All those combat-weary GI's wanted some action, and I gave it to 'em," he recalled in 1971. "My profits depended on a fast turnover, and I'd rush 'em in and rush 'em out on an assembly-line basis." After the war, he joined Medgar at Alcorn A&M, where within a few months he was confronted by the angry parents of three young women he had made pregnant. But as he told the *Playboy* interviewer years later, "can't stay in the sack *all* the time,"[7] so he began helping his brother in early voter registration work.

In Philadelphia, Mississippi, in the early 1950s, he ran a hotel, a cab company, and a burial insurance business. He was the first black disc jockey in the state, "on [his] way to becomin' a successful businessman with a healthy bank balance." Too successful. Local whites in that vicious little town ran him out, and in 1956 he landed in Chicago, down and more or less out. Angry and bitter, he worked nights as a men's room attendant at the Conrad Hilton Hotel, rolling white drunks when they came in. In the day he was a meatpacker in the stockyards. He got into the numbers racket as a policy runner, skimming off five hundred dollars a week. He resumed his old pimping ways.

All the while he kept in close touch with Medgar, sending him money but never telling him the source. "You can't *spend* civil rights," he would say later, "and a man ain't really free unless he has economic freedom as well as political and social freedom." In Chicago, he bought a few modest bars, ran a bootlegging operation, and got into the jukebox business. His life seemed to be going well.

The night Medgar was killed, he pulled up to his comfortable house in Chicago at 3:00 A.M. and all the lights were on. He knew something was wrong, and then his wife told him about the phone call from Mississippi moments before. Deeply grieving, he was on a plane to Jackson that morning. He threw himself into the details of his brother's burial, even going to the morgue with a barber to make sure Medgar's hair was cut in the right style. "God, it's still like a nightmare, jus' thinkin about it," he said in 1971.[8]

"I felt so guilty about not being with Medgar when they killed him that I wanted with all my heart to carry on his work": this explanation, given to the *Playboy* interviewer, does not quite cover the range of motivations Charles himself had adduced for the dramatic shift that took place in his life. The truth was that he and Medgar had been, in some respects, after the same thing: equality. His hustling had been a means to becoming, as he had put it, "really free." For now, with the death of his brother, he was abandoning his own methods to pick up Medgar's. A man who knew him well, the journalist Jason Berry, who was Evers's press secretary during the 1971 governor's race, says simply: "I think he wanted to be a better person. I think Medgar's death was a cathartic experience."[9] By the end of 1963 he had become the NAACP's clear leader in Mississippi, the source for a *New York Times* story on the "quiet progress" that blacks were supposedly making in the state. Medgar had been what John Salter called a "lone wolf" out of necessity; Charles was one by choice. His absolute unwillingness to play second fiddle asserted itself quickly; so did a conservatism integral to his individualism.

He distrusted the militants in SNCC and its child, the Mississippi Freedom Democratic party, the predominantly black party which challenged the legitimacy of the state's "regular," segregated Democratic party. He refused to work in the voter registration of Freedom Summer in 1964 and was impatient with the radicals among the Mississippi Young Democrats, a breakaway faction loyal (unlike the Regular Democrats) to the national party. "They are anti-anybody that comes in clean. They are anti-anybody that combs his hair," Evers told a reporter in August 1965.[10] For years, he has fiercely attacked black militants and separatists. Reminiscent of his brother, he maintains an unshakeable faith in integration.

By the end of 1965 he had carved out a role for himself as a kind of freewheeling, loner militant. He launched a series of boycotts in the tough small towns of southwestern Mississippi that transformed the region almost overnight. In May he had gone into Natchez with a small band, braved three hundred Ku Kluxers, and desegregated the hotels and stores.[11] In December a reporter spotted him singlehandedly facing down a mob of fifty armed whites during another boycott in front of the courthouse in the small, drab old cotton town of Fayette. "Negro Aide Defies Armed White Men" read the headline: the legend of his courage was growing.[12]

These were disciplined, military-style boycott campaigns. Evers would threaten to unleash his black firebrands on the local whites in power unless they cooperated with him. Almost always, they caved in. A team of about sixty-five young men, fanatically loyal, followed him about. His enemies called them the "goon squad" and claimed its members jostled blacks who dared enter the stores under boycott.[13]

It was in Fayette that Evers established his headquarters, in the very center of the region he had targeted in his boycott campaign. It seemed unpromising territory, one more redoubt of white militancy and black apathy, but to Evers, that was part of its appeal. Besides, it had a three-to-one black majority. Surrounding Jefferson County was the poorest in Mississippi: half its citizens lived below the poverty line, and one-third of the citizens were illiterate.[14] But to the bemusement of the local whites, Evers chose Jefferson and two neighboring counties as the launching pad for his own version of the black revolution.

Fayette had two traffic lights, three blocks of storefronts, a three-story hotel that had closed years ago, and about twenty-five hundred people. You could drive through town in less than five minutes. Reporters who came through repeated the same set of details to conjure the place up: the stray dogs wandering around town, the chickens pecking in the dust, the unemployed black men hanging around street corners.

Today it looks much the same. The line of stores is emptier, and the old Romanesque courthouse has burnt to the ground (a cataclysm that whites generally blame on the political incumbency of blacks). Fayette now looks about as vital as it did when Evers conquered it a quarter century ago.

For black people, it had historically been a deeply repressive place. If the sheriff saw black high school students on the streets, he would round them up and put them to work in R. J. Allen's cotton fields. Allen and the Strass family, Jewish merchants in Fayette, were the richest people in Jefferson County. The Strasses had a big cattle auction barn, and some black kids regularly missed every Monday of school to work in that barn.[15]

Evers moved the NAACP field office to the little town from Jackson primarily because of the huge black majorities in the Fayette area. "My feeling is that Negroes gotta control somewhere in America, and we've dropped anchor in these three counties," he wrote five years later. "We are going to control these three counties in the next ten years. There is no question about it."[16]

By the time those words were written, Evers had already achieved an intangible victory: in that small corner of Mississippi he had definitively pried the boot off the neck of the black man, for the first time ever in the state. Evers was nearing the culmination of a small-scale revolution, beginning in 1965 with an all-out voter registration campaign, and ending in his election as the mayor of Fayette in the spring of 1969. He was proceeding to an extraordinary reversal of power that left Mississippi whites wide-eyed.

At the end of 1965, black voters outnumbered whites two to one, thanks to Evers's registration drives. They had put teeth into demands for equal hiring and treatment in Fayette with a boycott that devastated the white business community. A visiting reporter noted the bewildered condescension of the elderly mayor toward this new force, and casually inserted a portentous phrase into his story: "Negroes and whites who have known one another for years have quite suddenly abandoned the old master–servant relationship and have begun to contest as political antagonists." [17]

In fact, this new relationship took several years to establish. In 1966, Evers got a black elected to the local school board, the first black elected official since Reconstruction. He established as a base for his expanding activities a hybrid operation at the edge of Fayette, a grocery–restaurant–registration center–teen dance hall in a modest two-story red brick building that he called the Medgar Evers Community Center. The opening of the Evers store coincided noticeably with the boycott of white stores he had himself launched.

Evers ran for Congress in early 1968, scaring the daylights out of whites when he led the field in the primary. The legislature promptly rushed through a law mandating a runoff if there was no majority in the primary. It was a race fueled by fifty-cent contributions, college student volunteers, and dinners at the roughest black honky-tonks he could find; in the end, Evers lost. [18]

By that time he had established a wide-ranging, loyal network of local NAACP branches in each county in the region. Each president was his deputy, and Evers would attend all the meetings. The organization was centered around him; he was the absolute, undisputed boss. [19]

It was all a prelude to a political triumph momentous in May 1969, but whose significance has by now been washed away by uncountable similar victories: Evers beat R. J. Allen, the incumbent mayor (nicknamed "Turnip Greens" because he was accustomed to giving away vegetables from his garden), by 386 to 255. He would later claim that he had managed to get 98 percent of eligible blacks to the polls. For the first time since Reconstruction, Mississippi whites found themselves under the governance of a black man.

The sheer novelty of this turn drew an incessant stream of reporters to Fayette. The omnipresence of the cameras and notepads and pesky Yankee voices raised the resentment level of the whites to bursting point. "If you expect anything out of me, you might as well turn around and go back where you came from," Allen snarled at one reporter later in 1969.[20]

Evers's riotous inaugural ball in Natchez was the coronation of a man who was now the undisputed mass leader of black Mississippians. The young militants grumbled about his materialism, and Mississippi's tiny band of white liberals were to become uncomfortable with his dubious past and autocratic present. But by the spring of 1969 no one else in Mississippi could command black allegiance like Evers, whose sheer toughness, reinforced by his imposing size, drew people. "He projected an image of self-confidence, and black folk needed that at that time," Robert Clark remembers. "Charles Evers would make a statement, something like, 'I'm 6'4 and 240, and I cover the ground I stand upon, and I'm not afraid of nobody.' He was the person we looked up to in the black community." In Fayette, the blacks worshipped him. He was "the big boss," and the times before 1963 were called "B.C."—Before Charles.[21]

Reporters from all over the country flocked to the inaugural, and so did the little folk who had followed Evers during his perilous registration drives. "It's hell on the town," a white woman told a reporter as cars full of blacks streamed into the antebellum river city. "All the motels are full of them." The home of Mississippi's most decadent aristocracy was suffering an ultimate indignity.

It was ninety degrees inside the rented auditorium. While white officials agonized over whether to come, the jubilant crowd inside listened to a band called the Soul Morticians. Many among them had been imprisoned in that same hall during the tumultuous boycott four years before.[22]

To the outside world, Evers's foray into public office was a fascinating spectacle. To Evers, it was a journey into the unknown. There was no precedent for his position. "Sure, I didn't know what to do," he says now. And so it would not be enough just to assume power under the existing laws; after all, whites had so often ignored those laws, simply to maintain Jim Crow. Fayette under a black mayor was a new frontier, where old, discredited laws would not be enough. The situation demanded that Evers assert himself and prove to whites that he was his own man.

And Evers had to assert himself to other blacks, too. Blacks in Jefferson County had never taken orders from a black either, and Evers wanted to show them who was boss as well. "Blacks were not used to blacks ruling," Evers says today. "They had to learn to accept directions." His past notwithstanding, Evers has always had a penchant for an oddly rigid, conservative moralism. Like other black Mississippians who aspired to middle-class status, he was repelled by the symptoms of poverty—the standing around on street corners, the cursing, the drinking, the quick resorting to violence. If Fayette was to be a model community, this kind of behavior had to be stomped out.

So Evers swung into office with a kind of freewheeling, frontier style that shocked both the whites and a black community stunned into torpor by decades of poverty and oppression. Mississippi had never seen anything remotely like this. He banned guns in Fayette but continued to carry one himself. He cracked down on public cursing and school delinquency. His black police force began strict enforcement of a twenty-five-mile-per-hour speed limit through the town. On the first day, he showed up at city hall forty minutes late, and thereafter he would bound into work wearing an olive green cotton jumpsuit, kissing the secretaries on the cheek as he headed to his office. Poor blacks got a quick hearing from him, while well-dressed white businessmen had to cool their heels in an outer office.

His staff included a twenty-eight-year-old city attorney whose miniskirt startled local sensibilities, and a weedy, mustachioed Yankee law student, Charles Ramberg, who came down for a few months and wound up staying a few years. They were just two of a small army of young, liberal white volunteers who resolutely trooped into Fayette to do battle on behalf of Evers. Many just as resolutely trooped back out in short order, disillusioned with Evers's interest in money and autocracy, which did not square with their image of a civil rights hero's priorities.[23]

In the meantime, white Fayette was to experience its own version of Freedom Summer, five years late and in miniature. It was definitely not enthusiastic. Student interns from the University of Southern California came through for a look and wrote earnest accounts in their student newspaper about the spirituality of the blacks and the wickedness of the whites. Ramberg would write home to his friends about the wondrous experiment taking place in Fayette, and they would come and stay with him, white and black, male and female. When a white girl hugged a black friend of Ramberg's on his front lawn that fall, Ramberg wrote home to a friend that he had "nearly shit" with anxiety.[24]

One day in September a Ku Kluxer rolled into town in a 1968 Mustang. He had a small arsenal of weapons in his car, and he wanted to kill Evers. A white man tipped off the mayor in time, and the Ku Kluxer was arrested. "I am a Mississippi white man," he said in explanation. Fayette was then treated to the breathtaking spectacle of this Mississippi white man in the hands of black dispensers of justice: a black judge, black policemen, and a black mayor. This too had never happened before. The Ku Kluxer had already gotten his own personal shock when Evers had sat down with him. "I wanted to find out what made him tick," as Evers told an interviewer several years later. "I think for a second there, I stopped bein' a symbol—some smartass sassy nigger lookin' for power—and almost became another human bein' to him."[25]

But on the whole, he was as much symbol as he was flesh-and-blood politician, to racists as well as liberals. Both saw him the same way: the ultimate tough-guy Southern black. On the wall of his office were the portraits of Medgar, the Kennedy brothers, and Martin Luther King, Jr. He had been an adoring supporter of Bobby Kennedy, with whom he had developed a distant friendship through the shared loss of a brother, and Evers was campaigning with him the day RFK was shot in Los Angeles. And Evers had known both JFK and MLK. To admirers, this gallery of martyrs was almost a challenge thrown out to the world, one more example of Charles's superhuman fearlessness. "Obviously, he's more emboldened than cautioned by their memory," one reporter wrote, himself momentarily jettisoning journalistic caution.[26] "A Toscanini of the Magnolia State, a gregarious bear of a man," is how another described him in a highly sympathetic account.[27]

Evers was conscious of the symbolic import of Fayette. "He hopes to turn the town into a kind of symbolic homeland for black people across the country," a reporter noted in the autumn of 1969.[28] In some ways this had already been achieved by the time of his election: Ed Cole, a Fayette native who was later to become Evers's economic development aide, remembers the sense of liberation he felt on crossing into the county after the first wave of elected blacks in 1966 and 1967. "Fayette is our Israel," Aaron Henry was fond of saying.

If that was so, then the whites of Fayette felt somewhat like beleaguered Arabs. They fought back, mostly in petty ways. The school board refused to let its property be used for Evers's swearing-in, so it had to be conducted in a parking lot. None of this discouraged Leontyne Price from coming down to sing the national anthem. There was a tense, sullen atmosphere in the little town six months into the Evers reign. Reporters caught the snarling mood of the whites and carefully reproduced their fractured grammar: "I don't hate no one, but I wouldn't put my arm around no nigger's neck," one man was heard to say. Significantly, this man was planning to stay in Fayette.[29]

The editor of the Fayette *Chronicle*, Marie Farr Walker, regularly excoriated Evers in print even as she tried to present a face of moderation to the outside world. The white citizenry in surrounding towns observed the goings-on in Fayette with fear and amazement. "I have watched with genuine sympathy the agony Fayette's white citizens have endured since that insufferable black oaf became mayor," one of Walker's colleagues, Mary Cain, wrote in her column for the newspaper in nearby Summit in October. The prominent whites used to socialize at city hall, but no more: "Now, most of us pay our bills by mail and give that place a good, wide berth," one white man said. One day in November, Evers and his black police chief stood on one side of U.S. Highway 61, and a group of whites stood on the courthouse steps on the other, staring and shaking their heads. Such open expressions of hostility were common. "They're cooperating because they haven't blown my head off. This is Mississippi," Evers said grimly at the end of 1969.

Evers kept the whites off-balance. They badly wanted to see him as a figure of black menace, but he would not give in to their typecasting. He was too much of an individualist—and too much of an integrationist—for that. So he would sound conciliatory and warlike by turns.

"My main reason for running is to prove to the world that blacks and whites can live and work together in rural Mississippi," he had said at one point during the campaign for mayor. But then he would angrily tell a reporter: "There's gonna be no more of their kind of brotherhood." He fought with the board of supervisors over his plan to put busts of the four martyrs—Martin Luther King, Jr., Medgar, and the Kennedys—on the courthouse square, and then he publicly hit the roof when his white city attorney announced her plan to marry a black policeman. "Like hell you are!" he shouted. "Get out! And I mean, get all the way out of Mississippi."

Fayette was too small to accommodate Evers's stand; that much had been clear from the beginning of his tenure, when he first began thinking about running for governor. To make that race would be an ultimate test of how far whites had come, and an ultimate example for blacks. For more than twenty years, ever since his massive defeat in 1971, Evers has provided one principal reason for his singular candidacy that year: "I ran for governor because if someone doesn't start running, there will never be a black man or a black woman governor of the state of Mississippi."[30]

It was a symbolic candidacy from the start, a proto–Jesse Jackson crusade forced to dazzle on the stump because real gains at the ballot box were so unlikely. And so he whirled around the state on a shoestring, sustained by cash from sales of buttons and his scandalous new autobiography, and drew crowds of blacks who listened enthusiastically to his inspirational down-home rhetoric and thin fringes of sullen whites who wished it would all go away. "When I'm governor we'll have rock concerts," he would tell the young people. His staff, young and naïve, put in twelve-hour days to make up for the lack of money and organization.[31]

The campaign seemed to have all the traditional apparatus—a manager, a press secretary, a schedule, contributions—but it was a flimsy superstructure. If it seemed slapdash, haphazard, and playful to the reporters covering it, it was. Evers veered gleefully between his roles of jokester, hustler, and crusader, equally at home in all of them. He would bound through the door of the campaign office on Lynch Street, bussing the secretaries on the cheek on the way in. "Darlin', you workin' for me today?," he would demand with mock seriousness. "I can't be no governor if my secretaries don't keep the office runnin' right."[32]

Where most politicians only have to contend with the problem of attracting voters, Evers had to reach back beyond that stage to overcome a more fundamental dilemma. "We gotta do more than just speak to our electorate," Cole, the campaign manager, explained to Berry, the press secretary, whose memoir unforgettably chronicles the quixotic Evers campaign. "We gotta make 'em realize they're an electorate."[33] They never quite managed it. The huge crowds at Evers's rallies adored him, but Evers wound up with only 22 percent of the vote, out of an electorate 40 percent black. "We're all just learnin'," he told Berry. "Politics ain't somethin' we gotta lot of experience in. Yeah, but b'lieve me when I tell you—this campaign's already makin' white folks confused."[34]

In fact, the campaign was full of moments that tested the limits of what white Mississippi would endure. The Evers caravan, in a spirit mixed of equal parts mischievousness and fear, continually careened against the age-old boundaries. That arch-representative of the old guard, the *Clarion-Ledger*, tried to ignore him by rarely covering his press conferences and campaign appearances. But Evers imposed himself.

He strode into an auditorium of two thousand whites at the annual Fisherman's Rodeo in Pascagoula, on the Gulf Coast. Suddenly, the hall was so quiet you could have heard "a piece of cotton fall on the floor," Evers said later. He was introduced on stage, and a man called out: "Go back home." Evers replied: "I am home." He preached his message of love and respect, and a fat white lady said loudly: "I can't love you." Evers: "You got to love me." Finally, the crowd applauded.[35]

Walking in the baking heat down the concrete sidewalks of Capitol Street in downtown Jackson with a few aides, Evers tried some impromptu campaigning with white women as they were walking to work. A reporter tagging along captured the awkwardness of the scene: "Some of the women blushed and murmured good morning to the Mayor in reply; some of them blanched, their faces tight with anger."[36]

At his kickoff rally on the steps of the county courthouse in Decatur, whites stood across the street from a large crowd of blacks and listened sullenly in the ninety-two-degree heat as Evers talked about joining hands and going forward together. The air was taut, made more so by the sound of a pickup truck loudly roaring up Main Street.

Later that day, to Evers's surprise, no local blacks showed up to hear him in the little town of Bay Springs. The fat, cigar-chomping chief coolly informed him that the "colored" had decided not to come, whereupon the candidate just as coolly thrust out his hand and said goodbye. "I don't shake hands with colored people" was the policeman's glacial response.[37]

In the smaller towns, the appearance of the Evers parade—sometimes as many as twenty-five cars—would throw the local police into a panic. In Mendenhall, Charles listened in on his police radio as the cops tried to figure out "what this big bunch of niggers is up to." Some of the police said the blacks were "going North"; when Evers's white aides were spotted, an officer radioed: "The hippies are coming." Eventually the order came down from the police chief: "Don't do anything. Stand by and report back what they're doing." This was political campaigning as high farce, overladen with a tinge of menace.

The campaign itself was imbued with a sense of play, not all due to the bunglings of white cops and officials. Was Evers's campaign a serious effort? It is hard to arrive at an unambiguous conclusion, twenty years later. There were times when Evers surprised people with the down-to-earth seriousness of his pitch: lower taxes for everybody, and especially, lower property taxes for the elderly; better health care; legalized gambling on the Gulf Coast. But then he could go and endorse the clownlike segregationist Jimmy Swan (see chapter 5) in the first primary, on the tortuous logic that whites would pick him, Evers, as the lesser of two evils in the fall. "This is politics," he explained to a mystified Bill Minor.[38] "Yeah, we had fun. I just cut [Swan's] nuts off," Evers says now, his eyes mischievously twinkling. The earnestness of such notables as John Lindsay, then mayor of New York, who jetted down to Mississippi to speechify about Evers as the representative of the "outsider," seemed beside the point next to these antics.

Even during the campaign some members of Mississippi's struggling black political set quietly grumbled that Evers was on an ego trip. He was hogging all the money and attention, they said, and his own race was hopeless. He should be helping them, all 269-odd black candidates, in their struggles for county supervisor, chancery clerk, or district court judge.

But he did not. And they, like Evers, lost big. Whites won 240 of those races, and the Jackson *Daily News* was able to proclaim contentedly: "The election, in our view, proves that an historic relationship of paternalism of the whites for the blacks still exists in Mississippi; that the blacks look upon the whites for leadership, for guidance, for favors, for loans, for friendship. The blacks in heavy numbers favored white candidates."[39]

The truth of that last assertion was doubtful; for one thing, there unquestionably had been electoral fraud, intimidation, and ballot stealing—the traditional Mississippi methods of suppressing black votes. Still, the losses looked like a heavy setback for the cause of black advancement. But in one sense—paradoxically, because it marked the beginning of the end for Evers—it was not.

"I think here he found people who said, yeah, come on over and be our king," says Kennie Middleton, the mayor of Fayette today. He has struggled with Evers for years, and Middleton adopts a tone of wary respect when discussing Evers. He wants to be liked by a man he regards as the master teacher of Mississippi black politicians. More than a decade ago, the pudgy, round-faced Middleton handed Evers his first political defeat in Fayette—the only jurisdiction in which Evers seemed invulnerable. As a teenager, he had marched for Evers and worshipped him like any of the other young black people in the town. As much as anybody, he had been prepared to assist in the coronation of Evers.

A king is what the civil rights years in Fayette needed, someone who gave orders and continuously challenged the whites, who "looked them eye to eye and said what needed to be said," as Middleton puts it. But a king does not need to hear the voices of his subjects, and Evers, the larger-than-life individualist in the sleepy little town, was not particularly inclined to listen anyway. Evers was an inspirational figure. But as the need for such inspiration diminished, and Evers's own autocratic tendencies grew, his position as what Clark called the "focal point" of the black community all over

Mississippi faded. This was a result of both idiosyncracy and changing times. The process began even before the 1971 race.

Four months into his term as mayor, in the first rash of newspaper assessments, the reports were full of rapturous quotes from blacks bursting with the Evers effect. "Well, I'm not afraid no more," Loupearl Jackson, a "Negro housewife," told the Memphis *Commercial-Appeal*. The whites could flail away and whine to their heart's content. "It's not good, healthy money," Marie Walker said, as the federal dollars flowed in. "I do think that by giving them this without them working for it, it is taking away their initiative."[40] The criticism did not matter as long as Evers had the support of his people.

But early in 1970, the first signs of trouble with the black constituents were evident. Four out of five of his policemen walked off their jobs, complaining they had been "treated like dogs" by the mayor. "I expect my policemen to keep their shoes shined. I don't want them laying around the cafe drinking coffee," Evers snapped. He was already telling reporters that the blacks of Fayette were "jealous" of him and would not reelect him mayor.[41] That was a doubtful explanation for what was really going wrong in Fayette. Unquestionably, the seeds of his downfall were already present.

From the start, many people had chafed under his peculiar homegrown morality scheme. As the judge in police court, Evers personally handed out fines for small infractions. "I didn't allow that, standing on the street cursing, didn't allow that. . . . I turned a lot of people against me," he remembers now. "He doesn't believe a black person can violate the civil rights of another black person," Middleton observed, accurately, in the early 1980s.

It was all part of the mayor's undeclared conception of Fayette as a personal fiefdom; democracy was not necessarily part of the Evers plan. Cole wanted to explain the mayor's actions at town meetings; Evers would remonstrate with him, telling Cole that explanations were not necessary. That four out of five of his aldermen were barely literate did not phase him—quite the contrary.[42] He was not particularly interested in their views, a fact that the increasingly wary Ramberg was recognizing. "One thing that Evers had was total control," Ramberg remembered in 1981. "I've got him on tape telling Fayette workers if they wanted to keep their jobs they were going to vote for him. I've seen him sit his aldermen down and treat them just like a first-grade classroom. . . . He's not much of a believer in democracy."[43]

Given the desperation of the setting, autocracy would have gone down more easily if the autocrat could have delivered prosperity. "Everything will come together," a smiling young black man told a reporter in Fayette in the fall of 1969.[44] Those kinds of hopes were sustained for a few years, as the federal grant money poured in and new buildings sprouted up among the old brick structures: subsidized housing, a $400,000 community center, a health clinic. Then the hopes disappeared entirely. "They came in with the great idea of creating utopia," says Middleton. "Eventually, it all fell apart." Evers's political friends in the North sent a stream of businessmen down to look at the great experiment, and virtually all left shaking their heads at the awful backwardness of the place.[45] "So you see that the millennium has not yet arrived in Fayette," Ramberg wrote a friend at the end of 1969. "We are waiting for the sun, and it seems we are in midwinter."

Finally, pushed by Ted Kennedy, ITT agreed to build a modest wire harness plant in Fayette. But having jobs for 150 people was not the answer to Fayette's problems; the simple truth was that Evers could not give everybody in town employment. In July 1981, when Middleton knocked Evers off his mayoral perch, Jefferson County had the highest unemployment rate in the state. In an advertisement that deeply affected the Fayette citizens, Middleton pointed out that 1981's high school graduating class had entered first grade the year Evers had became mayor, but "their prospects for employment" had not improved at all.[46]

From the start, whites had been cynical about Evers's venality. This was less a function of analysis than of predjudice, since most were inclined to see blacks as either crooked or dumb, or both. The boycotts of the 1960s, they said, were conducted so Evers could get more black business at his own store. Unfortunately for Evers, even other blacks began to believe these accounts. Already, by the end of the first year, Charles seemed to be spending less time in town and more time out on the road collecting lecture fees.[47]

Gradually, a vague distrust built up, fueled by occasional small improprieties and Evers's wild political gyrations. There was the time in the late 1970s when Evers used $5,300 in federal funds for permanent renovations to a day-care center, in a building he owned. He was using some of the center's federally paid employees for his private businesses, and he hired the town attorney, with federal money, to certify that he, Evers, was charging the government fair rent at the day-care center. "If my ways are a little unorthodox, that's just the way we've been taught," Evers told a reporter who came calling in Fayette.[48] But more than any specific episode, it was what Middleton calls the "cumulative effect of what appeared to be his self-enriching activities" that built up distrust.

The whites of Fayette wore a gleeful, I-told-you-so look when the IRS had Evers indicted in 1974 for not reporting $156,000 in income allegedly earned during the late 1960s. He was also accused of transferring some of Fayette's funds to a personal account in Chicago. Publicly, Evers affected unconcern: "It just shows that all blacks are not on welfare." His attorney adopted a novel defense, still the subject of wonderment among lawyers in Mississippi: yes, Evers had stashed money away, but he had done so long before the period specified in the indictment. And the lawyer admitted that it may have been earned during Evers's legendary Chicago vice lord days. In the end, a mistrial was declared on a technicality; the lawyer had to sue Evers to get his fee.

But for all the devil-may-care posing, this was a watershed; Afterwards, Evers never lost the taint. Minor wrote that the whole affair damaged Evers's "already sagging claim to being the coalescing figure of Mississippi blacks."[49]

Evers was becoming marginalized, partly because times had changed. Individual Mississippi blacks now had greater control over their own destiny than ever before, thanks to the voting and civil rights laws. So the moment of the unifying, inspirational, battering-ram leader had passed. In some ways, whites actually preferred the kind of black leader who could control people. Indeed, there are hints of nostalgia in Walker's reminiscences about the good old fights with Evers. Throughout Mississippi, local black leaders had been drawing allegiance away from Evers ever since Clark had first been elected to the state legislature in 1968.

Maybe Evers was unconsciously responding to the changing times, or maybe he was simply following his own predilections

(chiefly opportunism, his critics argued). And he has always liked
to shock people. But Evers's political course in the 1970s seemed to
be a willful moving away from his position as the boss. He visited
Richard Nixon in San Clemente after Watergate and defended Nixon's withholding of evidence. He went to see George Wallace and
boosted him for the vice-presidency. He supported the redneck candidate for governor of Mississippi, Cliff Finch, and campaigned
against William Winter, who had a long track record of racial moderation. Finch repaid the favor by making one of Evers's daughters
a receptionist at the Governor's Mansion. Four years later, Evers
enthusiastically embraced John Arthur Eaves, another barely repen-
tant segregationist. "Anybody can change. If he calls you a nigger,
then you a nigger," Evers said enigmatically.[50]

The final blow came when he endorsed Reagan in 1980, an
act that caused many blacks to write him off for good. "His Reagan
bit last fall was an Alice in Wonderland scene enacted right here in
Mississippi politics," Minor wrote. "Here was the once hated black
man, who used to regularly take a couple of thousand angry blacks
into the streets of Jackson to demand their civil rights, being embraced by the Republican fatcats at a Reagan rally in a Jackson
motel."[51]

Meanwhile, Evers kept losing political races, one after another. He lost a state senate race in 1975, carrying only two
majority-black counties. Three years later, he stood under the Bilbo
bust at the capitol and announced that whites would vote to put
him in the U.S. Senate. He lost that election disastrously and drew
enough votes away from the moderate Democrat to clear the way
for a Republican. In 1979 he told the local AFL-CIO man to stay
out of Jefferson County. Labor backed a white candidate against
Evers in another state senate race, and Evers was trounced in his
own backyard, a solid majority-black district; all candidates in
other races who had Evers's backing were also soundly defeated. He
was feuding with labor, he was feuding with Aaron Henry, and he
seemed to have no political friends left. Only an older generation of
rural blacks still had fond feelings for Evers, and even those supporters were rapidly falling away.

"He tries to control anything he has his hand in," said
Middleton in the summer of 1981, just after he defeated Evers in

Fayette. The event profoundly affected Evers, despite his usual bravado. He sounded almost like a hurt child: "There's no way he could have beat me if I tried, but I didn't try."[52]

From then on, the criticism from other blacks was unrestrained. "Any time he says something, people don't take it like they used to take it," said Phillip West, a black county supervisor in nearby Natchez, in 1982. "It used to be that people took him at his word. Now people are waiting to see."[53] Evers was losing his old movement colleagues. David Jordan, head of the Greenwood Voters' League, a powerful black organization in the Delta, urged black voters to stay away when Evers announced his candidacy for governor in 1983. By 1989, he had lost yet another race for mayor and had joined the Republican party, to savage criticism from fellow blacks.

None of the criticism seemed to bother Evers. "This meeting. This is a bore," he said after an NAACP banquet in 1985. "Too many banquets. Too much tea."[54]

CHAPTER SEVEN

BOBBY DELAUGHTER

N ot much baggage was attached to the Evers name when it first entered young Bobby DeLaughter's consciousness. Like many white teenagers in the hypernormal suburban world of Jackson in the 1970s, he knew about the Medgar Evers Homecoming, the raffish blues festival that Charles Evers put on every year in Fayette in tribute to his dead brother. Evers was a music promoter, not a politician, to the gangly teen. At that juncture, for some middle-class white teenagers, Evers had developed a certain cool. As early as 1971, he had been endorsed for governor by the newspaper of St. Joseph, a 90 percent white, private Catholic high school in Jackson, an event that touched off a small media ripple. Evers's black face had appeared on the cover of the school paper endorsing him, the lyrics of Neil Young's "Southern Man" superimposed on the picture.[1] For these earnest white Mississippi teenagers, hair almost as long as their northern contemporaries, he was clearly not the Great Nigra Peril.

DeLaughter was going to a public high school, and his hair was not long. But Evers was not a bogeyman for him either. Nor should he have been: by 1970 there were more than eighty black public officials, and if the sixteen-year-old DeLaughter had been aware of that statistic, Evers would have been lumped in with the rest of them. But he was not. The young man was coming of age in a curiously race-neutral world—a place where the old passions, to the degree he knew about them, were somewhat mystifying. To the young DeLaughter, Medgar was simply the dead brother of Charles, just a "slain civil rights leader." He uses that pat phrase now to invoke the memory of when he first heard about Medgar Evers.

DeLaughter himself felt no special sense of guilt or outrage about race relations. In that, he was not alone among members of his generation, and this was the sane response for young whites. To feel guilt meant rejection of one's family, of the very people who had cheered on Ross Barnett. For DeLaughter, who had intimate ties to the old regime, such rejection would have been virtually impossible. His great-uncle was Buddie Newman, Barnett's pug-like fixer in the legislature, a man known as the governor's "Little Switch." The youthful DeLaughter's wife was the daughter of Judge Russel Moore, one of the most militant segregationists on the state bench in the 1960s. A stalwart of the Citizens' Council, Moore was remembered as the man who sent blacks to jail for sitting in white waiting rooms. He had been a constant visitor to Beckwith's trial in 1964. DeLaughter was thus "a kid that was raised in the old-time bullshit," as his future boss, the Jackson lawyer Alvin Binder, put it.[2]

Righteous crusading, even if DeLaughter had considered it, was not a career option. For one thing, there was nothing to fuel outrage. He had not grown up thinking segregation was bad, and he had remained ignorant about the excesses of Jim Crow: at home nothing had been said on the subject. In school, the standard history textbooks had hardly dwelled on those excesses either. His own great-uncle was living proof that there had been no purge of old-guard foot soldiers—far from it, since Newman was rising to the state's most powerful political position, as the speaker of the house.

And yet DeLaughter was not trapped by this ignorance of the past. He was curiously liberated by it, neither outraged nor defensive about what had come before. It was an era when old relationships were being quietly overturned without much public acknowledgement or fury. Bill Waller was bringing blacks into state government (see chapter 5), and poor black and white voters banded together to elect his successor, Cliff Finch. Four months into his term, Finch even showed up at the Medgar Evers Homecoming. So by the time DeLaughter left the law school at Ole Miss in December 1977, it was the most natural thing in the world to think of blacks as co-citizens, more or less. They were to be objects neither of pity nor of predjudice.

In his apprenticeship, at Binder's Jackson law firm, DeLaughter found an incubating ground for these feelings. Binder, a Jew, had managed to stay adroitly at some remove from Mississippi's race agonies. Mostly, blacks were just clients to him. Binder's office on Pearl Street, in a faux–New Orleans–style building he had designed, was racial neutral ground. As for DeLaughter, *black* and *white* were words that defined his moral universe; as racial distinctions, they meant little to him. DeLaughter inhabited the law, a tool for sorting out right and wrong, and he eventually concluded that the best place to use that tool was the local district attorney's office.

DeLaughter was nine when Medgar Evers was shot. The event had as much chance of registering in his world as a military coup in Bolivia; young Southern boys were not normally preoccupied with the assassination of civil rights leaders. He was brought up in ignorance, like most other white children in that time and place. The other world, the world of black Jackson, could not have been more foreign to the private sphere of the DeLaughter household. Outside the house, the young boy could see that black people seemed to have their own schools, ride in a different part of the bus, and use different parks. For all he knew, it was like that everywhere else. His contact with the black world was minimal: "I mean, I knew from going out that there were black persons in Jackson," DeLaughter says now. Inside the house, the world of blacks penetrated even less than in other Jackson families—those of a more elevated socioeconomic rank. His parents were working people, his mother a clerk in the courthouse and his father a commercial artist in the advertising department of the now-defunct Jackson *State-Times* newspaper. For a brief period, they employed a black maid—that elemental status symbol—but DeLaughter cannot even remember the woman's name. He remembers no discussions of civil rights. "We were insulated from all that," he says.

DeLaughter was fifteen before he learned his world was not normal. That time was pivotal in Mississippi's history because of the integration of the schools. The Citizens' Council and even the state government were making it easy for white parents of modest means to send their children to the instant private schools, the "segregation academies." Young Bobby saw many of his old mates pulled away by the new schools, but Barney and Billie DeLaughter kept their sons in the public schools. Uncomfortable with change, they are hardly liberals. DeLaughter's father, now an insurance salesman, remains uneasy about Bobby's foray into the past, the re-indictment of Beckwith. He does not want to talk about his son, does not want to "get involved in that at all." And yet during those difficult years in the late 1960s they chose a course many race-obsessed white parents were rejecting.

It was the fall of 1969, and the DeLaughter family had moved to Natchez for the year. There were white schools and black schools—even more segregated an area than Jackson. Natchez was a tough town. The Klan had blown up Wharlest Jackson, a rubber company worker promoted to a job normally reserved for whites, in 1967, and memories of Charles Evers's boycott campaigns had not faded.[3] Over the Christmas holidays in 1969, DeLaughter received an unsettling message from the people at school: things would be different when he came back in January, blacks would be in some of his classes. For other classes he would have to get on a bus and go to what had been a black school. It was a moment of revelation for the young man. "That was the first time that I became aware that it's not like that, that it had not been segregated everywhere, and this is segregated." He had not been prepared for this moment of revelation about the old and new orders. Nor were his parents much help in figuring out what it was all about. For that, he had to read the newspaper, which told him that a mysterious entity called the federal courts was forcing the change.

Not that it bothered the teenage DeLaughter much. That first year in high school was also the year of Jackson's last major racial convulsion, when the Mississippi Highway Patrol fired four hundred bullets on demonstrating black students at Jackson State College, killing two young men. The subsequent whitewash was inspired by DeLaughter's future father-in-law, Judge Moore, who told the grand jury that killing demonstrators was justified in "suppressing any riot."[4]

But the passions of DeLaughter's elders on the subject of race were a mystery to him. "We didn't care," he says now. "It wasn't that big a deal." Racial problems were not rooted in anything rational; they were "in the minds of the adults," he says. Throughout his high school years, white school administrators could not shake their timidity over the new integrated order. By the time DeLaughter was a senior, back in Jackson at Wingfield High School, the school had canceled virtually all extracurricular events except sports. The Wingfield student body was only 5 percent black. But there were no social functions left—no dances, no meetings, no clubs—about which the students, black and white, were upset. DeLaughter was the president of the student body, "a real leader," principal D. T. Measells remembered, "bright" and "capable." He lobbied hard for the school administrators to change their policy. Finally, in 1972, in the spring of his senior year, while Waller was shaking up the legislature, DeLaughter got his integrated senior prom. It went off without a hitch.

The case against Beckwith would never have been pursued to its limit if not for DeLaughter. And yet for someone who has deliberately kicked over this rotting log of Mississippi history, he presents an awfully plain face to the world.

DeLaughter is a serious young man who rarely cracks a smile. Masklike, his expression does not change much, even in the middle of heated courtroom debate. The women who work in the circuit clerk's office at the Hinds County Courthouse know that kidding around does not get you very far with the quiet and undemonstrative DeLaughter, whom his friends stop just short of calling dull. His life revolves around his law books and his three children whom he raised alone after divorcing. He is the kind of man who can sit over a meal with you and not say anything for an hour. Once, in the mid-1980s, he went on a holiday to Mexico with his then–law partner, William Kirksey. After three days Kirksey called his wife and in desperation said, "Talk to me."[5]

The style of the Southern trial lawyer tends toward the back-slapping, the loud, the brash. Professionally, the lawyer needs to tell a dramatic story to jurors—fellow Southerners—reared in good storytelling. DeLaughter does not fit this mold. It is not so much that he doesn't command enormous respect. There are better lawyers in the state. But as a lawyer, his characteristic traits of intro-spection and restraint set him apart from his colleagues in the Mississippi bar. "He runs real deep," says Amy Whitten, a law-yer who worked with him. "He's got a very deep, quiet conviction about things."

His view of history—at least the one for public consump-tion—is diplomatic. It is influenced by DeLaughter's need to re-main part of his parents' world, a world that viewed the civil rights revolution with hostility. DeLaughter is careful not to make a moral distinction between insurgents and defenders: "It was one of those times in history that you had one group fighting as hard as they could to bring about some changes politically, socially and eco-nomically. And you had another group fighting just as hard to hang on to the way things had been." The 1960s, he says, involved a battle between competing groups of rights—not between privi-leges and rights. "It was a time of hurt, one group fighting for rights, another group fighting not to give up rights. It took time for the wounds to heal from that fight." DeLaughter's mission is not to right all the wrongs of history. He is nonetheless aware, in his diplomatic way, that not all the wounds have healed.

The blandness falls away abruptly when he recalls the scene of Medgar Evers's last moments, which remains vivid in his mind. His voice rises as he conjures up that scene:

> I feel indignant when I think about anybody being shot in the back from ambush in the driveway of their home with their

wife and small children inside. I feel indignant reading about these children coming out, crawling through a pool of blood in the carport and saying daddy, please get up. I get indignant about that.[6]

Clearly, there was something so wrong that it propelled De-Laughter through the weeks of discouragement, of dead-ends, of people telling him to give the case up. To be sure, he had other motivations—his political ambition; a gnawing sense that, in legalistic terms, justice had not been served in 1964; the desire of the district attorney (his boss, Ed Peters) to mend fences with Jackson's blacks. But overriding all was the sense that a terrible wrong had been perpetrated on a fundamentally decent human being, and DeLaughter found that hard to stomach.

Between DeLaughter's high school graduation and his return from the Ole Miss law school in 1978, Jackson's Americanization had proceeded rapidly. In the late 1970s the city looked and felt much like anywhere else, which slightly disappointed writers who remembered the feeling of danger they had once gotten from the place. It was now a city of small freeways and national chain stores, a "constant slither of merges and exits, alongside of which were most of the fast-food outfits and all the major motels . . . a string of A&P's open 24 hours, Master Hosts, Kentucky Fried Chicken . . . Bonanza Steak Joints."[7] The visiting writers usually recorded their astonishment at the change, and left.

In the summer of 1969, Myrlie Evers had come back to Jackson for the national NAACP's annual conference. It seemed remarkable enough that the event was taking place in Jackson at all, and at a downtown hotel that had recently barred blacks. But other things astonished her, such as friendly police and free access to restaurants. "It was hard not to be carried away with enthusiasm at all I saw," she wrote at the time. In fact, Jackson had simply become anytown: "I had to remind myself that this was the way things should always have been."[8]

But even liberals who had stayed on, people like Kenneth Dean, the head of the Mississippi Council on Human Relations, were surprised at what Jackson had become: very much like any other modest capital in the heart of a rural state. With the new network of interstate highways feeding consumer preoccupations, "the community ethos was against violence," says Dean. As early as 1971, Walter Cronkite had proclaimed the recent integration of Jackson's schools the model for the rest of the country; that turned out to be an exaggeration. But there was no denying the new wholesomeness of the place. Melvyn Leventhal, a pioneering civil rights lawyer who had come to Jackson in 1965, no longer rode around town with a rifle in the back seat of his car. Leventhal and another member of the lonely community of northern lawyers, Frank Parker, had scandalized white Jackson with their interracial marriages. (Leventhal was married to the writer Alice Walker.) For years, it had been dangerous for the couples to walk together down Farish Street, the main street of black Jackson.

Most astonishing to people who had been away, the troglodytic *Clarion-Ledger* and *Daily News* had come into the hands of an irreverent younger Hederman, Rea, who transformed the newspapers. Frankly embarrassed by their history, he left the racist old columnists to molder quietly in corners of the newsroom, hired earnest young reporters from all over the country, and announced his intention to make the Hederman family papers the best in the South. One editor hired by Rea Hederman remembers coming to the papers and finding a "small and awful staff" that played cards in the newsroom at night. Over eight years, Hederman hired more than three hundred reporters. In Jackson, they became known as "Rea's outside agitators" and the paper itself, the city's "foreign newspaper." To the embarrassment of the older Hedermans, the paper soon won a Robert F. Kennedy award for a series on poverty in the Delta.[9]

In the summer of 1977, DeLaughter came down from Oxford to clerk in Binder's law firm on Pearl Street. By January of the following year, he was working there full-time. Like so many career moves in Mississippi, DeLaughter's was dictated by family ties. Binder's law partner was Russel Moore, DeLaughter's new father-in-law. Still, for someone steeped in "the old-time bullshit," this was as close as DeLaughter could conceivably get to coming under the tutelage of one who had been exercised by racial injustice.

The skillful Binder gave DeLaughter much more than instruction in the craft of lawyering. There were, for example, lessons in coming to grips with Mississippi's past. Binder was in some ways the perfect teacher for the young DeLaughter. Although he could not possibly adopt Northerners' righteous indignation at Mississippi's ruling class—he had been too closely associated with it—Binder, as a Jew, had been forced to confront the injustices of white supremacy. And he had had his own private crises of conscience. (His one brush with national notoriety came when Wayne Williams, the black man convicted in February 1983 of a series of child murders in Atlanta, chose Binder as his lawyer on the recommendation of Mississippi civil rights figures.)

Binder, who died in the spring of 1993, occupied an ambiguous position in Jackson's political circles. The most prominent Jew in the city for much of his life, he was both of the establishment and outside it. Liberals considered him an "operator," as one put it. During the 1960s, he had been firmly identified with the segregationist power structure—as a city attorney prosecuting Freedom Riders; as an honorary member of Ross Barnett's staff; as a speaker for the Sovereignty Commission, defending the Mississippi way of life up North. A photograph from the 1960s of Binder standing between Barnett and his successor, Paul Johnson, at a ribbon cutting occupies a place of honor on his walls. A portly young man with thinning hair, Binder looks thoroughly at ease beside the grinning segregationists.

"Al's one of us. He's our Jew," is how the Mississippi establishment had thought of him for years, said Nancy Binder, his second wife. He was the "consigliere" (or councillor), according to a liberal Jackson lawyer, the Henry Kissinger of Mississippi. Binder himself did not hide the fact that, for the most part, he accepted the verities of the day: "You wouldn't think of having a Negro in your house," he said simply.[10]

His first wife, Paige Mitchell, wrote two potboiler novels set in the civil rights crisis years that feature a Binder-like character as the crusading central figure. They illustrate Binder's accommodationism. In *The Covenant* the Binder figure enunciates the resentment of outsiders that was white Mississippians' lingua franca: "They didn't need any more Yankee headlines, or any more invasions by cameras and questions. Black men and white men alike, who couldn't handle the problems in their own back yard, were the first to appear and tell the the South how to run its business."[11]

Paige Mitchell's novel faithfully mirrors the prevailing attitudes of Jackson's Jews. Jewish civil rights workers were not welcomed by the local community. "They were indifferent," said Leventhal. "They never made any effort to bring me into the congregation." His most meaningful encounter with Mississippi Jews was eating cheesecake at the Old Tyme Deli, which was run by Binder's parents. But Leventhal does not recall encountering Binder himself—indeed, has never even heard of him. Indifference shaded into fear of being associated with the outsiders. "It was just too dangerous to be friends with them," one Jewish woman said in the early 1970s.[12]

In truth, Jackson's Jews were no different from those in other Southern towns. Whatever their individual feelings about equal rights for blacks, the Jews' own sense of vulnerability barred them from adopting the cause. Some Jews even joined the Citizens' Council in those years, but others felt a persistent undercurrent of guilt. In *The Covenant*, the Jewish lawyer, prodded by his own guilt, ultimately takes the civil rights case.

Mississippi Jews showed no particular courage during the civil rights years. Still, a pre–civil rights legacy of fairness had prevailed in their dealings with blacks, and that continued as a faint background for relations between blacks and Jews into the 1960s. In his 1930s study *Caste and Class in a Southern Town* John Dollard had discovered this unexpected cordiality in Indianola, where gentile whites founded the Citizens' Council twenty years later (see chapter 3). All up and down the Delta, Jews owned most of the musty, sweet-smelling dry-goods stores. The Jews of the Delta, Dollard found, rarely insulted blacks and, unlike other whites, would bargain with blacks, always putting business before caste.[13] During Aaron Henry's growing-up years, "you would consider them the better of the white element that you had dealings with." Henry had known Binder for forty years, and other members of the Binder family even longer. In Henry's hometown of Clarksdale, Binder's parents owned a leading grocery store. And in the late

1930s the Clarksdale congregation, the largest Jewish congregation in the state for much of this century, had published a confident fiftieth-anniversary brochure that featured greetings from the leading merchants in town.

Binder may have been "their Jew," but he found it more difficult than his segregationist patrons to swallow things he saw going on around him. He had been a lawyer for the city of Jackson during the regime of Mayor Allan Thompson, who had done battle with Medgar Evers (see chapter 2), and Binder had prosecuted some of the Freedom Riders in 1961. One day, after a routine conviction had been successfully secured, he had turned to see the jury walking out the back door of the mayor's office: ritual congratulation for a job well done. "I thought to myself, My God. That's the day I quit being a city prosecutor. It was the most unethical thing."[14]

His anguish was quiet, and Binder never broke publicly with white supremacy's official upholders. Not until Jews themselves came under attack, in the Klan terror campaign of 1967, did Binder take a firm stand. There had always been a pugnacious streak in him. In the early 1950s, struggling to pay for his undergraduate schooling at Tulane University, Binder had taken to boxing for money. He sided with Perry Nussbaum, the liberal rabbi who wanted to hold integrated meetings in the temple, and Binder played a central role in raising money for Klan informants,[15] who would sneak into the Pearl Street law office during those years.

Binder's involvement was a matter as much of survival as of morality, as Binder himself was careful to say in an interview a decade later. "I was born in the South, where the KKK preaches that blacks don't deserve to live and Jews should be drowned. In situations where the white majority sits by and doesn't condemn that, you do what you have to do for self-survival or leave town and run."[16]

Asked how DeLaughter had gained the perspective that enabled him to go after Beckwith, Binder answered unhesitatingly: "He practiced law with me for eight years. I think I had an influence on him. He saw a lot of things over here. He knew I was active against the Klan." In Jackson, Binder was famous for his ego. In his version, the wily old attorney takes the overconfident young lawyer, exposes him to Mississippi's unpleasant realities, and turns him into a fearless prosecutor.

There is some truth in this. DeLaughter as a newly minted lawyer is remembered as full of himself; unquestionably, he was a different man when he walked out of Binder's office in the summer of 1982. But it is also true that by the time DeLaughter came to work for Binder, the Klan threat had long since been wiped out. Binder was more firmly entrenched in the power structure than ever, as legal counsel to the incumbent, Governor Finch, who was proving somewhat shadier than the norm. When Binder's old foes resurfaced now, the effect was grotesque rather than menacing. One day there was a commotion on the twentieth floor of the Sillers Building, where the governor had his offices and where Binder also kept an office. For Binder, it was like a bad dream of the shadowy war he had helped fight a decade earlier: there was Beckwith, demanding to see the governor. Binder threatened to have him thrown *off* the building; Beckwith left in a hurry.

What contact DeLaughter and Kirksey had with the 1960s came casually, in informal discussions around the office. It was a strangely quiet time in the public discourse about race in Mississippi, a time when people were pretending, with some strain, that race no longer existed. The *New York Times* could write in the spring of 1980: "Jackson is now the most changed and probably the most integrated—in schools, neighborhoods and politics—of the southern state capitals."[17]

The tales from the 1960s seemed to come from a different world. "We sat around the office talking about the sixties," Kirksey remembers. "Half the time I was in amazement." For the young lawyers, Binder's office opened their eyes to a new world, one that included Mississippi's Jews. Today, a decade after leaving Binder's employ, Kirksey refers to the older attorney as "my rabbi." Binder took DeLaughter and Kirksey to bar mitzvahs and Jewish weddings. He told them about getting rocks thrown at him as a lad growing up in the Delta. The Pearl Street office was not a place where the sort of casual racism typical of middle-class Mississippians was accepted. "If you're raised with any predjudice, you better leave it at the door," Kirksey recalls about Binder's office.

Binder not only raised DeLaughter's fledgling consciousness but also taught him about taking on unpopular cases. There was the Wayne Williams case, which dominated much of the last year of DeLaughter's tenure with Binder. There was the case of Marion "Mad Dog" Pruett, who had murdered a bank teller. And there were all those cronies of ex-governor Finch who had been hauled into the dock on corruption charges. It took a certain intestinal fortitude to withstand the nasty public sentiments these cases generated—a lesson that would serve DeLaughter in good stead later on.

The visits to Binder's office by Aaron Henry, then the NAACP president, were an important part of the new world for DeLaughter and Kirksey. Henry's tie to Binder was founded in a hometown bonding, something deeper than ideological affinity. Then, when the Klan synagogue bombings (chapter 4) pushed Binder into an overt stance against white supremacy, the relationship solidified further. Binder shared his hard-won intelligence on the Klan, gained from his informants, with the NAACP leader. In return, the state NAACP awarded Binder the association's Goodman-Schwerner-Chaney Award (named for the three slain civil rights workers).

Binder was a natural ally, a man who was part of the establishment and yet had credentials in the fight against a common enemy, the Klan. So Henry was an ideal civil rights figure to help raise the consciousness of the two young, traditionally raised Mississippians working with Binder. Not that Henry took any particular notice of DeLaughter; he was just one of Binder's employees.

Nor did DeLaughter take any great notice of Henry; the young man was not overly concerned with civil rights. DeLaughter had been hired because Binder had an instinct about him, a sense that this rather dry young man would prove to be a formidably meticulous legal researcher. Binder had taken his law partner's son-in-law with him on a couple of trials, and the admiration was mutual. "Bobby was hired primarily to get in them damn books," Kirksey remembers. "Al said, 'If we hire him, we'll never have to do any research.'"

And Binder proved to be right. "He was wonderful at it. He was amazing." There was a doggedness about the way he pursued cases that kept him looking for leads until he hit on the right nugget. "He would dig and dig until he could find something to support our side," remembers Nancy Binder. Binder set him to work on personal injury cases, Kirksey handled the lucrative divorces, and Binder kept to the big-ticket, big-publicity criminal cases. DeLaughter could take a case that everyone else in the office thought was hopeless and turn it into a moneymaker. In one case, he managed to suck $700,000 out of the giant papermaking concern Georgia-Pacific for a worker who had broken his back when a conveyor chain had snapped.

DeLaughter had an almost black-and-white sense of right and wrong. The law, with its precise codification of this distinction, was natural territory for him to inhabit. It was important to believe in the justice of his cause. Once he did so, he was able to exercise the fierce tenacity others see as his defining characteristic.

Criminal law, the domain of the mentor Binder, set out right and wrong with even greater clarity than did civil law. In the summer of 1982, Kirksey and DeLaughter decided to put into practice the lessons learned from their teacher. For the next five years De-Laughter threw himself into criminal defense, embracing it with such passion that the young firm literally went broke. He just was not interested in doing the routine but lucrative personal injury cases anymore. In one year, Kirksey and DeLaughter defended six men who were facing the death penalty. The attorneys put in eighteen-hour days to research the law on behalf of men who did not command much public sympathy. DeLaughter kept at it anyway, managing to gain lesser sentences in a celebrated murder case or two.

He loved the law, and he loved being in a courtroom. But with three children he was devoted to, earning a decent living by defending murderers proved next to impossible. He could have gone after more money by joining a large firm. Instead, in the spring of 1987, DeLaughter imposed what amounted to a pay cut on himself: he joined the district attorney's office, to stay close to criminal law.

As of 1987, Ed Peters had been the district attorney for over a decade. He was a dubious star for an ambitious young man to latch on to. The Hinds County D.A.'s office was not the place to which young legal talent in Jackson gravitated, and Peters had long had a sleazy reputation.

He had begun life in Waller's firm but had stayed barely over a year. In 1972 he had succeeded to Waller's old job, and for the next five years he would be caught up in a succession of scandals, some proved and others not. The acts he was linked to—small-scale extortion and fraud and shakedowns—were petty, more readily associated with a second-rate mobster than with Hinds County's top lawyer. But Peters had hung on, through several indictments, a scabrous column by the journalist Jack Anderson, and a judicial reprimand.

Peters had been indicted in 1975 for extorting $1,200 from an investigator in his office, and later he was indicted for continuing to collect legal fees after his election as district attorney; he was found not guilty in the first case, and charges were dropped in the second. In 1977 an undercover ex-mobster began poking into Jackson organized crime for the Mississippi attorney general. The undercover man apparently found more than his patron was looking for: he claimed Peters was trying to set up a prostitution ring. Anderson picked up the story, and sensational headlines appeared for a month. The district attorney emphatically denied it, and the attorney general said there was no evidence to proceed. The next year, Peters was found to have participated in a scheme to bilk credulous investors, shortly after becoming district attorney in 1974. A federal judge gave him a stinging rebuke, and he was reprimanded by the state bar association.

But Peters hung on, partly by not making enemies, never tackling anything controversial. He had married a rich woman, and some thought this instant wealth had sapped his ambition. He did not go after white-collar criminals and instead stuck faithfully to cases involving murderers, drug dealers, and so on. But as the memory of his misadventures in the 1970s faded, Peters's political base appeared more and more secure.

In one increasingly important segment of Jackson—the black community—Peters remained heartily disliked. As Hinds County turned majority black, this hole in his political base loomed ever larger. Blacks' dislike of Peters had festered for a long time. In

1978 the district attorney had gone after one of the young stars of the newest generation of black politicians, Bennie Thompson, the mayor of Bolton, a small town outside of Jackson. (Thompson is now a U.S. congressman.) Thompson's election had badly shaken up the local white establishment, and Peters convened a grand jury to look into the town's financial affairs. No improprieties were found, and the episode irreparably damaged Peters's standing among blacks.

For years, Charles Tisdale, the publisher of the black-oriented Jackson *Advocate*, had made Peters a target, printing wild, unsubstantiated stories about the district attorney's alleged drug abuse. Peters professed mystification at Tisdale's animus and even arranged a meeting with the publisher in 1986 at the Sun N' Sand motel in downtown Jackson. Under oath, Peters elaborately denied the drug allegations. Then, a local television station broadcast a thirty-minute special in which unidentified sources with darkened faces and distorted voices claimed that Peters had smoked marijuana and had accepted payoffs from drug dealers. None of this increased his standing among blacks.

In 1987, while prosecuting a capital murder case against a black man named Leo Edwards, Peters revealed that his long-standing practice in death penalty cases had been to exclude blacks from the jury. The reasons seemed obvious to him, and he made no secret of them: blacks were less "law-enforcement oriented" and less likely to vote for the death penalty. This seemed to him less a question of racism than of practical lawyering. Blacks have "been discriminated against," the district attorney explained, "they've been subjected to much crueler treatment at the hands of law enforcement," and so are "more likely to be against the system."

But this reasoning did not calm the storm that now blew up around him. Blacks in Jackson were furious. In fact, Peters was no more racist than any other white politician of his generation: one young black lawyer who worked for him in the early 1980s remembers the district attorney as being at least more outwardly correct than the other prosecutors in the office. But from the Edwards case on, Peters was routinely branded a racist.

Of course, DeLaughter's work was directly affected by whether or not Peters wanted any blacks on his death penalty cases. The young man was given exactly what he had been looking for: the murder detail, to be divided up with another assistant district attorney.

In the spring of 1987, as DeLaughter was taking up his new duties, another development was taking place, just up President Street in Jackson—one that would have a more subtle impact than Peters's jury-picking habits on DeLaughter's future course. In the capitol a transition was occurring that was as significant as any other in the previous twenty years—a rare break with the past, important not just symbolically but practically. Outside of Mississippi, few noticed the change, but some inside the state recognized it as a revolutionary development. The fall of the old order, in the person of DeLaughter's great uncle, Buddie Newman, had occurred within the confines of the prosecutor's own family.

CHAPTER EIGHT

DOWNFALL OF THE OLD ORDER AND REAWAKENING OF MEMORY

On one bright cold morning in January 1988 an unaccustomed bustle filled the marbled halls of the new capitol. A new governor, the youngest in the nation, had just been inaugurated in an eruption of optimistic plans for the future. There was a new legislature, and most important, a new kingpin for that legislature. For the first time in over a decade, the squat figure of Buddie Newman would not be shifting restlessly from side to side behind the speaker's podium of the Mississippi House of Representatives. Understandably, some in the remaining old guard were wandering around the building in a daze. Also looking startled that day were a group of visiting scholars from the Soviet Union who were touring the inner workings of this minor temple of American democracy in the pre-Yeltsin era. Glancing in the Soviets' direction as they walked down the hall, a leather-necked old legislator observed sourly, to no one in particular, "Hell, Buddie Newman ain't been gone a week, and they're already letting the Russians in."

The pain in the legislator's voice was real. Newman had been the last bulwark, and he had been a formidable one. Governors had come and gone, but Newman had kept rising to a position of immense power in the state. By the late 1970s, it had become axiomatic to describe Newman as the real boss of Mississippi. "It is emancipation day for Mississippi," a black legislator had crowed on January 9, 1987, the day Newman was brought down for good. "We are free at last."[1] Newman, the state's ultimate straw boss, represented that not-so-distant time when Mississippi was peopled by thousands like himself, little straw bosses dispensing the law in their little fiefdoms. The last important link to the Mississippi of Ross Barnett, Newman had served Barnett well and faithfully. Newman was the only surviving soldier of the old order to occupy a position of real power, and his political passing was epochal.

The young progressives who finally brought him down knew this and said glibly that he was a man who had outlived his time. Sitting in the house chamber in January 1988, they were radiant with the new order of things. To them, Newman was an authoritarian mastodon. Outside the legislature, the liberals in Jackson joked about Newman's bizarre friendship with Ferdinand Marcos. (In the Philippines, where Newman had fought during World War II and where he returned for visits, he was referred to publicly in the Marcos years as "the Speaker of the House in America.") But the joke was on all of them: Newman's power was such that he had managed to bring *his* time forward, well into the present.

For years, he had shaped Mississippi's course in the most mundane, invisible way imaginable. Under the rules solidified by his mentor, Walter Sillers, Newman had had absolute control over committee assignments in the legislature, doling them out to men he could trust absolutely. These men were in tune with Newman's view of the world: go slow; don't spend money; never raise taxes. "The number one responsibility of the governor, the lieutenant governor and every member of the legislature is to protect the fiscal integrity of the state," he said in 1982.[2] Mississippi was fine. Blacks could vote, so they had to be listened to, but politicians needed to be careful not to give them too much. That formula fit well with the natural inertia of Mississippi government.

Newman's lengthy political survival was testimony in part to his shrewdness. He had adapted himself with at least cosmetic nimbleness to the changes sweeping over the state. In one newspaper account from the late 1980s, he remained a segregationist until the end. But that he was able to make this confession to a group of black legislators was, in its own way, revealing: he was not trapped by ideological racism, as were other old segs.[3]

He lives in a plain brick ranch house hard by Highway 61 at the base of the Delta, a reminder that his roots are a good bit less elevated than those of the people he faithfully served during his long career. His father was a section foreman on the Illinois Central Railroad, and he was born in the foreman's house, on the tracks that now run through his backyard. Newman has preserved the simple little frame house, a reminder of how far he traveled. In tiny, rural Issaquena County, the elder Newman's job was a solid one, and he managed to get himself elected to the state legislature. Then young Buddie got a legislative page's job during the Great Depression. After the war, the son inherited his father's seat in the legislature, "the rawest, greenest redneck of those in the Senate," Bill Minor said years later.[4]

Real life for Buddie Newman began when he found his first master. He became a worshipful protégé of Speaker of the House Walter Sillers, an unquestioning supporter of all that the aristocratic Sillers stood for. There are suggestions of the Delta's rigid class divisions in the precise way Newman delineates his subordination to Sillers: it was at the older man's "knee," as Newman says, that he learned his trade as a legislator. Newman gratefully accepted the largesse that Sillers pitched his way. He unresentfully labored in obscurity during these years as he supported the majority position; occasionally made his own initiatives; and above all, took care to anchor his spot within the currents of received opinion. After the *Brown v. Board of Education* decision in 1954, Newman made sure the *Clarion-Ledger* knew about a "plan" he had submitted to the governor to circumvent integration. "We must not bow to the wishes of the Communist people of the Kremlin and Asia," Newman wrote in his plan, in which he recommended the closing of public schools "as a last resort."[5]

These exertions eventually earned him a place in Barnett's inner circle. In those palmy days, he only needed to "snap a finger," as Minor remembered later, and a highway patrol car or airplane would be his. He was one of four people sent by Barnett to Ole Miss the night of the riot over James Meredith's admission. Later, he flew back to Jackson and the Governor's Mansion, where he out-did the other hangers-on in urging the waffling governor to further defiance. (Newman himself had never attended any university.)[6]

Newman had always had a keen nose for shifting centers of power, so the black revolution did not catch him completely unpre-pared. In the spring of 1968, when Robert Clark was about to take his seat in the house of representatives, some of the legislators were in an incendiary mood and were weighing the attractions of causing a scene. Newman, then the powerful chairman of the Ways and Means Committee, took a few of them to the Patio Club, a dive near the capitol where he liked to hold court. He persuaded the legislators to be calm when the black man came into the chamber. Clark became a firm Newman ally, especially after Newman favored him with choice committee assignments. Newman played the same shrewd game in 1976 when he put together a peculiar coalition of old rednecks and younger, more reform-minded legislators to ma-neuver his way into the speaker's position.

Speakers of the Mississippi House generally stayed in office so long that they either retired or died at an old age. There was noth-ing to suggest the same would not be true of Buddie Newman. He never took controversial stands in public—rarely did anything in public—so the populace would not have had occasion to become angry with him. His own constituency was so tiny that he could easily keep everyone happy. The legislature was quiescent. The gov-ernor, Cliff Finch, was weak and preoccuppied with scandal. But by the end of the 1970s subtle changes were percolating up through the political order. This time, Newman was not quick enough to seize on the changes.

His supreme offering, throughout his career, had been to maintain the status quo. For as long as that had been synonymous with keeping the existing racial order, white Mississippians had been happy. But as the racial era was ending, Newman had nothing else to offer even as he maneuvered to gain the allegiance of black legislators. Into the vacuum of public preoccupations in Mississippi rushed one that would not have been out of place in a normal

American state: the condition of the schools. Some embarrassing statistics began to be iterated frequently, penetrating the indifference of a populace that had grown numb to such measures: when Mississippi boys tried to join the army, 35 percent were rejected for educational deficiencies; teacher pay was the lowest in the country; per-pupil spending was half the national average.

The man pounding these figures into the heads of his fellow citizens was the new governor, William Winter. He had spent a lifetime in Mississippi politics as one of the quiet moderates, silently disgusted by what he saw around him, but never raising his voice too loud. The tall and bony Winter, an amateur historian, took up the cause of the state's pitiful schools immediately on his accession in 1980. He made quietly urgent speeches on the rubber chicken-dinner circuit all over the state. By 1982 the legislature had beaten him back two years in a row: there just was not enough money, it was said, to pay for baubles such as public kindergartens. No money, said Newman in 1981—"that's just the way it is."[7] He knew what some of his white constituents were saying: kindergartens would be just a babysitting service for black kids.

But fatally, Newman did not see that Winter's campaign was having some effect. The great inert mass of the Mississippi public was getting itself worked up, as public opinion polls were proving. By the early 1980s, 91 percent of the people supported a mandatory-school-attendance law (one had been abolished during the height of the anti-*Brown* frenzy), 61 percent wanted state-supported kindergartens, and 70 percent wanted an increase in state and local spending for public education. That 80 percent of those under thirty supported school integration was not incidental; the schools could not survive unless they were integrated. And if nothing else, Mississippians were keenly interested in the survival of their schools.[8]

February 10, 1982, was Newman's Waterloo. For someone who had until then demonstrated such a sure political touch, Newman suffered a curiously self-inflicted defeat. The governor's kindergarten bill had been introduced for the third year in a row; a majority of the legislators knew the rising public emotion behind the issue, and they wanted the bill to pass. Newman did not. He was too shrewd to let on whether or not he considered kindergartens to be babysitting for blacks. But his right hand—the man who had his ear during the debate on education—was Bud Thigpen. Thigpen had maintained impeccable segregationist credentials: for years he was a member of the state executive committee of the Citizens' Council.[9]

Newman had other reasons for fighting Winter. For years, the speaker had occupied a vaguely defined position on the payroll of the Southern Natural Gas Company. It was not clear exactly what his duties were, but it was clear that the gas company considered him a "friend," as the president of the company obliquely put it in 1978.[10] Newman had pleaded the company's case in front of the state tax commission and had shepherded friendly legislation. Now, he was going to bat for Southern Natural once again: Winter wanted to pay for his kindergartens with an increase in the severance tax on natural gas.

It was the last day before the deadline, and late-winter dusk was gathering around the capitol. The kindergarten supporters—a tenuous coalition of blacks, liberal whites, and the old guard—were increasingly anxious. Two stood up and asked that the kindergarten bill be considered. Newman ignored them. Suddenly, the speaker called for a motion to adjourn. A chorus of dismayed no's broke out. A dozen-odd legislators stood up and called for a vote on whether to adjourn, as is required by the rules. But Newman ignored them all. He banged his gavel and strode off the podium. There was a surge of outrage on the floor, but kindergartens were dead.

Or so it seemed. Actually, Newman had banged the gavel down on old-style, personal rule, on Barnettism. With one stroke, he had clumsily created a symbol of his own resistance around which the reformists could rally. Winter went back on the stump in the summer of 1982; the education lobbyists gathered in Jackson; and, most importantly, ABC's "20/20" program did a devastating portrait of Newman as a dumb redneck politician who did not want children to have kindergartens. The old speaker even felt obliged to go out on the road to defend himself. But it was Winter's hour, and he seized it. To heighten the feeling of urgency, the governor demanded a special session of the legislature just before Christmas 1982; it was the most intense political moment Jackson had known in years. The teachers' lobbies, the oil and gas lobbies, the fundamentalists, and the private schools all demonstrated in the chill December air on the capitol grounds as the legislature tugged back and forth on Winter's proposals. This time, the governor won.

He immediately became something of a national guru on education reform. Walter Mondale said, "This guy is class," and hinted that Winter was on his vice-presidential short list. But for Newman, those December days were the beginning of a long downward spiral.

Inside the house chamber, dissent came into the open. A new crop of malcontents had been elected in 1983, adding to the few who had come in four years before. They were teachers and lawyers, and in less rural locales some of them would have been called yuppies, in the language of the time. People like Eric Clark, a bespectacled high school history teacher, and Mike Mills, a lawyer-activist who founded his own good-government group, had been teenage bystanders during the 1960s. Next to Newman, they looked and sounded as though they had come from a different country. When the 1984 session opened, they were spoiling for a fight. Immediately, they proposed the unthinkable: take away some of Newman's powers. It was risky, and when they were beaten after a short three hours of debate, Newman took away all their good committee assignments.

But they were not to be suppressed easily. All that year and the next, a band of twenty-six legislators, sometimes joined by the eighteen-member black coalition, gave Newman a hard time. There was open talk that he would not seek reelection, that his health would prevent him from doing so, that he was an impossible obstacle to progress. To prove to a nagging reporter that he was healthy, the sixty-three-year-old Newman teasingly jumped in the air and clicked his heels together.[11] Early in 1986 the *Clarion-Ledger* suggested in an opinion column, next to a photo of the speaker in a pensive mood, that Newman was in all likelihood one of the most unpopular men in Mississippi.

Later that year, the dissidents met at a legislator's Jackson home to plot Newman's downfall, in a "secret" meeting that was promptly reported in the newspaper. "I'm not vindictive at all. I'm a very sweet person," Newman smilingly told a reporter who asked him about it, and he promised no reprisals.[12] By the beginning of the next session, the dissidents were ready to strike. On January 9, spectators packed the house galleries. There would be a vote on whether Newman—and all of his successors—should be stripped of the traditional powers of the speaker. When the vote was taken, 75 legislators out of 122 had lined up against the old speaker. Eleven months later, Newman was clearing out his office in the state capitol.

On January 11, 1988, Ray Mabus was inaugurated governor. Newman was not at the inauguration; this was the first he had missed in forty years. He was hiding out in his rural lair, deep in the cotton fields of Issaquena County, so isolated and remote that you can look over miles and miles of flat land and not see a single building or other person. On that day, Newman was feeling the magnitude of what had happened. He peered disbelievingly at the television screen as the smooth young governor took the oath. He flipped the channel changer in the air and whistled softly to himself. "It's just absolutely shocking," he said quietly several times. What exactly was shocking? But Newman did not want to say. He pretended not to hear the question. Finally, he answered. "That this man was elected governor of Mississippi."[13]

It was possible that day, sitting in the low-ceilinged study of Newman's modest ranch house, to witness the full brooding retreat of the old order. Jumping up from behind a big desk that dwarfed his small frame, a pacing Newman seemed to feel the past slipping away. Sixty miles away in Jackson, optimistic crowds were streaming into the Governor's Mansion to greet Mabus. All during that time, from late morning until well into the afternoon, Newman described a political world that had been disappearing even as he had stood behind the speaker's podium. Almost a year after he had been brought down, Newman was still bewildered and hurt.

Newman's vanished world of Mississippi politics, and his slow rise in it, sounded like chapters from those old, abandoned history textbooks. Newman's progression was a featureless, patient chronology of endless committee assignments, small steps up a narrow ladder; he was a Mississippi apparatchik. The conflict of that supremely turbulent epoch in the state had been sucked away, just as in the old history books. "I started serving in the house in '52. My first leadership role was chairman of the County Affairs Committee. I served as chairman of County Affairs for eight years . . . " On and on Newman went, describing each little rise.[14]

Initiative and creativity, contention, and challenge to the leadership were not part of this story. "I was in the right places at the right time. I worked hard . . . Well then, I took my seat on the floor of the house, worked within the system, and I did right. I cooperated with the leadership. And the committee assignments started coming open." All that Newman had had to do was go along; and he had done so, unhesitatingly. His rise was predicated on a stolid unanimity possible only when there was just one real issue of concern: racial domination.

And yet that great motivating force, the issue that dominated all others for so many years of his service, was strangely absent from this narrative, just as it was from the textbooks. His were the small triumphs of the functionary, a fact he seemed gnawingly conscious of. He talked anxiously about destroying what he called "sectionalism"—the historic squabbling between the various regions of the state, principally the Delta against the others. He considered this his great contribution to Mississippi history, though in reality it was as much the result of the Delta's decline in economic importance as anything else. His pride is in having "never failed to rule on a point of order," in being "the only speaker that's ever made committee assignments the first week of the session."

The attempt to hold the line on racial domination is shunted aside in these recollections. "I'm the best friend blacks ever had in Mississippi, and this black woman back here will probably tell you that if you ask her," said one of segregation's leading foot soldiers, looking back to where his maid was preparing lunch. "I've already answered that question," he said testily when asked, for the first time, about whether the segregationists had been right. "The man's dead. I'm not going to be critical of Ross Barnett."

Or of any other politician: "I have never made a public statement of anybody, derogatory or critical, of anybody holding public office." That assertion, defiantly repeated, is partly a defensive turning the other cheek to his critics. But it is also the age-old vision of

Mississippi government as a club, a place where the men who run things never publicly criticize one another. He bursts with antagonism toward the young new governor, then quickly checks himself: "I don't want to be critical." He works himself up over a pay raise the legislature has handed itself in his absence, then stops himself: "I'm not going to say that. Let me take that off the record. I'm not going to be critical of the boys. They don't know any better." His wife, Betty, chuckles from the back of the room. Those same "boys" had let him down by voting for the change in the rules, violating the sacred quid pro quo under which he gave them small positions of power in exchange for loyalty. "Terribly disappointed and hurt," he was, "astonished, too."

He was still floating in a free fall of bewilderment: at newspapers that for years had been his servants, yet had turned fiercely against him; at men he had nurtured, who themselves had sensed the shifting winds and had turned on him; at a young governor who looked and sounded so different from any he had ever known that Newman was not sure whether he was still living in Mississippi.

One thing was certain: Mabus's Mississippi was a different place from Newman's. The new governor's identity was constructed around rejection of the past. There was nothing particularly unusual in a politician beating up on his predecessors, but a single-mindedness in Mabus's rhetoric—a sweeping rejection of the old political structure—was new. By the fall of 1987, deep into his campaign for governor, Mabus's rejection of the past had become the explicit centerpiece of his campaign speeches. As Mabus rolled into one dusty, worn-out town after another, the very contrast between the sharp look of his entourage and these drab places seemed an implicit reproach to the old guard.

Mabus's upbringing of relative privilege had separated him from some of Mississippi's earthier realities. He was a small-town boy not like many others in the state, the driven only child of a well-off timber-dealer and landowner, a businessman who owned the cotton gin and hardware store in Ackerman, Mississippi.[15] By the time he was nineteen, he had taken the Trans-Siberian railroad, and traveled with his beloved father to the Middle East, Central America, and Africa.[16] And then, after graduating first in the class of 1969, at Ole Miss, he had gone away, to Harvard Law School and the high-powered Washington law firm of which Kennedy in-law Sargent Shriver was a partner. He knew how things were in the wider world, knew how to present himself in a well-tailored suit with a sharp haircut.

It was not just this background, far outside the mold of the traditional Mississippi political backslapper, which set him apart. He had a coolness and a self-absorption that would later spell trouble for him; even smiling seemed to cost him some effort. Up close, he used the same measured, earnest tones as on the stump. The earnestness had set in early. As a boy, "he enjoyed fishing, but always threw his catch back into the water," says the promotional book published to celebrate his inauguration as governor, whose copyright Mabus holds.[17] At Ole Miss, a contemporary remembered, he would wear his ROTC uniform to the dances in an era—the late 1960s—when everybody else was shedding theirs as fast as they could. Running for state auditor in 1983, the then 35-year-old Mabus turned up all buttoned-up on a blazingly hot campaign day, a fellow politico remembers. He was sweating profusely, but trying hard not to show it. He won that race and immediately took on the county supervisors, the most powerful, deeply entrenched local politicians in Mississippi. He forced this statewide corps of straw bosses to stop paving driveways and digging graves for favored constituents and their families. When he uncovered financial abuse or stealing, he would call a press conference before the cases could make their way into court. "I really believe he is basically sincere," one local district attorney said in 1986. "But I think he's convinced himself he's the only honest person in the state."[18]

Mabus was filled with this zeal when he embarked on his campaign for governor in 1987. The previous occupants of this office, less worldly and righteous than himself, had left Mississippi in a fine mess, and it was up to him to rescue the state. He had, he told one audience, been "advocating a change in the complete system of government in Mississippi, from the state level down to the county level."[19] In his rhetoric he set himself up as the torchbearer of the new. The leaders of the past had failed Mississippians, he told one audience. "They grew cautious, they grew fearful of the risks, cowed by the possibility of change and the unknown. Each time they traded a better, brighter future for a safer, sadder past."[20] He even ventured into the dangerous territory of brandishing Mississippi's abjectness in front of the rest of the country and then promising that he would end it: "This time we tell the nation: Mississippi will never be last again." Over and over, he talked of the "old politics and politicians of the past," setting them up against "the children of Mississippi" whose "day has come."[21]

It was a generational pitch, but he was talking about himself more than anybody else. He was the "child" up against the old men of the past and the present, and it was his "day." But he was also telling people, though never explicitly, that he was a "child" of the new generation, the one that had been too young to fight blacks in the streets or cuss the Yankee newscasters in the evenings. He would not be burdened by that old bitterness. Privately, he told of two marking episodes in his childhood, when the quiet father he revered took him aside for calm chats about the lawlessness that seemed to be engulfing the state. In this way, Mabus learned about the riot at Ole Miss and the murders in Neshoba County, and he heard of them as shameful episodes that ought never to be repeated.

So Newman was right: it *was* shocking that Mabus had been elected. He had managed to reproach Mississippians for their past, tiptoe up to the edge of condemning them for it, and yet still win the governorship. Unprecedentedly, he made the same speeches to white audiences and black audiences. He had been able to avoid offending 40 percent of whites in the state—his percentage of the white vote. Wonderment emanated from many onlookers, not just Newman. "I think it was clear that our jubilation . . . rose out of a wonderful change in the public spirit," Eudora Welty wrote in the promotional book published for the inauguration, which carried the self-congratulatory title *Our Time Has Come: Mississippi Embraces Its Future*. "It expressed the conviction, and the gratification it brought, that we'd placed the right man in our highest office at the right time in our history. Our cheers were a long shout of welcome."[22]

The *Clarion-Ledger*'s coverage of the inaugural ceremony was just short of fawning, a special section full of color photographs of the new governor and the woman he had married just a year before. Julie Mabus looked positively Jackielike with her long black hair and stylish coat. A few weeks later a beaming Mabus showed up on the cover of the *New York Times Magazine*. The adulatory profile inside celebrated a new day in Mississippi and quoted a local enthusiast who said that Camelot had come to the state.[23]

In his inaugural speech on January 12, Mabus had laid out a bold challenge to Mississippi's ghosts. "History is something that should be controlled and not controlling. We in our generation can make the history of Mississippi. We are affected by the stream of events in other places, in earlier eras. But in the end, the only limitations we face are those we put on ourselves."[24] These were untested propositions; Mabus proceeded as though they were fact.

All the recent governors had been burdened by the state's past. He, Mabus, would be the master of history. He was anxious not to let the violence and crudity of his predecessors stain his own clean, technocratic sheen. A month before the inauguration, he had gone on a national media tour, stopping in at the *Washington Post* and the *New York Times* offices. "This is a state on the move, changing in an innovative way," he told the local reporters on his return. "Those that we talked to could see that there is a redefinition of Mississippi's image taking place." He was preoccupied with the *image* of Mississippi, an image that history had created. But under the new regime, Mississippi's image would be contiguous with the image of Mabus: it would be clean. Around the capitol, there were already resentful mutterings about the governor's Washington dreams.

The past could make the young governor look very good in the eyes of the nation—it already had. But if he was not careful, it could also be dangerous for him. Publicly, he was bravely proclaiming himself free of history, but it became clear that he was preoccupied with that history as well.

From his first day in office, Mabus had a clearcut plan to deal with the legacy of the past. There were four goals: revise the old 1890 state constitution (see chapter 3); reorganize state and local governments; give more money to the teachers (instead of tackling Winter's too-broad goal of reforming the education system, as Mabus's Yankee aides carefully explained). Image cleansing—throwing out the 1890 constitution in favor of a new one—topped the list. Almost all of its most outrageous portions had long since been struck, so the new governor's effort to scrap it was symbolic, as he admitted. And it was symbolism directed at the outside world, whose gaze Mabus felt constantly.

The initiative failed, as did most of the others. He seemed oddly to have forgotten that the Mississippi legislature would have to be a partner in creating this face-lift. And the legislators did not like him—not solely because he was cold and arrogant, scornful almost; or because he was a Harvard graduate; or even because his young aides went back to their offices and made cracks about those dreadful bumpkins in the state house. The legislators could even forgive his fondness for glittering fund-raisers in the Manhattan apartments of Mississippi exiles, or his passing up of the Democratic party's annual Jefferson-Jackson Day dinner—the first time a governor had missed it in nine years—in favor of Democratic party consultant Robert Shrum's Hollywood celebrity wedding, where Mabus rubbed shoulders with Warren Beatty and Henry Winkler.

What rankled most was his habit of placing himself at the center of the tableau, as the heroic deliverer of the state. Through his rhetoric, he had reduced his challenge to the past to a dragon-slaying contest. "Anytime you take on some of the deeply entrenched interests that I've taken on, you're going to get that sort of criticism pretty heavily that, well, this guy just doesn't understand us. If this guy understood us, he'd just go along," Mabus told an interviewer early in 1989.[25]

It dawned on the state's politicos that, just as important to Mabus as the actual taking on of "deeply entrenched interests," were statements that he was doing so. The quality of the rhetoric itself betrayed this. In these dismissive phrases he was consigning his opponents to moral oblivion. At the very least, this was not a very politic course. In the legislature, a tightness would come over the faces of the denizens when they were asked about the governor.

In his upbringing of upper-middle-class enlightenment, Mabus had been sheltered from the confrontations of the 1960s. This had left him strangely insensitive to the legacy of the black struggle, in particular. Interlocutors found him almost impatient with that history.[26] He clumsily tried to get rid of Ed Cole, Charles Evers's old aide, who had by now become the first black chairman of the Mississippi Democratic party. It was the most racially inflammatory action by a Mississippi governor in years. Cole, soft-spoken and conciliatory but no Uncle Tom, was one of the premiere symbols of black political achievement in Mississippi, the first black to work for Senators Stennis and Eastland. He was an object of pride.

The attack on Cole gave blacks an excuse to turn slowly away from Mabus, which would cost the governor his job three years later. They had never been quite as euphoric about the Mabus ascendancy as the white Mississippi liberals. In the legislature, they now talked about a "mass exodus" from the Democratic party. There was even discussion of reviving an independent party along the lines of the Freedom Democrats. "I do look for an independent movement by the black community," Aaron Henry said. Cole stayed in his job.

Mabus wanted to carry on inside Mississippi as if the old wounds were healed. At the same time, he seemed preoccupied with the possibility that the outside world might recognize the truth. All the governor's careful image burnishing might be for naught. Memory—particularly the memory of outsiders—might suddenly reassert itself.

The film *Mississippi Burning*, released at the end of 1989, was a fictionalized account of the murders of the three civil rights workers at Philadelphia in 1964 (see chapter 3), and it could have been Mabus's worst nightmare. The film was a crude caricature of the civil rights era, cheaply exploitive in its unrestrained sensationalizing of white violence, condescending in its portrayal of blacks as passive. It was the simple, demoniacal picture of Mississippi most Americans had in 1964, reified for the screen a quarter century later.

Mabus had not courted the film. Its production had begun under the governor's predecessor, Bill Allain. The new governor had no choice. It would have been a public relations disaster in the wider world to cancel cooperation with the English director, the ex–advertising man Alan Parker. There might even be benefit in going along with the Hollywood types, an enhancement to the smart image of the Mabus set. One of his aides dated the film's producer when the crew was filming in Jackson, and Mabus himself got to know well the stars, Gene Hackman and Willem Dafoe. The latter made slighting remarks about Mississippi at a favorite downtown watering hole; no matter.

The more the filming progressed, the clearer it became that its outcome was very far from what the governor might have hoped for. In the fall of 1988, Mabus was given an advance screening. He was horrified, "just sick," he remembers, and he canceled Orion Pictures' plan to have the premiere in Mississippi.

Suddenly, *Mississippi Burning* became a national phenomenon, partly because of the shock value from the blood that flowed in every scene. But critics and the public knew that whatever its flaws, the film was a rarity: Hollywood tackling something nasty, a bitter episode from the recent American past. *Mississippi Burning* wound up on the cover of *Time* magazine, and there were newspaper articles and talk-show discussions. Television crews descended on Mississippi, asking the old question: Had Mississippi really changed?

Mabus appeared to panic. He hired the public relations firm of Ogilvy and Mather to round up a roomful of well-known journalists in Washington, D.C., flew to Washington after the film opened there, and lectured the bemused reporters on how Parker's Mississippi was not the real thing.

That was a message for the governor's favorite audience, outsiders. For the people at home he had nothing. Politically, this was a mistake. At the Sun N' Sand, the seedy motel in downtown Jackson where much of the legislature puts up, there was a near-riot when word spread of Mabus's credit line in the Parker film. In diehards' redoubts, the past, like the legislature, still burned.

To Mabus, *Mississippi Burning* had been a crisis of public relations in the outside world. Inside Mississippi, however, the film served as the catalyst for an unmistakable reawakening of memory. Mabus himself was partly responsible: his frequent references to the bad old days were forcing people to think about history again.

In Jackson, people packed the theaters as the movie opened. At one 320-seat suburban theater, all four of the first day's showings were full, and people stood for more than two hours in the cold drizzle to attend the evening screening.[27] At another theater in Jackson, people had telephoned the manager all day for a week prior to the film's opening, wanting to rent out the entire theater for the first showings.[28] In those first days, some whites emerged from the theaters muttering angrily. But for the most part, the reaction was surprisingly muted, a stunned silence. In the old days it would have been easy: Yankee propaganda smearing us again. Things were not so simple now. Too much of the truth had seeped out, yet not enough of it was in the public domain to enable Mississippians to dismiss Parker's film as so much sensationalism. So whites were forced to watch it as documentary.

In Philadelphia, the site of the 1964 killings, the owner of the local movie theater at first took the old attitude, refusing to show it. He was forced to change his mind after an outcry. True, there were protests against the film. But strangely, they came not from Mississippi's whites but largely from blacks who objected to Parker's depiction of the black people as passive victims.

The movie was leaving an uneasy aftertaste. An inchoate feeling prevailed that something else needed to be done—not just to reassure the rest of the country but to reassure Mississippi. Hiring Ogilvy and Mather and flying to Washington was not enough. With whites silent, the field of public discourse was left to blacks and their liberal allies, principally the *Clarion-Ledger*. There were even calls for a prosecutorial reopening of the Philadelphia case, which, politically, could have been a highly risky course. The attorney general, Mike Moore, a young, telegenic Mabus ally, treated the problem through indirection by making vague promises and announcing that he was rereading the transcripts of the original trial. Mabus himself repeated his bland bromides about looking to the future instead of the past. Nothing ever came of it.

But the trouble stirred up by *Mississippi Burning* would not go away. It helped stimulate a mood of collective introspection about the past that year, expressed in the media, in speeches, and in private acts.

In 1989, this mood was evident to me, all the more so because I often shuttled back and forth between Mississippi and Alabama, where I lived. Alabama had been Mississippi's partner, its indistinguishable twin as an object of national scorn in the 1960s. Now, the moods seemed wholly different. In Alabama, there was an atmosphere of deadening silence about the past. There was no discussion of the former governor George Wallace and the harm his racialism had done to the state. Alabama's current governor, an inarticulate fundamentalist preacher whose shortcomings were never so painfully apparent as when he was next to his neighbor Mabus, refused to attend the dedication of a civil rights memorial, and he refused to pull down the Confederate battle flag from the state capitol. Alabama's political class ignored the state's real problems, such as its poverty and high rate of infant mortality. Mississippi, where politicians made frequent reference to the past and even attended civil rights commemorations, seemed enlightened by comparison.

One soggy May day I invited myself along on a countryside jaunt from Jackson with two men of the Mabus generation, a lawyer and a state bureaucrat. They had been planning this trip for some time, and they were hesitant about letting an outsider come along: private matters, they communicated indirectly, were going to be dealt with. And yet my curiosity about their purpose, and their own Southern politeness, overcame any mutual misgivings.

They were unquestionably men of decent instincts, unafraid in conversation to confront the more unsavory aspects of their state's history. Their parents had been conventional segregationists; as teenagers growing up in small rural towns in the 1960s, they had not been given to question the murderous defiance going on around them. That had come to their professions much later, after college and exposure to the wider world.

And yet it is one thing to converse freely with out-of-state reporters about one's not-so-proud heritage; it is another to wallow in that heritage, even for a day. That is what they were doing this day, and it seemed strange. They were taking the day off from work to visit all the sites associated with the single murderous act that had brought more shame to their state than even the killing of Evers: the Philadelphia murders. The movie had stirred their intense interest in the case. The lawyer had composed a little scorecard of people who had been indicted; his friend seemed to have encyclopedic recall of the details from a recently written history of it, entitled *We Are Not Afraid.*[29]

Riding down the highway, we joked about the incongruity of

Susan Akin, the wholesome blonde 1986 Miss America, being the granddaughter of the Klansman conspirator Bernard Akin, who had been in on the conspiracy to kill the rights workers, and we speculated on the possibilities of a friendly visit to Alton Wayne Roberts, the Klansman who had pulled the trigger on Goodman and Schwerner, and who supposedly could be found in a seedy nightclub in downtown Meridian. The sheer outlandishness of that era demanded that it be treated as a joke. And yet only so much lightheartedness could be applied. There was personal history to deal with, and it was not so funny. The lawyer's father was a county prosecutor who had strenuously worked to put the SNCC leader Bob Moses in jail; the bureaucrat's father, a hardware store owner, had fired a black employee for registering voters. These memories sobered up the mood in the car. We were getting ready to commune with the past.

This turned out to be difficult. The sign for Akin's Mobile Home Sales was modern, the interstate highway was new, and Bernard Akin, as it turned out, was dead. So we turned up Highway 19, the fateful route that Chaney, Goodman, and Schwerner had taken twenty-five years before, and hoped for a more evocative landscape. Gently rolling pastureland gave way to pine trees; nothing sinister marked the scene. The secondary road the boys had taken was not gravel anymore, and the few houses along it were modern. It looked like any other country road in the rural South. We passed Rock Cut Road, where the three had been taken to be shot. This time, we did not turn; the road seemed nondescript. Philadelphia itself, with its boarded-up businesses and cramped, raised sidewalk, was not reminiscent of anything more than a seedy Southern town. We passed the old Benwalt Hotel, where the hordes of reporters had stayed in 1964, and then the ex–city jail on our way to the rebuilt Mt. Zion Church.

These quiet places seemed to arouse no particular emotion in my friends. Outwardly at least, they regarded them with detachment. A prominent local lawyer, something of a liberal, had been our guide once we got to town, and he had been defensive and resentful, even of us. The first thing he showed us, on reaching his office, was an anti-Klan letter his grandfather had sent to the local newspaper in 1924. He spoke, with only a hint of self-consciousness, of occasionally sitting at breakfast with Cecil Price, the thuggish deputy sheriff imprisoned for his part in the killings and now fully reintegrated into the community.

Afterward my friends criticized the local lawyer. They evidently felt no need for defensiveness; they had frankly acknowledged to themselves the terribleness of what happened. At the same time, though, they seemed surprised by their own detachment and remarked on it when we had returned to Jackson.

I wondered about it myself. Their parents had bitterly cursed the civil rights workers and muttered that they had brought trouble on themselves. For these younger men, the episode could not, of course, have had the same impact. It had been most definitely consigned to history; their detachment made this plain. Still, it carried enough personal significance to impel them to drive out into the country on a weekday.

And yet the line between defensiveness and guilt is not rigid in Mississippi. Philadelphia, a town of five thousand people, was the locus for these feelings. There was growing dread among white Mississippians as the twenty-fifth anniversary of the murders approached in June of 1989. An unusual coalition of whites, blacks, and local Choctaw Indians decided that Philadelphia's sullen resentment, the usual face it presented to the snooping outsider, would not work this year. That these groups would get together at all was in itself a "pretty amazing occurrence," as Mississippi's secretary of state, Dick Molpus, the scion of Philadelphia's richest family, put it.[30]

Also a graduate of the Winter administration, the genial and down-to-earth Molpus was the guiding spirit behind what followed, which was even more remarkable: an officially sanctioned commemoration of a civil rights murder. To be sure, there was plenty of grumbling around Philadelphia's courthouse square about how the town was once again being unfairly picked on. Philadelphia's leaders were uneasy with the ceremony, too. But this year at least, there was no more fleeing from what had happened.

In sweltering June heat, hundreds of people gathered in a dusty lot at the Mt. Zion Church to dedicate a marker to the three boys. Ex-governor Winter, the men of the local chamber of commerce, and the mayor rubbed shoulders with Goodman's mother and Schwerner's widow. Mabus was there, looking buttoned-down and uncomfortable in a dark suit. But his remarks, prepared hastily that morning, were jumbled. The large crowd fidgeted. Then the native son, Molpus, got up. He had spent three weeks working on this short speech. His words were simple, contrition filled, and emotional.

"We deeply regret what happened here twenty-five years ago. We wish we could undo it," he said, with the relatives of the victims standing stoically by. The crowd became quiet and still.

"We are profoundly sorry that they are gone. We wish we could bring them back," Molpus continued. "My heart is full because I know that for a long time many of us have been searching for a way to ease the burden that this community carried for twenty-five years. But we have never known quite what to do or say. But today we know one way. Today we pay tribute to those who died. We acknowledge that dark corner of our past."[31]

It was a remarkable moment. Words like those had never before been uttered by a Mississippi politician. The press commentators were quick to realize that some sort of breakthrough had been achieved that afternoon. More significantly, no public attacks on Molpus occurred, no cries of outrage erupted. If anything, the stocky young man appeared to have strengthened his position as a leading candidate for the governor's office.

One month later, a Mississippi federal judge who was a conservative Republican and a Reagan appointee, wrote an opinion that repudiated an entire era in the state's political history, just as Molpus's speech had. In tough language, Judge William Barbour freed the Sovereignty Commission papers from their legislative seal. Barbour was of the small-town Delta gentry, from a prominent legal family, certainly part of the establishment. He had been away to school, to the Lawrenceville prep school and to Princeton and New York University. He had seen the wider world outside Yazoo City, and he had not returned to the state until 1967. He was too young to have been part of the old-guard political establishment.

Barbour had inherited the case from Judge Harold Cox, a segregationist who referred in court to blacks as "chimpanzees" and who had done his best to squelch the release of the papers. In this he was simply following the lead of the legislature. Everybody knew that at the very best, the papers did not paint a pretty picture of Mississippi. At the worst, there were fantastic stories linking the commission to everything from the assassination of Medgar Evers to the assassination of John Kennedy.

The legislature had not tried to thwart Bill Waller when he had killed the Sovereignty Commission in 1973. But its written record was another matter. Early in 1977 a fierce debate had arisen in the state house over what to do with the commission's files; many white legislators had voted to burn them. They had argued that opening them would be needlessly digging up the past. The state representative from Natchez, Walter Brown, had said the files should be burned, to "forever erase them from Mississippi." The handful of blacks in the house had opposed the move. "By your vote to burn those files you are, in my opinion, condemning those people you have worked along with," a black representative from Jackson had pointedly told his white colleagues. His arguments had been to no avail. The vote to destroy them had been overwhelming.[32]

But plenty of people such as Ed King, Medgar Evers's old ally (see chapter 2) knew that they had been spied on and covertly harassed, and they were not about to forget. For them, the ACLU had quickly filed an injunction against the destruction, and a lawsuit demanding possible damages from the state of Mississippi. Still, the legislature had had no intention of releasing the files. In March 1977 it passed a law sealing them for fifty years; even to talk about what was in the files became a crime. Six large filing cabinets full of Mississippi's dirty secrets had been shipped into a vault of the state archives building. Only three people from the archives department were allowed into the vault, and always two people at a time.[33] Two years after the legislature had buried the records, Cox, Senator Eastland's old ally, had thrown out the ACLU case. Reinstated by an appeals court, the case of the Sovereignty Commission papers had languished for a decade, slowed by hostile state attorneys general.

The legend of the papers had grown, fueled by the few plaintiffs who had seen them. There was more and more talk about who would be fingered as a stool pigeon—who among the blacks, who among the white civil rights community. Some of the plaintiffs— King and John Salter, a leader in the 1963 demonstrations in Jackson (see chapter 2)—had decided that the personal secrets dug up by the commission's gnomes were best left that way. Like others whose skulls had been bashed in the cause of civil rights, these two had had some difficulty reentering normal life. They had remained obsessed with the past, and protective of it. So they had back-tracked, split from the ACLU and aligned themselves with the state, and fought full disclosure of the records.

So when the case came to him in 1989, Barbour had several choices. He could side with the state and King and Salter, and not release the records. Or he could open them completely, which is what he did. "To leave the files closed would perpetuate the attempt of the state to escape accountability," he wrote. But the judge went much further. His words paralleled Molpus's and carried the same message of shame, though less emotionally:

> The state of Mississippi acted directly through its State Sov-ereignty Commission and through conspiracy with private individuals to deprive the plaintiffs of rights protected by the Constitution to free speech and association, to personal pri-vacy, and to lawful search and seizure, and statutes of the United States. . . . The final act of this tragedy was to cloak state actions in secrecy until those who had been harmed by these acts had died.

No member of the white Mississippi establishment had ever called the state's recent past a "tragedy." And yet no one publicly attempted to rebut these words, and no one—the civil rights veter-ans excepted—argued in public against releasing the files. To be sure, no one besides the *Clarion-Ledger* was publicly clamoring to see them either. In fact, the reaction to the ruling was muted. "Much to-do about nothing," Waller said dismissively. In the leg-islature, an attempt to hasten the opening up of the files—a bill to repeal the 1977 law sealing them—was made. But it aroused little interest, and a black committee chairman killed it. Blacks seemed even more unwilling to "open that can of worms" than whites, the legislator who introduced the bill recalled.[34]

Most of the records remained under lock and key, their release stymied by the appeal of the civil rights veterans, who remained worried about personal dirty laundry. But many trickled out—

some from ex-governor Paul Johnson's papers in Hattiesburg, some delivered right to the *Clarion-Ledger* by sympathetic sources. The newspaper, now owned by Gannett, was shaken out of its habitual torpor by this ready-made scandal from the past, complete with documents. Already that year, the paper had published stories based on leaked documents—the harassment of Tougaloo College, the infiltration of a COFO office in 1964. Now, week after week, the revelations piled up on the front page of the paper: Percy Greene, the editor of the black-oriented Jackson *Advocate* (see chapter 5), had been paid by the commission; it had spied on Mickey Schwerner and on the Freedom Democratic party.

Individually, each detail was not shocking. Unconsciously or otherwise, people who had lived through that era had approvingly absorbed the state's policies. Much of the commission's work, after all, had not been terribly secret: its small staff had met and corresponded continuously with all sorts of Mississippians—sheriffs, legislators, bankers. From Erle Johnston, the last living director of the commission, came pronouncements to the press about how benign his agency had been, how he had been engaged in "trying to help resolve local confrontations and bring about solutions." Never one of the ideological segregationists, he was an amiable old man living out his years in his rural hometown. "All this publicity is strengthening interest in my book," he said blandly.[35]

And yet in 1989, the cumulative effect of these documents was startling. To pore through the boxes of files in Hattiesburg, in particular, was to enter into a strange culture of paranoia difficult to reconcile with the placid contemporary surface of the state. "Having grown up in Mississippi during the '50s and '60s, I always thought of myself as an American," wrote the *Clarion-Ledger* columnist Danny McKenzie. "After reading the Sovereignty Commission documents, though, I felt like I'd grown up in Russia. It's a sickening feeling." In effect, the Sovereignty Commission papers had brought back another world, one that seemed distant.

The documents were irrefutable, documentary proof, far more credible than Parker's film. And the *Clarion-Ledger*, having been delivered a large trove of documents, kept that world on the front pages throughout the fall of 1989. It plunged into the past with a good deal more enthusiasm than it dug into the present.

CHAPTER NINE

THE PAST
DISINTERRED

District Attorney Ed Peters had never given much weight to the possibility of a new case against Byron de la Beckwith. In 1987, he was asked about it by a reporter, but he scornfully dismissed the idea. "There's no way under any stretch of the law that case could be tried again," Peters said. "Anyone having taken the first class in law school ought to know that." Any judge would be certain to block a new case, Peters continued. The reason seemed to him obvious: the then-eighteen-year interval since the dismissal of the indictment would amount to a violation of Beckwith's right to a speedy trial.[1]

That was the end of it, and DeLaughter remembers no discussion of Beckwith in the office. Even in the summer of 1989, with all the talk of reviving the Philadelphia murders case, the Evers affair was not mentioned. Busy with some of the higher-profile cases, DeLaughter was becoming known as someone with ambitions of his own. When his boss had announced in June 1988 that he would not run for reelection, DeLaughter was the first one called for comment. He would not say whether he wanted Peters's job.

On Sunday, October 1, 1989, the *Clarion-Ledger* put another revelation from the Sovereignty Commission files—this one, the most pungent yet—across the top of the front page. The commission, it turned out, had been recruited by Beckwith's lawyers to look into the potential jurors' backgrounds before the start of the second trial in 1964. The investigator's notes said one man was "believed to be Jewish." That man had not made the cut. Two more, the commission investigator had let Beckwith's lawyer know, were probably "fair and impartial." They had made it. Investigator Andy Hopkins, in fact, had written a detailed report on the prospective jurors, with information about occupations and membership in groups like the Citizens' Council. Most of it had been gathered from informal telephone calls to employers.[2]

This was a smoking gun. It was like Ross Barnett's visit to the courtroom, only worse: direct evidence that the white supremacist state had condoned, in a sly way, political murder. It had wanted to do whatever it could to help the man who was all but boasting of his feat. The *Clarion-Ledger* knew it had a good story, better than any of the other Sovereignty Commission revelations. Jerry Mitchell, the reporter who broke it and much of the other Sovereignty Commission relations, had invited the speculations of an Ole Miss law school professor on the import of the commission file. The verdict: possible jury tampering.

By Monday, Mitchell was on the phone with Myrlie Evers, now a member of the Los Angeles Board of Public Works. Interviewed often over the years, she offered pronouncements that had a ritualistic quality. In person, she was stiff and dignified, never letting her guard down. Almost inevitably, in the news stories she sounded less like a widow and more like a semiofficial keeper of the sacred flame. What should be done with this new evidence, the *Clarion-Ledger* wanted to know? Why, the case should be reopened, of course. Across the front page the next day, the headline proclaimed her desire: "Evers' Widow Says Files Justify Reopening Assassination Case."[3]

DeLaughter was noticing these stories. In the office that week, there was casual discussion of the newspaper's burgeoning campaign. A thought was forming in his mind. "Did you see the headlines in the paper this morning?" he asked Peters. "Do you think we ought to do something?"

The response was equally offhand. "Yeah, yeah. We probably would." More thinking. "Well, [so and so] is tied up on this and that."

DeLaughter's manner was hardly overeager. "Well, I'll do it if you need me to." Without pushing it, he had volunteered.

"Yeah, go ahead," said Peters.

Recollecting it eighteen months after the fact, DeLaughter was careful not to seem overly ambitious. "It was not like I was ordered to do it, yet it wasn't like I solicited it. We work as a team up here." At the same time, by portraying the decision as wholly casual, he was suggesting that political calculation had not gone into it.

What swayed the district attorney? DeLaughter's ambition played a part. But Peters had his own political accounts to settle. "The district attorney here has been fighting the black community for fifteen years," said Al Binder, who remained close to DeLaughter. "I think he said, 'This'll kick the fight I've had the last fifteen years in the ass, and show them I'm not against blacks.'"[4]

But if Peters had been thinking about reviving the case from the moment the headlines appeared in the *Clarion-Ledger*, as DeLaughter suggests, he gave no hint of that to the black politicians who now vigorously jumped on the issue. In Jackson, with its tiny white majority, there is constant jockeying for racial political advantage. Whites can only survive citywide by appealing to blacks, but not so much as to alienate a critical sliver of the white community. Black politicians, on the other hand, are always on the lookout for issues that will unite their constituency. The Medgar Evers case seemed to be ideal. A week after the first revelations, a county commissioner for Hinds County, Bennie Thompson—the same man Peters had unsuccessfully pursued a decade before (see chapter 7)—got up at a Hinds County Board of Supervisors meeting and introduced a resolution urging the authorities to pursue the case.

Thompson, the toughest black politician in Mississippi, is a large, unsmiling man who never shies from a bout of racial jousting with his white counterparts. Where others will make efforts to sound conciliatory toward whites, Thompson rarely does. Sixteen years old at the time of Evers' funeral, he was deeply impressed by the huge crowds. Later, at Tougaloo College, one of his teachers was an author of *Conflict and Change*. James Loewen left Thompson with an acute sense of Mississippi's tortured legacy.

In 1969, Thompson had been fired from his first job, teaching high school history, for telling his students not to trust the white-washed version of Mississippi history presented in the standard textbook by John K. Bettersworth (see chapter 1). When he was elected mayor of the small town of Bolton in 1973, the all-white police force resigned, and the city clerk refused to turn over any records. Thompson aggressively pursued federal grants and managed to rehabilitate the town's dilapidated housing and crumbling sewer systems.[5]

Thompson wanted to pay back his debt to Medgar Evers. But in October 1989, the resolution he introduced at the supervisors' meeting failed to draw support even from the other black county supervisor. But Thompson had forced the issue into the public arena, where it stayed. He met with an ally on the city council, Louis Armstrong, and they decided on a strategy of public pressure on Peters.

Late in October, Armstrong pushed through a city council resolution urging the reopening of the case, even picking up the support of one of the white council members. He sent Peters a copy of the resolution and got a frosty response questioning his motivation. Armstrong called a press conference. Within a week, Peters had announced, ever so hesitantly, that he would look into the possibility of jury tampering by the Sovereignty Commission in the second trial of Beckwith. He warned that the speedy-trial hurdle might be difficult to overcome.

For the cynics who thought Peters was simply throwing the dogs a bone, making a political gesture and nothing more, there seemed to be plenty of evidence in those first months. It was barely a month before discouraging words began emanating from the district attorney's office. Key evidence was missing, it was said: the murder weapon could not be found, in spite of a search of the FBI warehouse, and the trial transcript had somehow gotten lost. How could old witnesses be identified, much less tracked down? Mounting a case was going to be hard, if not impossible.

But this case would be difficult to drop. The black politicians in Jackson were watching Peters closely, and Armstrong demanded a meeting. The district attorney handed him over to his subordinate, DeLaughter. The prosecutor's explanations were delivered cordially, but the councilman was not convinced. Angry words were exchanged. They were afraid, politically scared, to reopen the case, Armstrong told DeLaughter. The young prosecutor took it as a personal insult, according to Armstrong. When Myrlie Evers flew to Jackson, she rated a meeting with Peters. But he was no more encouraging with her than DeLaughter had been with Armstrong.

Then, in mid-December 1989, DeLaughter had more discouraging news. What the Sovereignty Commission had done was "extremely unethical," he announced, but it was not illegal. Eleven of the twelve jurors from the second trial had been painstakingly interviewed. None had said themselves that they had been approached by the commission. Jury tampering could not thus be used as a lever to pry open the twenty-five-year-old case. Blacks, who saw this as one more excuse to be rid of the case, were skeptical of DeLaughter's assertion that he would continue to look at the case. "At no point was I convinced that the D.A.'s office was sincere," Armstrong says.

Admittedly, it did not look promising. But even by this time, a picture had formed in DeLaughter's head, a picture that made him mad every time he thought about it: the picture of the sniper lying in wait, of Medgar Evers lying in his own blood, of his children rushing out of the house on Guynes Street to watch him die. The other young prosecutors in the district attorney's office would look at DeLaughter with friendly skepticism, wondering why he was wasting his time. How would he find witnesses? Such a case was so far outside the realm of their drug-dealer and murderer experiences that they could hardly conceive of it.

But DeLaughter was puzzling out the problem methodically in his own mind, reminding himself of what he called "the basics." Suppose the evidence could be assembled again, as it once had been. What would be the excuse for not pursuing the case then? That it was too old, that it was "history"? But murder was murder; there was no statute of limitations on it. So even without having the evidence immediately in hand, to use "history" as an excuse to not look further clearly would not pass muster, legally or morally.

And then there was Medgar Evers. To DeLaughter, he was an easy person to admire. The prosecutor had come of age in a time when civil rights was identified with black militancy and nationalism, fearful entities. Evers represented something DeLaughter had never known, a nonviolent idealism that had the purity of myth. And as he himself became a target not just of skepticism in the office but of some hostility outside it, he had begun to empathize with Evers. "I imagine life was a daily hell for him, just from an emotional standpoint," the prosecutor said, a few months after Beckwith's indictment. "I would think it would be tough to get up every morning knowing there are a lot of folks that hate you. It's human to like to be liked."[6]

As for Beckwith himself, he was sitting up there on his mountain in Tennessee, cockily telling people, as he had the *Clarion-Ledger* early in November 1989, that he did not see much use in another trial. That made DeLaughter mad. And sometimes, not often, he would allow himself broader speculations about the meaning of Evers's death, the "heck of a gash" that "assassinating someone for what they believe in" caused to the social fabric. But he did not need such thoughts to keep himself going.

DeLaughter would ride a juggernaut in this case, swinging from great lows to great highs as the pieces of the puzzle assembled themselves. Never had he experienced anything like this. Slowly, slowly, the case came together, welded by a combination of doggedness and luck. The trust of Myrlie Evers would prove to be a great boon. They talked regularly on the telephone, and eventually she mailed him a vital element, a transcript of the first trial, unaccountably missing from the Hinds County court system. For almost thirty years she had kept it stored away in a trunk. A whole world was now opened up—witnesses, testimony, events, and recollections.

Armed with names, DeLaughter's investigator went all over the country tracking down the old witnesses Waller had used in 1964. He came up with many of the most important ones: Ines McIntyre, who had traded Beckwith the gun; John Chamblee and O. M. Luke, the Jackson police detectives; Ralph Hargrove, the police fingerprint expert; and one of the two cab drivers (see chapter 4). All agreed to testify, with varying degrees of cranky unwillingness. Then DeLaughter remembered something his ex-father-in-law, the now-deceased judge, had shown him in the early days of his now-faltering marriage to the judge's daughter Dixie—a gun from one of the old civil rights cases, which he had kept in a closet as a souvenir of that era. DeLaughter called his mother-in-law. Was it the gun from the Beckwith case? She did not know. He went for a look himself. The serial numbers matched. "I almost fell over," DeLaughter later told an interviewer.[7]

Old evidence would not be enough. DeLaughter needed new facts to justify putting Beckwith back in court. In the spring of 1990, DeLaughter came across an obscure book put out by a far-right publishing house about one Delmar Dennis, a Mississippi Ku Kluxer who had turned FBI informant. In the book, *Klandestine*, Dennis said he heard Beckwith confess to killing Evers at a Klan rally sometime in the mid-1960s. "Killing that nigger gave me no more inner discomfort than our wives endure when they give birth to our children," Beckwith is supposed to have said. Beckwith's past, it became apparent to the prosecutors, was littered with these little confessions: there were two women, Peggy Morgan and Mary Ann Adams, to whom Beckwith bragged about the killing in 1966, and also a man named Dickie Davis, who heard part of the story from Beckwith in 1969 in Florida.[8]

In March 1990, the *Clarion-Ledger* dug up Hollis Creswell and James Holley, the two ex–Greenwood policemen who had provided Beckwith with his critical alibi in 1964 (see chapter 4). They told the *Clarion-Ledger's* reporter that they were sticking to their story and would testify for Beckwith again. "If I see you or the blackest nigger in the country shortly after a murder happens, I'll testify to what I saw," Creswell said.[9] The case began to get attention outside the state. A team from ABC's "Prime Time Live" arrived in Jackson and came up with four witnesses who said they had seen Beckwith in Jackson on the night of the murder. They said they had seen him at the church rally attended by Evers that night. They had not spoken up before because they had felt certain that Jim Crow justice would have discounted their testimony.

DeLaughter was becoming the focus of public attention. People buttonholed him in stores and restaurants, some with praise,

many with angry remarks. The critics were discouraging. But De-
Laughter, a native son, could not be dismissive with them. He
would explain, in his methodical, plodding way, why he felt im-
pelled to go through with it. "I wouldn't prosecute this case, or any
case, if I felt we don't have enough evidence—not just to get an
indictment, but to convict," DeLaughter would begin. "No matter
what you think about a person's beliefs, you just don't go around
shooting people," he would continue. "And if the evidence is there,
aren't I doing the right thing? And if the evidence wasn't there, we
wouldn't have gotten as far as we've gotten." At that point, the
critics would sometimes back off.[10]

The evidence, old and new, was reaching a critical mass. In
the first weeks of December 1990, the Hinds County grand jury
was called back in session. Jackson was full of rumors that it was
considering the Beckwith case. Peters and DeLaughter would not
say, but as elderly, wizened witnesses trooped into the grand jury
room in the Hinds County Courthouse, the lawyers' hand was
tipped. There was Creswell, puffing fitfully on a cigarette, and
Holley, looking like he wanted to be somewhere else. Tight-lipped,
John Chamblee, the former detective (see chapters 3 and 4) and now
the state fire marshal, emerged. Late on the chilly evening of Friday,
December 15, the grand jury's work seemed to be winding down.
Myrlie Evers went into the room to testify. When she was finished,
there were few dry eyes among the ten blacks and eight whites on
the grand jury. She went upstairs, to Ed Peters's office, to wait anxiously for the verdict. "I don't have hatred," she said. "But I do have
the pain, the sorrow, the longing for Medgar."[11]

When Delaughter emerged from the grand jury room with
a faint smile on his usually impassive face, the waiting reporters knew.

For Delaughter, the case had become a test of his own state.
Seeing it through to prosecution was the only way of proving that
the transformation of Mississippi, which he and others believed in,
was real. "If Mississippi has truly changed, then we shouldn't be
afraid to try a case like this at all," he said later. "If we've got to the
stage where we prosecute cases based on the law and the evidence,
not on race and political reasons, then this case should go to trial."[12]

BECKWITH IN JACKSON

More than three years passed. The elderly Beckwith fought his extradition from Tennessee. His court-appointed lawyers, grimly conscientious, raised serious constitutional challenges. There was indecision over where to hold the trial and where to pick the jury—Jackson now was judged tainted because of all the publicity. The months dragged on. Trial dates were set, then canceled.

The powerful fact of the indictment remained. But the case itself languished, inertia settling over it. Meanwhile, just keeping it together was a nightmare for Ed Peters and Bobby DeLaughter. Old, infirm witnesses were getting older and sicker. There was talk that everybody involved hoped Beckwith would have the uncharacteristic good grace to die before a trial could occur. Plenty of whites were not growing any fonder of this prosecution, and whenever the case reemerged in the newspapers, DeLaughter would hear from them. At the beginning, when the angry letters came in to the district attorney's office, he felt obliged to answer them. But the criticism never let up, and DeLaughter could not escape it. As he walked downtown, went to lunch, or attended sporting events with his children, angry citizens—even "church people," as he said later—would buttonhole him.

He never stopped thinking he was doing the right thing. But DeLaughter was not living in a vaccuum; he wanted to be part of his community. At times the reactions were demoralizing, he acknowledged later. He would wonder: Will these people ever leave me alone? Is this ever going to pass? Am I ever going to get over it?[1]

It wasn't only the haters and the racists who were estranged from the case. People I had seen quietly celebrating in the downtown bar the night of Beckwith's indictment had grown indifferent. Even those convinced he was guilty began to have doubts about a fair trial after so many years.

For months, it seemed as though the doubters might hold sway. In the summer of 1992, Beckwith's lawyers appealed to the Mississippi Supreme Court to stop the trial from going forward (privately, they found their client "despicable," according to a Jackson attorney who knows both). Of course, their legal perspective was not informed by speculations about historical change in the state. But they asked obvious, potentially troubling questions: Why had the state not brought Beckwith to trial in the five years between 1964 and 1969, when the indictment was dismissed? And why had it then waited another twenty-one years to reindict him? Shorter delays, in other cases, had been found to violate the constitutional right of defendants to a speedy trial. Compellingly, they argued that the long stretch of years had severely damaged Beckwith's chances of mounting an effective defense. Thus, his due process rights would be violated. The lawyers pointed out that many of the key original witnesses were dead: several of the FBI agents, the man who had traded Beckwith the Goldenhawk sight for his rifle, one of Beckwith's alibi witnesses, the chief of Jackson detectives, and one of the cab drivers who claimed to have spotted Beckwith at the bus station (see chapter 4). Of course, the transcript of their 1964 testimony remained, and it had been officially certified by the judge when the case was reopened. But obviously a transcript cannot be cross-examined in court—an important point now that the defense had access to previously unavailable 1963 Jackson police reports which indicated, for instance, confusion on the part of one of the cab drivers about the physical characteristics of the man at the bus station. Evidence was missing—namely, the bullet that had killed Medgar Evers.[2] And two of Beckwith's three original lawyers had died. The only survivor, the growly octogenarian Hardy Lott, said he had long since destroyed all his files. And then there was Beckwith himself. For all the hints that his memory was selective, he was undeniably old, sick, and unable to help his lawyers as well as he might have twenty-nine years before. Certainly, it was one of the oldest murder cases ever to be prosecuted in the United States.

Time had demonstrably harmed Beckwith's defense; there was no real rebuttal to this. But Beckwith was an odious, voluble racist. (When he took the witness stand at a hearing in 1992, one of his lawyers shouted to Beckwith, in full view of spectators, to keep his mouth shut.) Whites troubled by his legal position could not defend his views. And too many blacks wanted to see him prosecuted. For the moment (and among Jackson's whites it was a moment rife with rumors—all utterly unfounded—that blacks would riot if Beckwith went free) the issue of the old man's rights would be postponed. The state supreme court ducked it altogether, as well as DeLaughter's high-minded legal brief arguing that political assassination must not go unpunished, and that the climate of "the times" (he cautiously put the phrase in quotation marks) had made a fair trial impossible in the 1960s.[3]

Just over a week before Christmas 1992, a bare majority of the Mississippi Supreme Court justices voted that the case must go forward. The ruling was narrowly technical: only after a trial and conviction could Beckwith's lawyers properly raise the constitutional issues. Clearly, this was too sensitive a case to be stopped now. The state's chief justice, Roy Noble Lee, dissented violently, calling his colleagues' decision "the worst pronouncement of the law during my tenure on the Mississippi Supreme Court Bench, and [an] egregious miscarriage of justice." Lee, seventy-seven years old and nearing retirement, had been admitted to the Mississippi Bar in 1939. He blithely ignored (like his colleagues in the majority) historical truths about the recent inequities of Mississippi justice: "My examination of the record before us does not support the statement that the prosecution did not obtain a fair trial" three decades before, he wrote.[4] Ten months later, the U.S. Supreme Court upheld the majority.

The constitutional issues raised by the indictment had not been settled, but Beckwith, now seventy-three, would stand trial. Early in December 1993, the first subpoenas went out: the trial would begin January 18, 1994. The jury was to be picked in Panola County, 140 miles north of the state capital, and testimony would be heard in the courthouse at Jackson. DeLaughter told his hard-working investigator that if the trial did not come off this time, it would never happen. Indeed, one of his key witnesses, a Jackson policeman, suffered a severe stroke that very month.

The disapproval of DeLaughter's critics was not letting up. Even after jury selection had begun, on a frigid day in the plain-featured country town of Batesville, he continued to receive hate letters and postcards, delivered to him in the courtroom. Somewhat milder sentiments along the same lines were to be heard every day from among the five hundred summoned for jury duty. "This trial is not about justice; it's about politics," said James Sullivan, a forty-one-year-old white man. "This deal happened thirty years ago," said Danny Ray Berry, another white man. "It's been tried several times. He's seventy-something years old. In my mind, it's just senseless." Just politics, said the druggist on the town square, Donald Davis—nothing but politics, and what a waste of the taxpayers' money. These feelings were not confined to whites. A number of blacks in the jury pool were equally adamant that the whole process was a waste of time. They knew little about the defendant, but he was clearly an old man—why not leave him alone?

After eight days of rigorous winnowing, the lawyers found eight blacks and four whites who said they did not feel this way: a maid, a school cook, several maintenance workers, two factory workers, a truck driver, a bus driver, a minister, and a secretary. None had completed college. And eight had been infants when Evers was shot.

Two weeks later, the night before his case went to these seven women and five men, I ran into Beckwith at a small Greek restaurant in north Jackson. He was dining *en famille*—Thelma, Little

Delay (Beckwith's son), and his chubby grandson. I walked in. He fixed me with his stare. "There's that Jewish fellow," I heard him say grimly. I sat down across from his table. Beckwith, staring at me, went through the story of our encounter, guffawing about his attempt to make me say the Hail Mary (see chapter 1).

A tension hung in the little dining room, but the old man soon became jovial and avuncular; just a regular citizen. Holding forth in a cherry-red jacket, he flirted with the waitresses and ordered baklava. A white couple walked in, and the woman spotted Beckwith. "I think we'll go somewhere else," she said sharply to her husband, and they walked out. Presently, the Beckwith family got up to leave. Walking past my table, the old man stood behind me. For a moment, he made a crossing gesture with his fingers over my back—the sign of the cross, perhaps (so said the other reporter I was with). Beckwith walked toward the door. "We gonna win this," he boomed out. A well-wisher had gotten up from her table. "I hope so," she said softly, putting her hand on Beckwith's shoulder, before he strode off into the night.

"How old are you, honey?" Those in the courtroom heard the unmistakeable idiom of a vanished era, a question never meant to be repeated again out loud. On February 3, 1994, the words were spoken once more, thirty years later, by a man reading the part of Bill Waller to a woman reading the part of a seventeen-year-old carhop. By then, Beckwith's third trial was six days old. But the shock of being jolted back into the world of Jackson, 1963, had not worn off, and so the ephemeral words provoked titters from the courtroom audience members. They had been taken to a world where President Kennedy made speeches on television, where bored teenagers on a Saturday night in Jackson went to the airport to watch planes or hung out around the magazine rack at the neighborhood store, where drive-ins had carhops, and carhops were called "honey." During those days in Jackson, the courtroom seesawed disorientingly, from that early 1960s world to 1994 and back again, over and over.

This was a most unusual experiment in history, memory, and the law. Long-dead or missing witnesses spoke through the 1964 trial transcript, read out in court as in the exchange between Waller and the carhop; old men wrestled with fading memories; the old En-field rifle, looking more like an antique than a murder weapon, be-came the familiar icon of the event, propped up by the witness stand; attitudes toward a dead concept, segregation, were probed; and members of a moribund organization, the Ku Klux Klan, spoke.

The peculiarities of the new case against Beckwith not only had constitutional implications. They determined the character of the trial itself. Over the course of the week the affair came to seem less a judicial proceeding than a theatrical reenactment, and a stum-bling one at that. The transcript readers—employees of the district attorney's office or of the defense—rushed awkwardly through their lines, as though conscious that giving the old speech dramatic in-flexion might give the game away. In this context, the fact that the stage setting was identical (the same courtroom as in 1964) and that the trial began on January 27, thirty years to the day after the opening of the first, appeared more than coincidential—inside jokes, almost.

Still, this trial-as-theater, with its strangely didactic air, turned out to be oddly appropriate. Over those bright days in January and February it became clear that the trial had as much to do with dispensing history as with dispensing justice. The need for a history lesson had been made manifestly evident during the days of jury selection. To the prosecutors' surprise, ignorance about Evers among the potential jurors—blacks as well as whites—was nearly univer-sal. "I was shocked, actually, how few people knew him or knew what he stood for and who he was," Peters told reporters during a break in Batesville one day.[5] When the district attorney asked a panel of fifteen potential jurors, plain-looking country people in bargain-store clothes, whether anyone knew anything of Evers, no one raised a hand.

In Jackson, the courtroom was hardly crowded at first. But the crowds increased steadily, the line waiting to get into the vaulted courtroom snaking deeper back into the marbled second-floor cor-ridor as the week wore on. There were plenty of young people, black and white students from local high schools and colleges; middle-aged, middle-class, smartly dressed blacks; elderly black men of Evers's generation and older in Homburgs and dark suits; and a substantial scattering of whites of all ages as well.

A few of Beckwith's friends skulked grimly about (the no-

nonsense Hinds County sheriff, recognizing an old Ku Kluxer lurking in the courthouse basement, firmly showed him the door). DeLaughter saw his old Boy Scout master in the crowd; the man refused to speak to him. Most of the whites said they came because it was history; blacks, to see history *and* justice. On the fourth day, two high school–aged black girls waiting patiently together, said they would not have missed this chance for a historical lesson, adding sharply that Beckwith *was* indeed guilty. On the fifth, a small troupe of white students from a local Christian school was led by a sour-faced teacher, who dragged her protesting charges away at the break; on the sixth, Sam Bailey, Evers's old friend (see chapter 2), showed up, beaming and satisfied. On the last day, an open-faced young white man wearing a ball cap brought his young son for the show. The proud owner of a small construction company, he was sure of Beckwith's guilt. Still, he said amiably, thirty years was a long time . . .

From the first moments it was apparent that this trial was a world removed from the everyday logic of the courtroom. Every trial, and particularly a murder trial, tells a story. But it is usually a story in the raw, a story unfolding for the first time. Whether one side, defense or prosecution, can develop it into a memorable narrative has much to do with that side's ultimate success.

At Beckwith's trial, the narrative had discernably been in existence for years. Myrlie Evers was the state's first witness, just as she had been in 1964. She looked elegant and commanding in a handsome gray coat, and she delivered her lines—she had told the story many times—with a practiced fluidity absent from normal courtroom testimony. Here was the painful tale yet again. She heard the sound of the car motor in the driveway. The Evers children shouted "Here's Daddy!" Then, "this horrible blast," and the children fell to the floor, as Medgar had taught them. Myrlie ran out, calling vainly.

The words themselves, delivered in a calm, even tone, sounded as though they had already been spoken: the hug Medgar gave her on the last day was a "very special embrace"; after he had been shot, she had screamed "uncontrollably." Even her comments to the reporters at the end of that first day sounded prepared. "It's thirty years to the day that we find ourselves back in the same courtroom . . ."

The rest of the trial's story unfolded much as it had in 1964: Medgar's neighbor hearing the shot, the policemen arriving, the ride to the hospital, the Jackson detectives and their investigation, the sniper's hiding place; Beckwith's rifle in the honeysuckle, his fingerprint on the scope, the witnesses from the grocery store and the drive-in who saw his white Plymouth Valiant. The old evidence pointed clearly to Beckwith's guilt, just as it had thirty years before (see chapter 4). But this time it struggled to assert itself through a thick fog of time and memory. The age of the case asserted itself visually, over and over.

A string of elderly witnesses trooped uncertainly up to the stand, an extraordinary procession of white- and gray-haired men who had long since retired. There was Willie Quinn, Medgar's neighbor, gray, bent, and confused-looking, making his way haltingly. The quavering voice of B. D. Harrell, once a Jackson police officer, followed; a few witnesses later, a white-haired Forrest Bratley, the doctor who had performed the autopsy on Evers, spoke shakily, followed by John Chamblee, the detective who had discovered the sniper's perch, gaunt and balding now. "I can't remember all the details," he said apologetically. "There's a lot of things about this murder case I wished I could remember. But I'm sorry. I can't," he told the lawyers. There was Ralph Hargrove, the police department's identification expert, who had lifted Beckwith's fingerprint from the scope. He hobbled to the witness stand with a cane and needed the questions shouted.

The few witnesses who had been young in 1964 were disorienting. They jerked the context back to the present, as if the events could in fact have happened recently. There was a middle-aged and paunchy Kenneth Adcock, who as a teenager had heard the shot while strolling with his girlfriend, but now looked bewildered to be back in the courtroom after so many years. And a surprisingly trim and fit Thorn McIntyre, the man who as a twenty-six-year-old farmer in the Delta had traded Beckwith the .30/06 Enfield rifle, testified with a confidence that seemed incongruous in this context.

In this theater, Beckwith himself was the principal prop. He was a spectral, disengaged presence at his own trial. Frail and wizened, he leaned back distractedly from the defense table, yawning frequently. Often, he stared without expression into the distance. He seemed to have little interest in what was being said. Sometimes

he put into his ear the amplifying device that helped him hear, then
stroked his chin as he listened. But often, he left the device out. He
looked like a feeble old man.

This was a shadow of the weirdly insouciant personality that
had dominated the first trial's stage. There was a gap between the
heavy historical freight carried by Beckwith (and which DeLaughter
alluded to, for the jurors' sake, in his opening argument: he was the
"self-proclaimed rabid racist . . . on a one-man mission to rid society" of integrationists) and the pathetic spectacle he presented in
the courtroom.

Some of Beckwith's harebrained, frothing letters were read out
in court, presented by Reed Massengill, the nephew of Mary Louise
and the author of a scandalous new biography of the old man. Massengill's surprise appearance was the occasion for one of Beckwith's
few periods of alertness, the uneasy-looking young man studiously
avoiding his kin's gaze. In one of the letters, sent from jail to his
son the day Kennedy was shot, Beckwith had written: "That fellow
sho' done some fancy shooting didn't he HAW HAW HAW. I'll bet
Medgar Evers said I thought you'd get down here pretty soon boss.
HA HA HA."

All this had a grotesquely comic ring to it. As the symbol of
1960s white violence, he was no longer very convincing. In this
he resembled nothing so much as those Nazi war criminals who
have proven unsatisfactory, small and pathetic, when brought to
judgment. (Hannah Arendt had found Adolph Eichmann to be a
"clown" at his trial in Jerusalem in 1961;[6] to the writer Ted Morgan, Klaus Barbie, at his 1987 trial in Lyon, was an "elderly bald
fellow with . . . bent head, weary eyes and humble body language."[7]) All of these men, like Beckwith, seemed smaller than
their world-altering crimes. The latter's ludicrous extremism, now
provoking derisive snorts rather than fear, made him even more
improbable (in his hometown of Greenwood, people agreed, right
up to the third trial, that the outlandish Delay *couldn't* have done
it, which demonstrated only that their attitudes had shifted, while
Beckwith's had not). History had magnified the assassination of
Evers into a mythic event, so that it was now difficult to connect it
to a mere mortal, much less a pathetic one like Beckwith.

Evers's status at the trial paralleled Beckwith's. While Beckwith was in some way absent, Evers was a martyr-symbol, larger

than real life. It is second nature for prosecutors in a murder trial to bring the victim to life as much as possible. But from Myrlie and the district attorney, the jury learned only about the symbolic Evers: he wanted to integrate schools and swimming pools, wanted blacks "to be able to go into department stores and try on hats," wanted courtesy titles and school-crossing guards. He was the representative of goals broad and small, all now so much a part of daily life that the jurors were astonished when Peters asked, during jury selection, if these goals had justified Evers's murder.[8] DeLaughter called Evers the "focal point" in his opening argument—"the focal point of everything this defendant hated."

The tension of an ordinary murder trial was absent. There was no taut sense of one life recently taken, and another life in the balance. This absence was not made up for by the gruesome photographs of Evers's newly exhumed body—the prosecution had wanted a new medical examination—startlingly well preserved after thirty years. It was this lack of tension which gave reason for doubt, as the prosecution's case was winding up, whether the accumulation of old evidence and testimony would be enough. Much of that testimony, having been read out loud from an old transcript, seemed weightless. And the elderly prosecution witnesses did not always inspire confidence.

But Beckwith was an inveterate fouler of his own nest. At the end of its case, the prosecution presented the confessional boasts he had left behind over thirty years. They tipped the balance, as Peters later acknowledged.[9] The witnesses, none of them elderly, who presented these savage confessions had the effect of moving the story nearer the present, of suggesting that it had not ended in 1963.

Those boasts were plausible, but they still lacked the last measure of solidity: two of the witnesses who had reported hearing Beckwith boast about killing Evers had been Ku Klux Klan informants, and two others had drinking and psychiatric problems, respectively. A fifth, though obviously an upstanding citizen (she worked for the IRS), admitted that she had not been able to remember Beckwith's exact words in her initial contacts with DeLaughter. So the appearance of the district attorney's last witness seemed providential, a saving god descending in ancient theatrical fashion on the stage, literally from a machine.

In this case the machine was television. The witness was a stolid, red-headed junior executive from Chicago named Mark Reiley, who, while snowbound at home, had been watching CNN the Friday before. A report came on about the trial, and a memory from another life emerged. He called the district attorney's office in Jackson that same day and was soon on a plane south.

Fifteen years before, Reiley had been a young guard at the Louisiana State Penitentiary. Beckwith, doing time for the bomb plot against A. I. Botnick (see chapter 4), had befriended the guard he called "Young Blood." Reiley, at twenty-one the youngest guard by far, cut off from his family and lonely, had at first seen Beckwith as a father figure. But this strange inmate had seemed distinctly less paternal on closer acquaintance. Once, Beckwith had angrily demanded the removal of a black nurse, saying: "If I could get rid of an uppity nigger like Medgar Evers, I can get rid of a no-account nigger like you." And Reiley remembered that the man had called blacks "beasts of the field" and had declared that no guilt attached to their killing. Beckwith had held himself out to the young guard as a man of importance. "He told me that if he was lying and didn't have the power and connections he said he had, he would be serving time in prison for getting rid of that nigger Medgar Evers."

Reiley provided the trial's only new drama, and it was significant. The weight had shifted decisively to DeLaughter and Peters. They were aided greatly by the defense case, which was even more perfunctory than in 1964. Its centerpiece, one of the Greenwood policemen who had given Beckwith his alibi, looked uneasy as he was forced to tell the story again. Wearing a buzz-cut so close he seemed to have been coiffed for a Hollywood drama about the 1960s, the beefy ex-cop, James Holley, was distinctly a relic. In 1963 men such as he had patrolled Mississippi's streets with billy clubs, and they had commanded a certain authority with the citizenry. Now, they seemed simply foolish.

Had it been right to reach back into history, to dredge up so old and so obviously troubled a case? What, finally, had been the point? A man in his sixties from Greenwood, one of the more thoughtful of that town's citizens, observing the proceedings, mused about the wisdom of one generation using the courtroom to judge the conduct of another. He seemed to feel that his own generation had been on trial during the week, though he himself had hardly been implicated in its misconduct. But then he agreed: murder was murder, no matter how much time had passed.

This lesson had not been at all explicit during the previous days. It was up to DeLaughter to make it so. On the last day, the courtroom was packed, the expectant crowd spilling over into the press gallery upstairs. DeLaughter had so far been subdued, allowing witnesses to go on (sometimes far too long) during the days of testimony without obvious efforts to shape the story. The more spectacular interventions had come from Peters, who even provoked the crowd to laughter on the last day as he mocked the hapless Holley's responses.

But this day, the summing-up day, was DeLaughter's. He had to make sense of the strange farrago of history, theater, memory, and evidentiary minutia to explain more publicly than ever before why he had undertaken a course so many of his fellow Mississippians found obnoxious. The normally unexpressive DeLaughter rose to the occasion. His closing argument to the jury was filled with an understated passion, an intensity of feeling that put the case sharply into focus. With simple language he drew out all the human and social significance of the case. Those accustomed to DeLaughter's low-key courtroom performances agreed that he had surpassed himself on this day.

What was the case all about? "An unarmed man, arriving home in the late hours of the night . . . and being shot down by a bushwacker from ambush . . . his three children, stating over and over, 'Daddy, please get up.' A man being shot down, not being able to face his self-appointed judge, jury, and executioner." DeLaughter went on: "This assassination by a sniper from ambush is timeless. It spans the races. It is something that should sicken every decent human being, regardless of race. This is about civilized society versus the vile. This is about the state of Mississippi versus Byron de la Beckwith."

The prosecutor presented a brief exposition of the evidence and a sketch of Beckwith, and continued, deliberately colloquial: "His gun, his fingerprint, his car, his scope. And last but not least, his mouth. When he thought he had beaten the system, he couldn't keep his mouth shut. He wants to take credit . . . but he just don't want to pay the price for it.

"Why did this happen? Why did any of this happen? Why was Medgar Evers assassinated? For his beliefs. To go in a restaurant. To vote. For wanting some degree of equality for himself and his fellow human beings. This kind of murder . . . there is just a gaping wound laid open in society. We have to learn from the past, folks. Where justice is never fulfilled . . . all it does is just fester and fester over the years."

Then, he made the prosecutor's ritual plea to the jury. But this time the words carried a special moral point. He seemed to be answering all the critics who had sneered over the months. "It's right, it's just, and Lord knows, it's just time," DeLaughter said to the jury. "Is it ever too late to do the right thing? For the sake of truth and justice, I hope it's not."

He was asking for a verdict of guilty. That evening, there were anxious moments as the jury deliberated five hours, then returned wearily to its hotel without a decision. But the joyous shouts in the courthouse the next morning, when the guilty verdict came in, seemed almost inevitable, given the certainty of DeLaughter's conclusions.

For the reporters at the press conference immediately afterward, he delivered the predictably pious hope that the case could be "a focal point for all the races to come together and work for the betterment of our community and our state." [10] But a few days later, after a stoic exposition of the difficulties his stance had caused him with his fellow citizens for the last three years, DeLaughter sounded less pious, less hopeful, less certain: "It remains to be seen what we do with it," he said simply. [11]

NOTES

PREFACE

1. Interview with John T. Hester, December 1992.

CHAPTER ONE: CONFRONTING HISTORY IN
MISSISSIPPI

1. Erle Johnston, *Mississippi's Defiant Years, 1953–1973* (Forest, Miss.: Lake Harbor Press, 1990), p. 95.

2. *Clarion-Ledger,* February 28, 1978.

3. Letter courtesy of Reed Massengill.

4. See Robert Moore, *Two History Texts: A Study in Contrast* (New York: Racism and Sexism Resource Center for Educators, n.d.).

5. *James Loewen et al. vs. John Turnipseed, Mississippi State Textbook Purchasing Board,* U.S. District Court, Northern District of Mississippi, Court reporter's transcript of the defendants' proposed post-trial findings of fact and conclusions of law, 1975.

6. In a telephone interview, January 1992.

7. Telephone interview with Neil McMillen. *Dark Journey* went on to win the Bancroft Award, a top prize for historians.

8. James W. Silver, *Mississippi: The Closed Society* (New York: Harcourt, Brace, 1964), p. 150.

9. *Clarion-Ledger,* September 9, 1984.

10. John R. Salter, *Jackson, Mississippi: An American Chronicle of Struggle and Schism* (Hicksville, N.Y.: Exposition Press, 1979), p. 187.

CHAPTER TWO: MEDGAR EVERS

1. Myrlie Evers, with William Peters, *For Us, the Living* (New York: Doubleday, 1967), p. 31.

2. Interview with Charles Evers.

3. *New Orleans Times-Picayune,* June 16, 1963.

4. Papers of the National Association for the Advancement of Colored People, III, Library of Congress.

5. Evers, with Peters, *For Us, the Living,* p. 248.

6. Tape of responses to televised speech, May 20, 1963, WBLT-TV, Jackson, Miss. Courtesy of Sharon Stallworth of the *Clarion-Ledger.*

7. "John Salter," oral history interview (Jackson: Mississippi Department of Archives and History, January 6, 1981), p. 32.

8. Ibid.

9. Walter Lord, *The Past That Would Not Die* (New York: Pocket Books, 1967), p. 83.

10. Interview with C. B. Needham, Decatur, September 1991.

11. Charles Evers, *Evers* (New York: World, 1971), p. 77.

12. M. Evers, with Peters, *For Us, the Living,* p. 20.

13. "No alcohol": M. Evers, with Peters, *For Us, the Living,* p. 23; "trips to revivals": C. Evers, *Evers,* p. 31.

14. C. Evers, *Evers,* p. 11.

15. M. Evers, with Peters, *For Us, the Living,* pp. 14, 19.

16. Interviews: Charles Evers, August 1991; C. B. Needham, September 1991; and Elizabeth Jordan, October 1991.

17. C. Evers, *Evers,* p. 25.

18. Needham interview

19. C. Evers, *Evers,* p. 47.

20. Telephone interview with Liz Jordan, October 28, 1991.

21. C. Evers interview.

22. Ibid.

23. Needham interview. (In Charles Evers's version, his father

brandished broken glass at the storeowner, forcing him to back off [C. Evers interview]).

24. Interviews: Y. Z. Walker, September 1991; and Needham.

25. Needham interview.

26. C. Evers, *Evers,* pp. 44, 54, 81.

27. M. Evers, with Peters, *For Us, the Living,* pp. 24, 25.

28. Needham interview.

29. M. Evers, with Peters, *For Us, the Living,* p. 26.

30. Ibid., p. 27.

31. Ibid., p. 33.

32. Evers, *Evers,* p. 96; M. Evers, with Peters, *For Us, the Living,* p. 28.

33. M. Evers, with Peters, *For Us, the Living,* p. 10.

34. Denton Watson, *Lion in the Lobby: Clarence Mitchell's Struggle for the Passage of Civil Rights Laws* (New York: Morrow, 1990), p. 487.

35. James C. Cobb, *The Most Southern Place on Earth: The Mississippi Delta and the Roots of Regional Identity* (New York: Oxford University Press, 1992), pp. 81, 112–13.

36. Interview with Thomas H. Moore, August 1991.

37. M. Evers, with Peters, *For Us, the Living,* p. 91.

38. Interview with Aaron Henry, Clarksdale, Miss., August 1991.

39. Neil R. McMillen, *Dark Journey: Black Mississippians in the Age of Jim Crow* (Urbana: University of Illinois Press, 1989), p. 229.

40. Roy Wilkins, *Standing Fast: The Autobiography of Roy Wilkins* (New York: Viking Press, 1982), p. 23.

41. Ibid., pp. 105–106.

42. McMillen, *Dark Journey,* pp. 314–16.

43. M. Evers, with Peters, *For Us, the Living,* p. 98.

44. Letter to the author from Gloster B. Current, August 18, 1993.

45. Dixiecrats were the segregationist Southern Democrats who broke from the national Democratic Party in 1948 because they opposed the party's civil rights platform.

46. Moore interview.

47. Current letter, August 18, 1993.

48. M. Evers, with Peters, *For Us, the Living,* p. 100–118.

49. NAACP Papers, Library of Congress, III.

50. Erle Johnston, *Mississippi's Defiant Years, 1953–1973* (Forest, Miss.: Lake Harbor, 1990), p. 34; *Howell Raines, My Soul Is Rested* (New York: Penguin, 1983), p. 132.

51. NAACP Papers, III.

52. John Dittmer, "The Politics of the Mississippi Movement, 1954–1964," in *The Civil Rights Movement in America,* ed. Charles Eagles (Jackson: University Press of Mississippi, 1986), p. 69.

53. Letter from John Salter to Polly Greenberg, September 27, 1966, John Salter Papers, Mississippi Department of Archives and History, Jackson.

54. Associated Press, June 12, 1991.

55. *Citizens' Council,* January 1959.

56. Interview with Sam Bailey, August 1991.

57. Letter from Salter to Greenberg, Salter Papers.

58. M. Evers, with Peters, *For Us, the Living,* p. 226.

59. Ibid.

60. Ibid., p. 235.

61. John R. Salter interview transcript, December 26, 1990, John C. Stennis Oral History Project (Starkville: Department of History, Mississippi State University, 1990), p. 16 (hereafter cited as Salter interview, Stennis Project).

62. Dittmer, *Mississippi Movement,* p. 71.

63. Elizabeth Jacoway and David R. Colburn, eds, *Southern Businessmen and Desegregation* (Baton Rouge: Louisiana State University Press, 1982), p. 239, 249.

64. Salter interview, Stennis Project, p. 14. Was there a deliberate NAACP policy to go slow in Mississippi in the late 1950s? Salter asserts that there was and that Medgar Evers told him about it. To Evers's disgust, according to Salter, the NAACP had entered into a "gentleman's agreement" with the Eisenhower administration that it would not pursue "direct action" or even school desegregation in Mississippi because the state was so "volatile." Evers's boss, Gloster Current, vigorously disputes Salter's assertions. "John Salter, no friend ideologically of the NAACP, is wrong," writes Current, who turned eighty in the spring of 1993. "There was no policy to 'go slow' in Mississippi in the late 1950s. Nor was there any 'agreement' with the Eisenhower administration. . . . The employment of Medgar Evers attests to the intention of NAACP [sic] in Mississippi to press for desegregation." [letter to author, August 18, 1993]

65. Letter from Salter to Greenberg, Salter Papers.

66. Interview with John Herbers, December 1991.

67. *New York Times,* June 20, 1963.

68. Salter interview, Stennis Project, p. 32.

69. NAACP Papers, III.

70. Interview with Sam Bailey, August 1991.

71. M. Evers, with Peters, *For Us, the Living,* p. 159.

72. Ibid., p. 225.

73. *New York Times,* June 13, 1963.

74. Letter from Salter to Greenberg, September 27, 1966, Salter Papers.

75. M. Evers, with Peters, *For Us, the Living,* p. 248.

76. "Story of Greenwood, Mississippi," Smithsonian Folkways Records, FD 5593.

77. John Salter, *Jackson, Mississippi: An American Chronicle of Struggle and Schism* (Hicksville, New York: Exposition Press, 1977), p. 160.

78. Ibid., p. 39.

79. Ibid., p. 105.

80. Ibid., p. 109.

81. Ibid., p. 120.

82. Response to Medgar Evers speech, May 20, 1963, WLBT-TV, Jackson, Mississippi; tape courtesy of Sharon Stallworth of the *Clarion-Ledger.*

83. Anne Moody, *Coming of Age in Mississippi* (New York: Bantam/Doubleday, 1976), p. 268. For three hours that day, Salter and four Tougaloo students had endured taunts, mustard and ketchup squirted on them, and finally beatings by a mob of young whites at the lunch counter in the downtown Woolworth's.

84. M. Evers, with Peters, *For Us, the Living,* p. 257.

85. Ibid., p. 258.

86. Ibid., p. 262.

87. *New York Times,* June 4, 1963.

88. Salter, p. 156.

89. M. Evers, with Peters, *For Us, the Living,* p. 273.

90. U.S. Department of Justice, Federal Bureau of Investigation, *FOIPA #312,109—Medgar Evers.*

91. *State of Mississippi vs. Byron de la Beckwith,* in the Circuit Court of the First Judicial District of Hinds County, Mississippi, Court reporter's transcript of first trial, 1964, p. 6 (hereafter cited as Transcript of First Trial); M. Evers, with Peters, *For Us, the Living,* p. 302.

92. M. Evers, with Peters, *For Us, the Living,* p. 303.

93. Transcript of First Trial, 1964, p. 46.

94. Transcript of First Trial, 1964, p. 143, 158.

95. *New York Times,* June 13, 1963.

96. *New York Times Magazine,* June 23, 1963.

97. Ed King, "Life in Miss. VIII Beckwith Trial. Winter, Spring 1964" (personal file, courtesy of Ed King).

CHAPTER THREE: THE WHITE SUPREMACIST STATE

1. Willie Morris, *North Towards Home* (Oxford, Miss.: Yoknapa-tawpha Press, 1982), p. 319.

2. *New York Times,* March 30, 1961.

3. Papers of the National Association for the Advancement of Colored People, III, Library of Congress.

4. *New York Times,* June 1, 1963.

5. John Salter, *Jackson, Mississippi: An American Chronicle of Struggle and Schism* (Hicksville, New York: Exposition Press, 1979), p. 152.

6. Interview with Joe Wroten, November 1991.

7. *New York Times,* February 17, 1962.

8. James W. Silver, *Mississippi: The Closed Society* (New York: Harcourt, Brace, 1964), p. 48.

9. Quoted in ibid., p. 147.

10. *New York Times,* December 1, 1964.

11. Salter, *Jackson, Mississippi.*

12. *New York Times,* June 14, 1963.

13. *New York Times,* April 6, 1963.

14. John Dollard, *Caste and Class in a Southern Town* (New York: Doubleday Anchor, 1957), p. 5.

15. Ibid., p. 14.

16. Ibid., pp. 11, 19.

17. Anthony Lewis and the *New York Times, Portrait of a Decade* (New York: Random House, 1964), p. 204.

18. Silver, *Closed Society,* p. 154.

19. James W. Silver, *Running Scared: Silver in Mississippi* (Jackson: University Press of Mississippi, 1984), pp. 64, 58.

20. "James Silver," oral history interview (Jackson: Mississippi Department of Archives and History, 1981) p. 13.

21. Ibid., p. 88.

22. *New York Times,* November 8, 1963.

23. Silver, *Running Scared,* p. 90.

24. *New York Times,* November 8, 1963.

25. 'Silver," oral history.

26. *New York Times,* November 8, 1963.

27. Silver, *Closed Society,* p. XX.

28. *Clarion-Ledger,* April 13, 1964.

29. Silver, *Running Scared,* pp. 96–97.

30. Ibid., p. 101.

31. Ibid., p. 112.

32. Robert Penn Warren, *Who Speaks for the Negro?* (New York: Random House, 1965), p. 113.

33. Ibid., pp. 44, 47.

34. Nicholas Von Hoffman, *Mississippi Notebook* (New York: White, 1964), p. 37.

35. Ibid., p. 54.

36. Calvin Trillin, "Letter from Jackson," *New Yorker*, August 29, 1964, pp. 81–101.

37. *New York Times Magazine*, April 28, 1963.

38. *U.S. Commission on Civil Rights, Hearings before the Commission on Civil Rights, Jackson, Mississippi, vols. 1–2* (Washington, D.C.: U.S. Government Printing Office), p. 124.

39. Steven F. Lawson, *Black Ballots: Voting Rights in the South, 1944–1969* (New York: Columbia University Press, 1976), p. 284.

40. *Commission on Civil Rights*, pp. 79–82.

41. Ibid., p. 181.

42. David Sansing and Caroll Waller, *A History of the Mississippi Governor's Mansion* (Jackson: University Press of Mississippi, 1977), p. 112.

43. Albert Kirwan, *Revolt of the Rednecks: Mississippi Politics, 1876–1925* (Lexington: University of Kentucky Press, 1951), p. 88.

44. Richard Wright, *Black Boy* (New York: Harper & Row, 1966), pp. 162–64.

45. Neal R. Peirce, *The Deep South States of America* (New York: Norton, 1974), p. xx.

46. Eudora Welty, *Photographs* (Jackson: University Press of Mississippi, 1989), p. 800.

47. *Saturday Evening Post*, "The Cities of America: Jackson, Mississippi," October 9, 1948, p. 34.

48. Silver, *Closed Society*, p. 21.

49. *Jackson Capitol Reporter*, September 4, 1981; Peirce, *Deep South States*, p. 199.

50. Robert Sherrill, *Gothic Politics in the Deep South* (New York: Grossman, 1968), p. 186.

51. *Clarion-Ledger*, June 10, 1962.

52. *Wall Street Journal*, May 29, 1963.

53. Erle Johnston, *Mississippi's Defiant Years, 1953–1973*, (Forest, Miss.: Lake Harbor, 1990), p. 397.

54. Unpublished manuscript in file labeled "T.M. Hederman, Sr.," Mississippi Department of Archives and History, Jackson.

55. *Washington Post*, April 25, 1983.

56. Silver, *Closed Society,* p. 30.

57. Johnston, *Defiant Years,* p. 388.

58. Peirce, *Deep South States,* p. 220.

59. *Eyes on the Prize, Part 2,* "Fighting Back" (Boston: Blackside, Inc., Henry Hampton, 1986), television documentary.

60. Walter Lord, *The Past That Would Not Die* (New York: Pocket Books, 1965), p. 167.

61. Salter, *Jackson, Mississippi.*

62. William F. Holmes, *The White Chief: James Kimble Vardaman* (Baton Rouge: Louisiana State University Press, 1970), p. vii.

63. Neil R. McMillen, *Dark Journey: Black Mississippians in the Age of Jim Crow* (Urbana: University of Illinois Press, 1989), p. 237.

64. *New York Times,* November 8, 1963.

65. James W. Loewen and Charles Sallis, eds., *Mississippi: Conflict and Change* (New York: Pantheon, 1980), p. 154; Eric Foner, *Reconstruction: America's Unfinished Revolution, 1863–1877* (New York: Harper & Row, 1988), pp. 370–71.

66. Foner, *Reconstruction,* p. 560; Kirwan, *Revolt of the Rednecks,* p. 4; Loewen and Sallis, *Conflict and Change,* p. 161.

67. Kirwan, *Revolt of the Rednecks,* p. 66.

68. Wigfall Green, *The Man Bilbo* (Westport, Conn.: Greenwood Press, 1976), p. 93.

69. Holmes, *White Chief,* p. 88.

70. Hortense Powdermaker, *After Freedom: A Cultural Study in the Deep South* (New York: Viking, 1933; reprint, New York: Atheneum, 1968), p. 52.

71. McMillen, *Dark Journey,* p. 245.

72. Dollard, *Caste and Class,* pp. 364–89.

73. Johnston, *Defiant Years.*

74. *Citizens' Council,* May 1957.

75. Howell Raines, *My Soul Is Rested* (New York: Penguin, 1983), p. 298.

76. *New York Times,* September 28, 1962.

77. Neil R. McMillen, *The Citizens' Council* (Urbana: University of Illinois Press, 1971), pp. 322, 326.

78. Myrlie Evers, with William Peters, *For Us, the Living* (New York: Doubleday, 1967), pp. 164–65.

79. *New York Times Magazine,* November 12, 1961.

80. *Wall Street Journal,* May 29, 1963.

81. McMillen, *The Citizens' Council,* p. 328.

82. Ibid.

83. Ibid., p. 334.

84. Ibid., p. 125.

85. Ibid.

86. *New York Times,* March 30, 1961.

87. "Mrs. Jane Schutt," oral history interview, February 2, 1981, Mississippi Department of Archives and History, Jackson.

88. *Citizen,* November 1961.

89. *Race and Reason Day* (Jackson: Council Forum Films, Mississippi Department of Archives and History), filmstrip.

90. *Clarion-Ledger,* November 26, 1989.

91. Initials are used to protect the identities of those who may still be living.

92. Sovereignty Commission report, April 16, 1965, copy in Paul B. Johnson Papers, University of Southern Mississippi, Hattiesburg.

93. Silver, *Closed Society,* 2nd ed. (New York: Harcourt Brace, 1966), p. 278.

94. *New York Times,* July 13, 1964.

95. *New York Times,* July 19, 1964.

96. Elizabeth Jacoway and David R. Colburn, eds., *Southern Businessmen and Desegregation* (Baton Rouge: Louisiana State University Press, 1982), p. 241.

97. *New York Times,* June 14, 1963.

CHAPTER FOUR: BYRON DE LA BECKWITH

1. R. W. Scott, *Glory in Conflict: A Saga of Byron de la Beckwith* (Camden, Ark.: Camark Press, 1991), p. 120.

2. Jeannine Heron, "Notes on the Beckwith Trial," *Nation,* February 24, 1964, p. 179; Harold M. Martin, "The Trial of Delay Beckwith," *Saturday Evening Post,* March 14, 1964, p. 36.

3. *New York Times,* February 7, 1964.

4. Scott, *Glory in Conflict.*

5. Ibid., p. 181.

6. Ibid., p. 83.

7. Ibid., p. 101. For years, Beckwith had been trying to enlist a writer to tell his story, even paying several people. R. W. Scott, the Arkansas resident who finally took on the task, was an old acquaintance and political soulmate of Beckwith's, according to David Pitts, the Greenwood antiques dealer who distributed the book. Beckwith and Scott have a mutual friend: the attorney who defended the Little Rock school system during its desegregation crisis. Scott paid for the publi-

cation himself, according to Pitts. It has a distinctly amateur feel about it, with crude typography, printing, and photographs. The brief biography of Scott on the back notes that the author "enjoys a comprehensive range of interests including history, Constitutional Law, and a large assortment of hobbies."

8. *Memphis Commercial-Appeal,* February 6, 1964.

9. *New Orleans Times-Picayune,* November 26, 1963.

10. Scott, *Glory in Conflict,* pp. 63, 78.

11. *Knoxville News-Sentinel,* December 20, 1992.

12. *New York Times,* July 9, 1963.

13. *Knoxville News-Sentinel,* December 20, 1992.

14. *New York Times,* February 8, 1963.

15. *State of Mississippi vs. Byron de la Beckwith,* Circuit Court, First Judicial District, Hinds County, Court reporter's transcript of 1992 hearing, p. 44 (hereafter cited as 1992 Hearing Transcript).

16. James Cobb, *The Most Southern Place on Earth: The Mississippi Delta and the Roots of Regional Identity* (New York: Oxford University Press, 1992), pp. 32, 131.

17. William C. Harris, *The Day of the Carpetbagger: Republican Reconstruction in Mississippi* (Baton Rouge: Louisiana State University Press, 1979), p. 82.

18. Albert Kirwan, *Revolt of the Rednecks: Mississippi Politics, 1876–1925* (Lexington: University of Kentucky Press, 1951), p. 237.

19. Malvina Scott Sykes, comp., *Our Family* (Washington, D.C.: privately printed, 1947), p. 80; Thomas B. and Mary D. Edsall, *Chain Reaction: The Impact of Race, Rights and Taxes on American Politics* (New York: Norton, 1991), pp. 43–44.

20. Scott, *Glory in Conflict,* p. 41.

21. *Knoxville News-Sentinel,* December 20, 1992.

22. Scott, *Glory in Conflict,* pp. 21–22.

23. *Knoxville News-Sentinel,* December 20, 1992.

24. Scott, *Glory in Conflict,* p. 23.

25. Ibid., p. 28.

26. Ibid., pp. 25–38.

27. Ibid., p. 45.

28. Ibid., p. 40.

29. Martin Russ, *Line of Departure: Tarawa* (Garden City, N.Y.: Doubleday, 1973), p. 70.

30. Reed Massengill, *Portrait of a Racist* (New York: St. Martin's Press, 1994), p. 67.

31. Scott, *Glory in Conflict,* p. 47.

32. *New York Times,* June 25, 1963.

33. Martin, *Saturday Evening Post,* March 14, 1964.

34. *Clarion-Ledger,* November 3, 1991.

35. *Jackson Daily News,* ca. 1957, clipping in Bill Minor Papers, Mississippi State University, Starkville.

36. House Committee on Un-American Activities, *Hearings before the Committee on Un-American Activities,* 89th Congress, 2nd sess., January 12, 1966, pp. 2667–83.

37. *New York Times,* July 19, 1963.

38. Cobb, *Most Southern Place,* p. 232.

39. Taylor Branch, *Parting the Waters: America in the King Years, 1954–1963* (New York: Simon & Schuster, 1988), p. 633.

40. Sally Belfrage, *Freedom Summer* (New York: Viking, 1965; reprint, Charlottesville: University Press of Virginia, 1990), p. 118.

41. See especially Cobb, *Most Southern Place,* p. 237.

42. House Committee, *Un-American Activities,* p. 2929.

43. *New York Times,* April 6, 1963; Branch, *Parting the Waters,* p. 718.

44. Belfrage, *Freedom Summer,* p. 108.

45. Branch, *Parting the Waters,* p. 724.

46. "Story of Greenwood, Mississippi," Smithsonian Folkways Records FD 5593.

47. Scott, *Glory in Conflict,* p. 61.

48. *Saturday Evening Post,* March 14, 1964.

49. *State of Mississippi vs. Byron de la Beckwith,* in the Circuit Court of the First Judicial District of Hinds County, Mississippi, Court reporter's transcript of first trial, 1964, pp. 464, 883 (hereafter cited as Transcript of First Trial).

50. Interview with Reed Massengill, January 1993.

51. House Committee, *Un-American Activities,* p. 2668.

52. Transcript of First Trial, p. 471.

53. *New York Times,* June 25, 1963.

54. Transcript of First Trial, pp. 427–28.

55. Ibid., p. 509.

56. Ibid., pp. 462–485.

57. Ibid., p. xxx.

58. Myrlie Evers, with William Peters, *For Us, the Living* (New York: Doubleday, 1967), p. 305.

59. Transcript of First Trial, p. 31.

60. Ibid., pp. 55–96.

61. Interview with Bill Waller, March 1992.

62. Bill Minor, typescript of story for *Newsweek,* in Bill Minor Papers, Mitchell Memorial Library, Mississippi State University, Starkville.

63. Transcript of First Trial, p. xxx.

64. Martin, *Saturday Evening Post,* March 14, 1964.

65. Robert Penn Warren, *Who Speaks for the Negro?* (New York: Random House, 1965), p. 45.

66. Martin, *Saturday Evening Post,* March 14, 1964.

67. Quoted in Warren, *Who Speaks for the Negro?,* p. 46.

68. James W. Silver, *Mississippi: The Closed Society* (New York: Harcourt Brace, 1964), p. 239.

69. *New Republic,* May 23, 1964; Belfrage, *Freedom Summer,* p. 121.

70. Circuit Court of the First Judicial District, Hinds County, Miss., *Hearing on Speedy Trial Issues,* July 1992, pp. 80–81.

71. *Knoxville News Sentinel,* December 20, 1992; Bond hearing, Circuit Court of the First Judicial District, Hinds County, Miss., November 12, 1991.

72. *Byron de la Beckwith vs. Mary Louise Williams Beckwith,* Leflore County Chancery Court, September 1965.

73. Huie, interviewed in Howell Raines, *My Soul Is Rested* (New York: Penguin, 1983), p. 393.

74. *New York Times,* November 15, 1964.

75. *New York Times,* November 12, 1964.

76. Jack Nelson, *Terror in the Night: The Klan's Campaign against the Jews* (New York: Simon & Schuster, 1993), pp. 26, 62–63.

77. House Committee, *Un-American Activities,* p. 2938.

78. Wyn Craig Wade, *The Fiery Cross: The Ku Klux Klan in America* (New York: Simon & Schuster, 1987), p. 334.

79. House Committee, *Un-American Activities*

80. Scott, *Glory in Conflict,* p. 178.

81. House Committee, *Un-American Activities,* p. 2700.

82. Nelson, *Terror in the Night,* p. 219.

83. *Speedy Trial Hearing,* p. 38.

84. *New Orleans Times-Picayune,* September 29, 1973; *Jackson Daily News,* October 1, 1973.

85. Interview with Al Binder, Jackson, Miss., December 1992; Nelson, *Terror in the Night,* p. 250.

86. *New York Times,* January 21, 1974.

87. Scott, *Glory in Conflict,* p. 217.

88. 1991 Bond hearing, p. 63.

89. *Jackson Daily News,* June 13, 1983.

CHAPTER FIVE: BILL WALLER

1. Myrlie Evers, with William Peters, *For Us, the Living* (New York: Doubleday, 1967), p. 351.

2. "William L. Waller, " oral history interview, November 14, 1971 (Hattiesburg: Oral History Program, University of Southern Mississippi), p. 1.

3. Interview with Bill Minor, March 1992.

4. Interview with Robert Pritchard, March 1992.

5. Jeannine Heron, "Notes on the Beckwith Trial," *Nation*, February 24, 1964, p. 36.

6. *New York Times*, January 30, 1964.

7. Erle Johnston, *Mississippi's Defiant Years, 1953–1973* (Forest, Miss.: Lake Harbor, 1990), p. 340.

8. Steven F. Lawson, *In Pursuit of Power: Southern Blacks and Electoral Politics, 1965–1982* (New York: Columbia University Press, 1985), p. 92–93.

9. Vertical Files and Audio-Visual Collection, Mississippi Department of Archives and History, Jackson.

10. Interview with Bill Waller, Jackson, Miss., April 1992; "Waller," oral history, p. 11.

11. *Jackson Daily News*, April 25, 1967.

12. *Jackson Daily News*, June 8, 1967.

13. Bill Minor, *New Orleans Times-Picayune*, April 11, 1971.

14. Jason Berry, *Amazing Grace: With Charles Evers in Mississippi* (Saturday Review Press, 1973; reprint, Baton Rouge: Legacy, 1978), pp. 48, 118.

15. Ibid., p. 119.

16. *New York Times*, November 3, 1971.

17. "Waller," oral history, p. 15.

18. Bill Minor, *New Orleans Times-Picayune*, August 21, 1971.

19. *Jackson Daily News*, March 6, 1972.

20. "Waller," oral history, p. 11.

21. *Jackson Daily News*, December 28, 1972.

22. Roy Steinfort, editor of the *Aberdeen Examiner*, quoted in the *Jackson State-Times*, August 30, 1959.

23. *Clarion-Ledger*, September 25, 1966; *Jackson Daily News*, September 26, 1966.

24. "Karl Wiesenburg,"oral history interview (Jackson: Mississippi Department of Archives and History, 1976).

25. "Wilson F. Minor," oral history interview, July 22, 1974 (Jackson: Mississippi Department of Archives and History, 1974).

26. Ibid.

27. Minor interview.

28. *New Orleans Times-Picayune,* April 1, 1973.

29. Ibid., October 21, 1973.

30. Minor interview.

31. *New Orleans Times-Picayune,* January 25, 1976.

32. Ibid., March 3, 1974.

33. "Waller," oral history, p. 3.

34. *New Orleans Times-Picayune,* August 31, 1975.

35. *Capitol Reporter,* October 20, 1977.

36. Interview with Gerald Blessey, April 1992.

37. "Waller," oral history, p. 35.

38. *New Orleans Times-Picayune,* March 9, 1975.

CHAPTER SIX: CHARLES EVERS

1. Thomas Powers, "Letter From A Lost Campaign," *Harper's,* March 1972.

2. William Bradford Huie, *True Magazine,* May 1970.

3. Powers, "Letter From A Lost Campaign."

4. "Playboy Interview: Charles Evers," *Playboy,* October 1971.

5. Interviews: Doris Allison, August 1991; Aaron Henry.

6. Interview with Charles Evers.

7. *Playboy,* October 1971.

8. Ibid.

9. Interview with Jason Berry.

10. *New York Times,* August 16, 1965.

11. Charles Evers, *Evers* (New York: World, 1971), pp. 130–131.

12. *New York Times,* December 25, 1965.

13. *New York Times Magazine,* August 4, 1968.

14. *New York Times,* October 26, 1969.

15. Interview with Ed Cole, May 1992.

16. Julian Bond, *Black Candidates: Southern Campaign Experiences* (Atlanta: Southern Regional Council), May 1969.

17. *New York Times,* December 23, 1965.

18. *New York Times Magazine,* August 4, 1968.

19. Ibid.

20. *Memphis Commercial Appeal,* November 9, 1969.

21. *New York Times Magazine,* August 4, 1968.

22. *New York Times,* July 9, 1969.

23. Cole interview.

24. Ramberg Collection, Mississippi Department of Archives and History, Jackson.

25. *Playboy,* October 1971.

26. *New York Times Magazine,* October 26, 1969.

27. *New York Times,* August 15, 1969.

28. *Memphis Commercial Appeal,* November 9, 1969.

29. *New York Times Magazine,* October 26, 1969.

30. Interview with Charles Evers.

31. Jason Berry, *Amazing Grace: With Charles Evers in Mississippi* (Saturday Review Press, 1973; reprint, Baton Rouge: Legacy, 1978), p. 26.

32. Ibid., p. 27.

33. Ibid., p. 75.

34. Ibid., p. 19.

35. Associated Press, October 31, 1971.

36. Ibid.

37. Berry, *Amazing Grace,* p. 73.

38. Ibid., p. 120.

39. *Jackson Daily News,* November 4, 1971.

40. *Delta Democrat-Times,* June 11, 1973.

41. *Los Angeles Times,* January 22, 1970.

42. Cole interview.

43. *Clarion-Ledger,* May 1981.

44. *New York Times Magazine,* October 26, 1969.

45. *Wall Street Journal,* March 18, 1970.

46. *Capitol Reporter,* July 2, 1981.

47. Huie, *True Magazine,* May 1970.

48. *Clarion-Ledger,* September 24, 1979.

49. *New Orleans Times-Picayune,* August 25, 1974.

50. *Capitol Reporter,* July 19, 1979.

51. Ibid., May 14, 1981.

52. Ibid., July 2, 1981.

53. *Clarion-Ledger,* July 5, 1982.

54. *Clarion-Ledger,* November 9, 1985.

CHAPTER SEVEN: BOBBY DELAUGHTER

1. Jason Berry, *Amazing Grace: With Charles Evers in Mississippi* (Saturday Review Press, 1973; reprint, Baton Rouge: Legacy, 1978), pp. 253–55.

2. Interview with Alan Binder.

3. Southern Poverty Law Center, *Free at Last: A History of the Civil Rights Movement and Those Who Died in the Struggle* (Montgomery, Ala.: SPLC, n.d.), p. 90.

4. *New York Times Magazine,* March 21, 1971.

5. Interview with William Kirksey.

6. Interview with Bobby DeLaughter.

7. Fred Powledge, *Journeys through the South* (New York: Vanguard, 1979), p. 119.

8. *Ladies Home Journal,* October 1969.

9. Interview with Bob Gordon, January 1993; *Washington Post,* April 25, 1983.

10. Interview with Alan Binder.

11. Paige Mitchell, *The Covenant* (New York: Atheneum, 1973).

12. Eli Evans, *The Provincials* (New York: Atheneum, 1973), p. 125.

13. John Dollard, *Caste and Class in a Southern Town* (Garden City, N.Y.: Doubleday Anchor), p. 129.

14. Interview with Alan Binder.

15. See Jack Nelson, *Terror in the Night: The Klan's Campaign against the Jews* (New York: Simon & Schuster, 1993).

16. *Atlanta Journal-Constitution,* November 9, 1981.

17. *New York Times,* March 21, 1980.

CHAPTER EIGHT: DOWNFALL OF THE OLD ORDER

1. *Clarion-Ledger,* January 10, 1987.

2. *Clarion-Ledger,* March 14, 1982.

3. Bill Minor, *Clarion-Ledger,* April 15, 1987.

4. *Vicksburg Evening Post,* April 19, 1987.

5. *Clarion-Ledger,* June 11, 1954.

6. Minor, *Clarion-Ledger,* April 15, 1987.

7. *Clarion-Ledger,* February 15, 1986.

8. Dale Krane and Stephen D. Shaffer, *Mississippi Government and Politics* (Lincoln: University of Nebraska Press, 1992), pp. 65–67.

9. Bill Minor, *Clarion-Ledger,* December 11, 1983.

10. *Jackson Capitol Reporter,* March 19, 1981.

11. *Clarion-Ledger,* March 24, 1985.

12. *Clarion-Ledger,* September 19, 1986.

13. Interview with Buddie Newman, January 1988.

14. Ibid.

15. Carroll Brinson, *Our Time Has Come: Mississippi Embraces Its Future* (Jackson, Miss.: Oakdale Press, 1988), p. 47.

16. Ibid., p. 49; *New York Times Magazine,* February 26, 1988, p. 40.

17. Brinson, p. 48.

18. *Clarion-Ledger,* June 29, 1986.

19. *Memphis Commercial-Appeal,* February 17, 1987.

20. Ray Mabus Basic Speech, Gubernatorial Campaign Press Office, 1987.

21. Ray Mabus Neshoba Fair Speech, Gubernatorial Campaign Press Office, 1987.

22. Brinson, p. 1.

23. *New York Times Magazine,* February 28, 1988.

24. *Clarion-Ledger,* January 13, 1988.

25. *Clarion-Ledger,* January 15, 1989.

26. For more on this, see Tony Dunbar, *Delta Time* (New York: Pantheon, 1989), chap. 9.

27. *Clarion-Ledger,* January 14, 1989.

28. *Jackson Daily News,* January 11, 1989.

29. Seth Cagin and Philip Dray, *We Are Not Afraid: The Story of Goodman, Schwerner, and Chaney and the Civil Rights Campaign for Mississippi* (New York: Macmillan, 1988).

30. Interview with Dick Molpus, June 1989.

31. *Atlanta Journal-Constitution,* June 22, 1989.

32. Erle Johnston, *Mississippi's Defiant Years, 1953–1973* (Forest, Miss.: Lake Harbor, 1990), p. 380.

33. Ibid.

34. Interview with Mike Mills, October 1992.

35. Interview with Erle Johnston, August 1989.

CHAPTER NINE: THE PAST DISINTERRED

1. *Clarion-Ledger,* August 17, 1987.

2. Erle Johnston, *Mississippi's Defiant Years, 1953–1973* (Forest, Miss.: Lake Harbor, 1990), p. 414.

3. *Clarion-Ledger,* October 3, 1989.

4. Interview with Alan Binder.

5. Frank Parker, *Black Votes Count* (Chapel Hill: University of North Carolina Press, 1990), p. 165.

6. Interview with Bobby DeLaughter, February 1991.

7. *New York Times Magazine,* May 17, 1992.

8. *State of Mississippi vs. Byron de la Beckwith,* in the Circuit Court of the First Judicial District, Hinds County, Court reporter's transcript of hearing, August 3, 1992, p. 31.

9. *Clarion-Ledger,* March 11, 1990.

10. Ibid.

11. *Atlanta Journal-Constitution,* December 15, 1990.

12. Interview with Bobby DeLaughter, February 1991.

EPILOGUE: BECKWITH IN JACKSON

1. Interview with Bobby DeLaughter, February, 1994.

2. *Byron de la Beckwith vs. State of Mississippi,* Supreme Court of Mississippi, Brief of appellant, no. 91-KA-1207, p. ix.

3. *Byron de la Beckwith vs. State of Mississippi,* Supreme Court of Mississippi, Brief of appellee, no. 91-KA-1207, pp. 14, 18.

4. Supreme Court of Mississippi, Dissent of Roy Noble Lee, no. 91-KA-1207, pp. 1, 6.

5. *Washington Post,* January 21, 1994.

6. Hannah Arendt, *Eichmann in Jerusalem: A Report on the Banality of Evil* (New York: Penguin Books, 1977), p. 54.

7. Ted Morgan, *An Uncertain Hour* (New York: Morrow, 1990), p. 26.

8. Associated Press, February 8, 1994.

9. Associated Press, February 5, 1994.

10. Ibid.

11. Interview with Bobby DeLaughter, February, 1994.

BIBLIOGRAPHY

BOOKS CONSULTED

Arendt, Hannah. *Eichmann in Jerusalem: A Report on the Banality of Evil.* New York: Penguin Books, 1977.

Baker, Lewis. *The Percys of Mississippi.* Baton Rouge: Louisiana State University Press, 1983.

Bass, Jack, and Walter DeVries. *The Transformation of Southern Politics.* New York: Basic Books, 1976.

Berry, Jason. *Amazing Grace: With Charles Evers in Mississippi.* Saturday Review Press, 1973; reprint, Baton Rouge: Legacy, 1978.

Belfrage, Sally. *Freedom Summer.* New York: Viking, 1965; reprint, Charlottesville: University Press of Virginia, 1990.

Black, Earl, and Merle Black. *Politics and Society in the South.* Cambridge, Mass.: Harvard University Press, 1987.

Black, Patti Carr, ed. *Documentary Portrait of Mississippi: The Thirties.* Jackson: University Press of Mississippi, 1982.

Bond, Julian. *Black Candidates: Southern Campaign Experiences.* Atlanta: Southern Regional Council, 1969.

Branch, Taylor. *Parting the Waters: America in the King Years, 1954–1963.* New York: Simon & Schuster, 1988.

Brinson, Carroll. *Our Time Has Come: Mississippi Embraces Its Future.* Jackson: Oakdale Press, 1988.

Cagin, Seth, and Philip Dray. *We Are Not Afraid.* New York: Macmillan, 1988.

Carson, Clayborne. *In Struggle: SNCC and the Black Awakening.* Cambridge, Mass.: Harvard University Press, 1981.

Carter, Hodding. *So the Heffners Left McComb.* New York: Doubleday, 1965.

Carter, Hodding III. *The South Strikes Back.* New York: Doubleday, 1959.

Cobb, James C. *The Most Southern Place on Earth: The Mississippi Delta and the Roots of Regional Identity.* New York: Oxford University Press, 1992.

Davis, Allison, Burleigh B. Gardner, and Mary R. Gardner. *Deep South.* Chicago: University of Chicago Press, 1941.

Dollard, John. *Caste and Class in a Southern Town.* New York: Doubleday Anchor, 1957.

Eagles, Charles, ed. *The Civil Rights Movement in America.* Jackson: University Press of Mississippi, 1986.

Edsall, Thomas B., and Mary D. Edsall. *Chain Reaction: The Impact of Race, Rights and Taxes on American Politics.* New York: Norton, 1991.

Evans, Eli. *The Provincials.* New York: Atheneum, 1973.

Evers, Charles, with Grace Maisell, ed. *Evers.* New York: World, 1971.

Evers, Myrlie, with William Peters. *For Us, the Living.* New York: Doubleday, 1967.

Foner, Eric. *Reconstruction: America's Unfinished Revolution, 1863–1877.* New York: Harper & Row, 1988.

Green, A. Wigfall. *The Man Bilbo.* Westport, Conn.: Greenwood Press, 1976.

Harris, William C. *The Day of the Carpetbagger: Republican Reconstruction in Mississippi.* Baton Rouge: Louisiana State University Press, 1979.

Holmes, William F. *The White Chief: James Kimble Vardaman.* Baton Rouge: Louisiana State University Press, 1970.

Jacoway, Elizabeth, and David R. Colburn, eds. *Southern Businessmen and Desegregation.* Baton Rouge: Louisiana State University Press, 1982.

Johnston, Erle. *I Rolled with Ross.* Baton Rouge: Moran, 1980.

————. *Mississippi's Defiant Years, 1953–1973.* Forest, Miss.: Lake Harbor, 1990.

Key, V. O., Jr. *Southern Politics in the State and Nation.* Knoxville: University of Tennessee Press, 1984.

King, Martin Luther, Jr. *Why We Can't Wait.* New York: Signet, 1964.

Kirwan, Albert D. *Revolt of the Rednecks: Mississippi Politics, 1876–1925.* Lexington: University of Kentucky Press, 1951.

Krane, Dale, and Stephen D. Shaffer. *Mississippi Government and Politics.* Lincoln: University of Nebraska Press, 1951.

Lamis, Alexander. *The Two-Party South.* New York: Oxford University Press, 1984.

Lawson, Steven F. *Black Ballots: Voting Rights in the South, 1944–1969.* New York: Columbia University Press, 1976.

————. *In Pursuit of Power: Southern Blacks and Electoral Politics, 1965–1982.* New York: Columbia University Press, 1985.

Lemann, Nicholas. *The Promised Land.* New York: Vintage, 1991.

Loewen, James W., and Charles Sallis, eds. *Mississippi: Conflict and Change.* New York: Pantheon, 1980.

Lewis, Anthony, and the *New York Times. Portrait of a Decade: The Second American Revolution.* New York: Random House, 1964.

Lord, Walter. *The Past That Would Not Die.* New York: Pocket Books, 1967.

Maier, Charles S. *The Unmasterable Past.* Cambridge, Mass.: Harvard University Press, 1988.

Mars, Florence. *Witness in Philadelphia.* Baton Rouge: Louisiana State University Press, 1977.

McAdam, Doug. *Freedom Summer.* New York: Oxford University Press, 1988.

McLemore, Richard Aubrey, ed. *A History of Mississippi,* vol. 2. Jackson: University Press of Mississippi, 1973.

McMillen, Neil R. *Dark Journey: Black Mississippians in the Age of Jim Crow.* Urbana: University of Illinois Press, 1989.

————. *The Citizens' Council: Organized Resistance to the Second Reconstruction, 1954–1964.* Urbana: University of Illinois Press, 1971.

Meier, August, Elliot Rudwick, and John Bracey, Jr., eds. *Black Protest in the Sixties: Articles from the "New York Times."* New York: Wiener, 1991.

Meredith, James. *Three Years in Mississippi.* Bloomington: Indiana University Press, 1966.

Mississippi: A Guide to the Magnolia State. New York: Viking, 1938.

Mitchell, Paige. *The Covenant.* New York: Atheneum, 1973.

Moody, Anne. *Coming of Age in Mississippi.* New York: Bantam Double-day Dell, 1976.

Moore, Robert B. *Two History Texts: A Study in Contrast.* New York: Racism and Sexism Resource Center for Educators, n.d.

Morgan, Chester. *Redneck Liberal: Theodore G. Bilbo and the New Deal.* Baton Rouge: Louisiana State University Press, 1985.

Morgan, Ted. *An Uncertain Hour.* New York: Morrow, 1990.

Morris, Willie. *North Towards Home.* Oxford, Miss.: Yoknapatawpha Press, 1982.

———. *Yazoo.* New York: Ballantine, 1972.

Murphy, Reg, and Hal Gulliver. *The Southern Strategy.* New York: Scribner's, 1971.

Naipaul, V. S. *A Turn in the South.* New York: Knopf, 1989.

Neilson, Melany. *Even Mississippi.* Tuscaloosa: University of Alabama Press, 1989.

Nelson, Jack. *Terror in the Night: The Klan's Campaign against the Jews.* New York: Simon & Schuster, 1993.

Parker, Frank. *Black Votes Count.* Chapel Hill: University of North Carolina Press, 1990.

Peirce, Neal R. *The Deep South States of America.* New York: Norton, 1974.

Peirce, Neal R., and Jerry Hagstrom, *The Book of America.* New York: Norton, 1983.

Powdermaker, Hortense. *After Freedom: A Cultural Study in the Deep South.* New York: Viking, 1933; reprint, New York: Atheneum, 1968.

Powledge, Fred. *Journey through the South: A Rediscovery.* New York: Vanguard Press, 1979.

Raines, Howell. *My Soul Is Rested.* New York: Penguin, 1983.

Rousso, Henry. *The Vichy Syndrome: History and Memory in France since 1944.* Cambridge, Mass.: Harvard University Press, 1991.

Russ, Martin. *Line of Departure: Tarawa.* Garden City, N.Y.: Doubleday, 1973.

Salter, John. *Jackson, Mississippi: An American Chronicle of Struggle and Schism.* Hicksville, N.Y.: Exposition Press, 1979.

Sansing, David G., and Carroll Waller. *A History of the Mississippi Governor's Mansion.* Jackson: University Press of Mississippi, 1977.

Scott, R. W. *Glory in Conflict: A Saga of Byron de la Beckwith.* Camden, Ark.: Camark Press, 1991.

Sellers, Cleveland. *The River of No Return.* Jackson: University Press of Mississippi, 1990.

Sherrill, Robert. *Gothic Politics in the Deep South.* New York: Grossman, 1968.

Silver, James W. *Mississippi: The Closed Society.* New York: Harcourt Brace, 1964 and 1966.

———. *Running Scared: Silver in Mississippi.* Jackson: University Press of Mississippi, 1984.

Sims, Patsy. *The Klan.* New York: Dorset Press, 1988.

Smead, Howard. *Blood Justice: The Lynching of Mack Charles Parker.* New York: Oxford University Press, 1986.

Smith, Frank. *Congressman from Mississippi.* New York: Capricorn, 1967.

———. *The Yazoo River.* New York: Random House, 1954; reprint, Jackson: University Press of Mississippi, 1988.

Southern Poverty Law Center. *Free at Last: A History of the Civil Rights Movement and Those Who Died in the Struggle.* Montgomery, Ala.: SPLC, n.d.

Sterne, Emma Gelders. *They Took Their Stand.* New York: Crowell-Collier, 1968.

Sutherland, Elizabeth, ed. *Letters from Mississippi.* New York: McGraw-Hill, 1965.

Sykes, Malvina Scott, comp. *Our Family.* Washington, D.C.: privately printed, 1947.

Viorst, Milton. *Fire in the Streets: America in the 1960s.* New York: Simon & Schuster, 1979.

Von Hoffman, Nicholas. *Mississippi Notebook.* New York: White, 1964.

Wade, Wyn Craig. *The Fiery Cross: The Ku Klux Klan in America.* New York: Simon & Schuster, 1979.

Warren, Robert Penn. *Segregation.* New York: Random House, 1956.

———. *Who Speaks for the Negro?* New York: Random House, 1965.

Watson, Denton L. *Lion in the Lobby: Clarence Mitchell's Struggle for the Passage of Civil Rights Laws.* New York: Morrow, 1990.

Watters, Pat. *Down to Now.* New York: Pantheon, 1971.

Welty, Eudora. *Collected Stories.* New York: Harcourt, 1982.

———. *Photographs.* Jackson: University Press of Mississippi, 1989.

Whitfield, Stephen J. *A Death in the Delta.* New York: Free Press, 1988.

Wilkins, Roy. *Standing Fast: The Autobiography of Roy Wilkins.* New York: Viking Press, 1982.

Williamson, Joel. *The Crucible of Race.* New York: Oxford University Press, 1984.

Woodward, C. Vann. *The Burden of Southern History.* Baton Rouge: Louisiana State University Press, 1986.

Wright, Richard. *Black Boy.* New York: Harper & Row, 1966.

Zinn, Howard. *The Southern Mystique.* New York: Simon & Schuster, 1972.

ORAL HISTORIES

Minor, Wilson F. [Bill]. 1974. Mississippi Department of Archives and History (MDAH), Jackson.

Salter, John R. January 6, 1981. MDAH.

Salter, John R. December 26, 1990. John C. Stennis Oral History Project, Department of History, Mississippi State University, Starkville.

Salter, John R., and Rev. Edwin King. January 6, 1981. MDAH.

Schutt, Jane. February 2, 1981. MDAH.

Silver, James W. 1981. MDAH.

Waller, William L. November 14, 1971; April 21, 1976; July 21, 1982. Mississippi Oral History Program, University of Southern Mississippi, Hattiesburg.

Wiesenberg, Karl. 1976. MDAH.

Wroten, Joe. June 1965. Millsaps College, Jackson.

Wroten, Joe. July 7, 1976. MDAH.

MANUSCRIPT SOURCES AND LIBRARIES

Johnson, Paul B. Papers. University of Southern Mississippi, Hattiesburg.

King, Ed. "Life in Mississippi. VIII Beckwith Trial. Winter, Spring 1964." Unpublished manuscript.

Minor, Bill. Papers. Mississippi State University, Starkville.

National Association for the Advancement of Colored People. Papers, III. Library of Congress, Washington, D.C.

Right-Wing Ephemera Collection. Tulane University, New Orleans.

Salter, John. Papers. Mississippi Department of Archives and History (MDAH), Jackson.

Southern Regional Council Clipping Files, Atlanta.

Vertical Files. Amistad Research Center, Tulane University, New Orleans.

Vertical Files and Audio-Visual Collection. MDAH.

GOVERNMENT DOCUMENTS AND COURT PAPERS

Bobby DeLaughter vs. Dixie DeLaughter. Hinds County Chancery Court. 1991.

Byron de la Beckwith vs. Mary Louise Williams Beckwith. Leflore County Chancery Court. 1965.

Byron de la Beckwith vs. State of Mississippi. Supreme Court of Mississippi. Briefs of appellant and appellee, September 1992.

Federal Bureau of Investigation. *FOIPA #312,109—Medgar Evers.* (Courtesy of Lance Hill.)

James Loewen et al. vs John Turnipseed, Mississippi State Textbook Purchasing Board. U.S. District Court, Northern District of Mississippi, 1975.

State of Mississippi vs. Byron de la Beckwith. Circuit Court of the First Judicial District, Hinds County, Mississippi. Court reporter's transcript of first trial, 1964.

State of Mississippi vs. Byron de la Beckwith. Circuit Court of the First Judicial District, Hinds County, Mississippi. Proceedings on motion for bail, November 12, 1991.

State of Mississippi vs. Byron de la Beckwith. Circuit Court of the First Judicial District, Hinds County, Mississippi. Hearing on motions, August 3, 1992.

U.S. Commission on Civil Rights. *Hearings. U.S. Commission on Civil Rights: Jackson, Mississippi,* vols. 1–2. 1965.

U.S. House Committee on Un-American Activities. *Hearings before the Committee on Un-American Activities,* part 3. 89th Congress, 1966.

OTHER MATERIALS

Bailey, Ron. *Remembering Medgar Evers . . . For a New Generation.* Oxford: Civil Rights Research and Documentation Project, University of Mississippi, 1988.

Eyes on the Prize, "Mississippi: Is This America?" Televised film series.

"Story of Greenwood, Mississippi." Folkways Records. FD 5593.

Tape of responses to Medgar Evers's televised speech, May 20, 1963, WLBT-TV, Jackson, Miss., Mississippi Department of Archives and History, courtesy of Sharon Stallworth.

INTERVIEWS BY THE AUTHOR

Alford, Virginia. January 1991 (telephone).

Allison, Doris. August 1991, Jackson, Miss.

Armstrong, Louis. October 1992, Jackson, Miss.

Bailey, Sam. August 1991, Jackson, Miss.

Barber, Frank. November 1991, Jackson, Miss.

Beckwith, Byron de la. July 1992, Jackson, Miss.

Berry, Jason. April 1993, New Orleans.

Binder, Al. November 1991–December 1992, Jackson, Miss.

Binder, Nancy. August 1992, Jackson, Miss.

Blessey, Gerald. April 1992 (telephone).

Carter, Hodding III. December 1992 (telephone).

Cascio, Vincent. January 1991, Greenwood, Miss.

Clark, Robert. May 1992, Jackson, Miss.

Cole, Ed. May 1992, Jackson, Miss.

Current, Gloster. October 1991, New York.

Dean, Kenneth. September 1992 (telephone).

DeLaughter, Bobby. February 1991 and February 1994, Jackson, Miss.

Dillard, Chet. March 1992, Jackson, Miss.

Ditto, Jack. January 1991 (telephone).

Edwards, Wayne. March 1992 (telephone).

Evers, Charles. August 1991–May 1992, Jackson, Miss.

Fox, John. March 1992, Jackson, Miss.

Gordon, Bob. January 1993 (telephone).

Hawkins, Loran. August 1991, Mound Bayou, Miss.

Henry, Aaron. August 1991–September 1992, Clarksdale, Miss.

Herbers, John. December 1991, Washington, D.C.

Hester, John T. December 1992 (telephone).

Jordan, Elizabeth. October 1991.

King, Ed. August 1991, Jackson, Miss.

Kirksey, William. August 1992 (telephone).

Lackey, Gordon. December 1992, Greenwood, Miss.

Ladner, Joyce. September 1991, Washington, D.C.

Lawrence, Ken. November 1991 (telephone).

Leventhal, Melvyn. September 1992 (telephone).

Lott, Hardy. January 1991, Greenwood, Miss.

Mabus, Ray. October 1992, Jackson, Miss.

Massengill, Reed. January 1993 (telephone).

Measells, D. T. October 1992 (telephone).

McMillen, Neil. January 1992–April 1993, Hattiesburg, Miss., and on
    telephone.

Mills, Mike. October 1992 (telephone).

Minor, Bill. March 1992, Jackson, Miss.

Molpus, Dick. June 1989 (telephone).

Moore, Thomas H. August 1991, Mound Bayou, Miss.

Needham, C. B. September 1991, Decatur, Miss.

Newman, Buddie. January 1988, Valley Park, Miss.

Pritchard, Robert. March 1992, Pascagoula, Miss.

Rundles, John. March 1992, Jackson, Miss.

Rutledge, Steve. October 1991 (telephone).
Smith, R. L. T. December 1990, Jackson, Miss.
Stone, Ben. April 1992 (telephone).
Sweet, Dennis. August 1992 (telephone).
Thompson, Bennie. October 1992, Jackson, Miss.
Truly, Farrar. May 1992 (telephone).
Walcott, DeWitt. January 1991 (telephone).
Walker, Marie Farr. May 1992, Fayette, Miss.
Walker, Y. Z. September 1991, Decatur, Miss.
Waller, Bill. August 1991–March 1992, Jackson, Miss.
Waller, Carol. March 1992, Jackson, Miss.
Waller, Don. March 1992, Jackson, Miss.
Walt, Thatcher. December 1992 (telephone).
Watkins, Hollis. August 1991, Jackson, Miss.
Wheatley, Seth. December 1992, Greenwood, Miss.
Whitten, Amy. August 1992 (telephone).
Wroten, Joe. November 1991, Aberdeen, Miss.
Zellner, Bob. September 1991, New Orleans.

INDEX

Monk, Ladd, 18
Moorehead (Mississippi), 4
Moorehead, Yerger, 115–116
Moore, Mike, 229
Moore, Russel, 196, 199, 202
Moore, Thomas, 39, 40–41
Morgan, Peggy, 243
Morgan, Ted, 253
Morphew, Richard, 103
Morris, Willie, 66
Moses, Bob, 57, 72, 231
Mound Bayou (Mississippi), 37–38, 42, 175
Mt. Zion Church, 231, 232
Myrdal, Gunnar, 89

N

NAACP. *See also* Civil rights movement
Doris Allison and, 22, 54
Beckwith's opposition to, 119
black's fear of, 45–46
conservative nature of, 58, 60
Council of Federated Organizations (COFO) and, 4
Charles Evers's work for, 179–181
Medgar Evers's national speeches for, 51–52
Medgar Evers's work for, 26, 27–28, 39, 42–51
Aaron Henry as leader of, 6–7, 38, 207
Legal Defense Fund of, 56
in Mississippi, 39, 40–51, 262 n.64
national acceptance of, 39–40
relationship to other civil rights organizations, 27, 50–51
whites' intimidation of members of, 45–46

Natchez (Mississippi), 179, 182, 198, 234
Nation, 93, 106, 154
National Association for the Advancement of Colored People. *See* NAACP
National Committee to Elect Charles Evers Governor, 175
National Rifle Association, 123
Nazism
Medgar Evers's encounter with, 36
in Mississippi, 67–68
NBC-TV, civil rights reports on, 84
Needham, C. B., relationship to Medgar Evers, 32, 33, 34, 36
Neff, Thelma. *See* Beckwith, Thelma de la
New Deal Tobacco Company, 107, 117–118
Newman, Betty, 222
Newman, Buddie
Ross Barnett and, 214, 215–216, 221
on changes in Mississippi politics, 220–222
Robert Clark and, 216
Bobby DeLaughter and, 196, 211
education reform and, 217–219
political career of, 213–220
Walter Sillers and, 214, 215
New Orleans (Louisiana), 139
New Orleans Times-Picayune, 84, 152, 160, 165
Newsweek, 75
New Yorker, 76